A Guide to
Serial Bibliographies
for Modern Literatures

A Guide to Serial Bibliographies for Modern Literatures

Second Edition

William A. Wortman

THE MODERN LANGUAGE ASSOCIATION OF AMERICA
New York   1995

Library of Congress Cataloging-in-Publication Data

Wortman, William A., 1940–
    A guide to serial bibliographies for modern literatures / William
A. Wortman.
        p. cm.
    Includes bibliographical references and index.
    ISBN 0-87352-965-0 (alk. paper).—ISBN 0-87352-966-9 (pbk. :
alk. paper)
        1. Literature, Modern—Bibliography—Periodicals—Bibliography.
    2. Bibliography—Bibliography—Literature, Modern.
    3. Bibliography—Bibliography—Periodicals. I. Title.
    Z6519.W67   1995
    [PN695]
    016.805—dc20   95-33134

Book design by Charlotte Staub. Set in New Baskerville. Printed on
recycled, acid-free paper

Published by The Modern Language Association of America
10 Astor Place, New York, NY 10003-6981

Contents

6. *Authors* 241

Preface

This revised edition of *A Guide to Serial Bibliographies* (1st ed., 1982) maintains the volume's original purpose—to list all current serial bibliographies likely to be needed by students, faculty members, teachers, librarians, and others interested in any of the modern literatures and related subjects—and is revised only in having listed half again as many bibliographies, slightly expanded the range of subjects covered in chapter 5, and improved the cross-references. More than one colleague questioned whether a second edition was even necessary: "Haven't computers changed the way research is done?" they asked. My answer, for the moment, is that the major change brought by computerization seems mainly to have been the creation of more serial bibliographies. Whether computerization has made it easier for bibliographers to practice their craft or harder for scholars to find what they need in the great, turbulent sea of citations, the immediate result is that instead of one huge database of scholarly information from which any of us can draw whatever we might want, there are many, many specialized bibliographies, some quite sophisticated and almost all of them very useful and important. This may be the age of theory, but it is also the era of bibliographers, and the bibliographic craft are certainly very hard at work. There are 777 unique serial bibliographies in this edition as compared with 504 in the first, a fifty-four percent increase; counting cross-references there are 1,268 entries overall (an example of a cross-reference is the *Keats-Shelley Journal*, listed under Byron, Hazlitt, Hunt, Keats, Mary Shelley, and Percy Shelley and under the sections on the Romantic period for English and the Continental literatures). In addition, about one hundred titles of cumulations and earlier versions are buried in the annotations. Because this area is so changeable I plan to establish and maintain an Internet file titled "Serial Bibliographies" (http://lib.muohio.edu/serial-bibliographies) in which additions and corrections to this guide will be regularly listed.

Although the most widely used serial bibliographies are listed in the standard guides to literary study, such as James L. Harner's *Literary Research Guide* (2nd ed., New York: MLA, 1993) and Michael J. Marcuse's *A Reference Guide for English Studies* (Berkeley: U of California P, 1990), and a very thorough list of them was compiled by Richard Gray in *Serial Bibliographies in the Humanities and Social Sciences* (Ann Arbor: Pierian, 1969), the first edition of *A Guide to Serial Bibliographies* was the first up-to-date and comprehensive list of current serial bibliographies in all the modern literatures. Because literary studies is a broad field and of interest to a wide range of people, this guide is also in effect a record of serial bibliographies in the humanities and social sciences.

Being concerned with breadth of coverage, I have had to look far afield, and, therefore, I want to acknowledge the work of bibliographers, librarians, and information scientists who have created specialized bibliographies, accessible collections, and sophisticated databases. I did much of my work using the collections, bibliographies, and electronic indexes and databases of the Miami University libraries. There I was able to examine journals and bibliographies, search the *MLA International Bibliography*, *Humanities Index*, OCLC's *Worldcat* and other electronic resources, and use the Internet to reach online catalogs in other libraries. I have depended on the fine collections there as well as at the University of Cincinnati, Ohio State University, Columbia University, and the New York Public Library.

To identify resources is of little point if one cannot get one's hands on them. Crucial to my work have been interlibrary loan, in particular the help of Scott Van Dam, former head of Miami University's Interlibrary Loan Department; financial assistance from Miami's Committee for Faculty Research; and time, for which I thank Richard Quay, head of the Humanities and Social Sciences Department; Barbara Galik, assistant university librarian for Information and Research Services; and Judith Sessions, dean and university librarian. Several individuals helped with specific points: Martha Evans with French, Ming Gu with Chinese, Heike Mitchell with German, Bob Junke with computerization of the index, Alice Peo with typing, and Sue Wortman with computerization and Russian.

The readers James L. Harner and James R. Kelly encouraged me in this second edition and offered many helpful suggestions and leads, and the copyeditor James Poniewozik of the MLA did a heroic job on a manuscript full of complex bibliographic detail. The spirit of scholarly completeness and accuracy is strongly alive, whatever its actual manifestation here at my hand.

I dedicated the first edition to the previous generation, my parents-in-law; this edition is for the next generation, Emily and Alice.

Chapter One

Introduction

This guide is intended to include all current serial bibliographies that cover national literatures, literary periods, genres, themes and subjects, and literary authors. It also includes the major humanities and general periodical indexes and many bibliographies and indexes for subjects related to literature, literary study, and the literary profession as it is today.

DEFINITION AND COVERAGE

Serial bibliographies are bibliographic compilations and indexes that are published serially, whether as part of a journal, separately, or electronically. The checklist in the *James Joyce Quarterly* is an example of the first; the *MLA International Bibliography*, the *Arts and Humanities Citation Index*, and the *International Arthurian Bibliography* are separately published serial bibliographies; and *Ethnic Newswatch* and *Chicano Index* are only available as electronic serial bibliographies.

"Current" means 1960 to the present, and this guide should include all relevant serial bibliographies that have been published during the past thirty-five years, whether ceased or continuing. A number of items listed here started only in the 1990s, and a few have been running since the 1890s and before. The direct predecessors of current serial bibliographies are also included; these are the earlier versions or venues, such as the *Bibliothèque d'humanisme et Renaissance* that became the *Bibliographie internationale de l'humanisme et de la Renaissance* and the three different journals that published the bibliography *The Romantic Movement* from 1937 to 1979 before it became a separate publication. Cumulations or compilations of extended runs of a bibliography are also included.

The national literatures, literary periods, literary genres, and authors covered are those included in the *MLA International Bibliography*. Although there is an Anglo-American bias here, every effort has been made to identify and include all the significant and most of the lesser bibliographies for all the world's modern literatures. The literary periods are the major European movements or eras, from the medieval through the Renaissance, eighteenth-century, Romantic, and Victorian periods to the twentieth century.

Subjects include not only distinctly literary subjects, such as genres, creative writing, literary theory, and stylistics, but also area studies (e.g., African American, Caribbean, classics, medieval, Renaissance, and women's studies); other disciplines (e.g., history, philosophy, psychology, religion, and the social sciences); related interests (e.g., film, folklore, libraries, and printing); and related professional activities (e.g., composition, rhetoric, linguistics, and journalism). Chapter 5, "Subjects," is by far the longest because the term *subjects* accommodates the broad interests of the profession.

Contemporary literary scholars, students, teachers, and librarians have a remarkably wide range of interests, as any annual meeting of the MLA and most college curricula attest. In addition to traditional literary concerns with biography, bibliography, criticism, and literary history, there are the current concerns with new critical approaches and newly recognized authors and genres, the workaday concerns of pedagogy and professional survival, and the more or less extraliterary concerns with such matters as linguistics, libraries, and the book trade or the relations between literature and science (or art, psychology, history, Christianity, etc.). The people for whom this guide is intended are increasingly specialized yet increasingly multidisciplinary and varied in their interests.

KINDS OF BIBLIOGRAPHIES

Serial bibliographies are basic tools of research and are essential at all levels of literary work. Where there are scholars and scholarship there is scholarly communication, and where there is communication there is also someone trying to record and preserve it, organize it, and make its compilation useful. Serial bibliographies exist as checklists, abstracting services, bibliographic essays, catalogs, classified or selective bibliographies, and indexes, each form having a different origin, different organizing and governing principles, and different ways of being useful. These terms are not employed consistently, however, and conditions often alter intentions; despite the bibliographic spirit that aims at completeness, the compiler's time, energy, and resources are inevitably limited.

Abstracting services list abstracts or summaries of articles in scholarly publications, usually with subject indexing or in a classified arrangement and usually covering a predetermined, fixed set of publications.

Bibliographic essays evaluate current literary and scholarly production, sometimes narrowly, such as those in *Old English Newsletter*, sometimes broadly, such as those in *The Year's Work in Modern Language Studies*, but are necessarily limited in the number of items they can record and comment on.

Bibliographies carry the presumption of thoroughness and classification in their compilation. Many are thorough within stated limits, of course, and so are selective, and most display an explicit classification scheme that does not merely organize the materials cited but also classifies the subject these materials record. A bibliography reaches beyond the immediate, local collection and tries to record all known, relevant publications.

Catalogs record the materials gathered in a particular place, like a library, a private collection, or an organization's central offices, and presumably collected fairly diligently and purposefully. The emphasis is probably more on the totality of the collection than on its currentness.

Checklists list relevant publications, generally recent, usually arranged alphabetically by author, and sometimes subdivided for date, form, or broad topic. They can be quite thorough or can be limited, perhaps by genre or language or simply the compiler's energy, and are designed more to alert the interested student than to identify the full range of resources comprehensively.

Indexes are both tools with which to reach more accurately and surely into a field of information and, like classification schemes, conceptual organizations of that information. Periodical indexes, as a distinct kind of serial bibliography (which includes indexes to collections such as Festschriften and to specialized materials such as the dissertations and abstracts listed in *Dissertation Abstracts International*), can be very thorough and cite virtually every element in each issue of a periodical, or can restrict themselves to the major articles. They index in various ways, using keywords in titles of articles, using hierarchical concepts (divisions and subdivisions) derived from the contents of articles, and using subject descriptors attached to each article. Indexing has been greatly enhanced by computers, which make it possible to tag and record additional fields (such as the language, the date, or the citations, as in the *Arts and Humanities Citation Index*), to develop subject strings (as in the *MLA International Bibliography*), and to use Boolean logic in combining subject terms and strings, keywords, field tags, and other elements of indexing.

Contents of Entries

Each entry should provide several items of information: (1) title of the bibliography or of its parent journal; (2) publisher and place of publication; (3) dates of publication of the bibliography and of the years covered by it (the former are noted in the citation, the latter in the annotation); (4) frequency of publication; (5) electronic formats, if any; (6) character of the coverage and the means of access to it (the terms used to describe these characteristics are explained below); (7) titles of direct predecessors and cumulations, if any. If I have not been able to examine the bibliography, this fact is indicated in the citation.

Terms

Most terms in the guide's annotations are self-explanatory, but some might cause confusion and so need a brief explanation.

Annotated. Annotations are abstracts or descriptive comments about items cited; if the annotations are lengthy, this length is noted.

Articles. Most indexes and bibliographies that cover periodicals confine their coverage to major articles and omit notes, letters, illustrations, and other features. If coverage is broader than just articles, that fact is noted.

Author list. Items are listed alphabetically by their authors' names.

Bibliographic essay. An evaluative essay that surveys current scholarship and criticism on a subject or author.

Books. Includes both monographs and the chapters in collective volumes such as Festschriften, conference proceedings, and essay collections.

Boolean. Boolean logic allows the complex linking with *and, or,* and *not* functions of multiple subject terms, keywords, fields of a bibliographic record (such as language and date), and other indexing elements.

Classified. Items in the bibliography are arranged under a variety of subject headings or in subject categories. Part 1 of the printed edition of the *MLA International Bibliography* is an example.

Comprehensive. The bibliography covers a wide range of subjects or the wide range of a large subject's many aspects. The *MLA International Bibliography* comprehensively covers modern literatures, folklore, and linguistics; the *Linguistics Bibliography* covers the broad subject of linguistics comprehensively.

Dates. When the years covered by the bibliography are different from those of its publication, both dates are noted.

Dissertations. Dissertations, the major research component of doctoral study, are frequently included in bibliographies, but master's theses are not; if they are, the coverage is noted. See also the section for dissertations and theses in chapter 5.

Electronic formats. The two formats now widely available are CD-ROM and online databases. Entries note publisher and dates of coverage, but because this is a fluid area, not necessarily all available examples have been noted. The publisher is frequently a commercial firm different from the actual producer of the database; the information in the *MLA International Bibliography*, for example, is produced by the MLA but published, as of this writing, in CD-ROM by SilverPlatter and online by OCLC. Further information is given in the appendix.

Extensive. Most comprehensive bibliographies are also extensive in coverage: they list a great many items. Many less comprehensive bibliographies are also quite extensive in the number of items listed.

Indexes. The more extensive and comprehensive serial bibliographies ought to have author indexes and, where feasible, subject indexes. *Author index* refers to authors of scholarship, not authors of primary material; if the latter are indexed and confusion is possible, a distinction is made between critics and primary authors.

International. The bibliography covers publications from more than one country (with the United States and Canada considered as North America). In practice, *international* generally means North America, Great Britain, and western Europe.

Reviews. Book reviews. If reviews of other materials such as films, theater productions, software, and educational materials are included, this coverage is mentioned specifically.

Subject Author. The literary author who is the subject of the bibliography.

COMPUTERIZATION

This guide includes over sixty bibliographies that appear in electronic format, CD-ROM and online, several in only this format but most in both print and electronic versions. Entries note the type of format. For convenience, all the bibliographies with electronic formats are also listed separately in the appendix, with place of publication.

Computerization has improved but not yet transformed the world of serial bibliography and has had major effects in five areas. It has made possible the creation of massive bibliographic databases, such as OCLC (Online Computer Library Center), RLIN (Research Libraries Information Network), and online library catalogs. Accompanying these has been the development of standardized description of items listed (using MARC [machine-readable cataloging] conventions) and display of information about them. Computerized typesetting has made it possible to produce and print large, complex bibliographies relatively quickly. The *MLA International Bibliography* certainly benefits from computerized typesetting, which among other things allows its printed format to be reasonably up-to-date and makes possible the string indexing in its subject index; and printed indexes such as the *Arts and Humanities Citation Index* and *Dissertation Abstracts International* depend on computerized typesetting for citation and keyword-in-title indexing as well as for currentness.

Alternatively, the printing process can actually be bypassed and bibliographies made directly available online or in CD-ROM by electronic publishers and distribution services. These electronic publishers, such as H. W. Wilson and SilverPlatter, and database services, such as RLIN, Dialog, and OCLC FirstSearch, now provide a useful range of bibliographies, although not yet many that are exclusively literary in coverage. Computerization also has enhanced indexing, especially for electronic databases, by making possible free-text searches for any word, keyword-in-title indexing, citation indexing, string indexing, and field indexing of complex records with a rich range of elements (not only the author, title, and source but also subject terms, language, publication type, year, and other identifiers), all combined with Boolean-logic searching.

Finally, computerized telecommunications enable us to transmit bibliographic data, gain access to catalogs and documents virtually anywhere in the world, and exchange texts and information through the Internet. Already the Internet offers electronic journals with bibliographies, e-mail communication among scholars about bibliographic information, and the ability to transfer bibliographic and other files using File Transfer Protocol (FTP). No doubt the next step in serial bibliography will be to make bibliographies available through the Internet, and the next edition of this guide will doubtless be full of Internet addresses and FTP instructions. Even more likely, in fact, the next edition of this guide will itself be electronic rather than print. As noted in the preface, I will create and maintain an Internet file titled "Serial Bibliographies" (http://lib.muohio.edu/serial-bibliographies) in which new bibliographies and changes and corrections in current ones will be recorded. But computerization has not eliminated the need for serial bibliographies. The adequate recording of scholarly writing, print or electronic, and the ability to identify and gain access to it will still depend on the kind of controls that define good bibliographies today—a clear plan, appropriate thoroughness, standard citation formats, ease of use, and consistent execution.

EXCLUSIONS AND LIMITATIONS

Although I have tried to include all relevant serial bibliographies, there are some deliberate exclusions and limitations.

Trade and national bibliographies. These bibliographies are so numerous as to require a separate book and are adequately covered in the *Guide to Reference Books* (D402).

General periodical indexes. Except for those listed in chapter 2 and a few listed in chapters 3 and 4, these indexes are not included. Like trade and national bibliographies, they are listed in the *Guide to Reference Books*.

Journals that regularly publish bibliographic articles on various subjects. Omitted. The coverage of such journals as *Bulletin of Bibliography* and *Modern Fiction Studies* can be found easily in many of the bibliographies cited here.

Lists of books received. Omitted, with a few exceptions in which the lists are comprehensive or systematic.

Reviews of reviews. Omitted. Formerly common, these listings of tables of contents of related journals have been eclipsed by periodical indexes and other serial bibliographies. One exception: *Current Contents: Arts and Humanities* (A7).

Irregular bibliographies and bibliographic series from such publishers as Borgo, Garland, G. K. Hall, Kent State University Press, and Scarecrow. Omitted.

Bibliographies of current creative writing. Limited to North American writing and bibliographies, for which there is an extensive section in chapter 5. Bibliographies of creative writing in other countries are not listed unless they also carry criticism and scholarship.

ARRANGEMENT AND USE

The arrangement of the bibliographies here is generally from most comprehensive to most specialized. Thus, chapter 2 lists those few bibliographies that cover all literatures, as well as the general and humanities periodical indexes. Chapters 3 and 4 list bibliographies for individual national literatures and literary periods. Chapter 5 lists subject bibliographies dealing with literary themes, topics, genres, and related issues or with broad cognate fields (e.g., history, psychology, religion), and chapter 6 covers specialized author bibliographies.

To find items in this guide, follow the classified arrangement, which includes introductory and explanatory paragraphs, cross-references, and titles of predecessors and cumulations; scan the subject and author headings in chapters 5 and 6; and use the subject and title index that cites every occurrence of every title and allows more precise subject access than does the arrangement of chapter 5. Within individual sections the most comprehensive or most usable bibliographies are listed first. Although foreign language bibliographies are certainly listed, English-language and North American bibliographies are given priority on the assumption that both they and the items cited in them are more likely to be available to scholars in North America.

In using serial bibliographies, one ought to move from the general to the specific. Start with the *MLA International Bibliography* in one of its electronic formats (not neglecting to scan relevant sections of its print edition) and then move on to the major bibliographies for relevant topics followed by the related or appropriate specialized bibliographies, depending on one's subject, the bibliographies' coverage and their classification and indexing, and the degree of thoroughness required. Frequently, a given topic will be covered in several different bibliographies. Someone working on William Blake, for example, should start with the *MLA International Bibliography* on CD-ROM or online and then go on to use at least the *Annual Bibliography of English Language and Literature* and the *Year's Work in English Studies, Blake: An Illustrated Quarterly*, the eighteenth-century and Romantic movement bibliographies, perhaps the *Art Index* and *Bibliography of the History of Art*, and the *Arts and Humanities Citation Index* and *Periodical Abstracts* or the *Humanities Index* and *Infotrac*, all before considering additional bibliographies in which to conduct a more thorough search for dissertations and theses, foreign language publications, and newspaper stories and media materials. It is not possible, of course, to suggest all possible bibliographies for all possible topics, but I do try throughout this guide to remind readers that more comprehensive or more specialized ones exist and need to be consulted. The amount of literary material available is enormous and the range of serial bibliographies daunting, but one can select them systematically and use them with confidence.

Chapter Two
Comprehensive Bibliographies and General Indexes

Although the *MLA International Bibliography* (A1) is now the most comprehensive bibliography for all the modern languages and literatures, its coverage is complemented, and in some areas surpassed, by other bibliographies that can be more current, more specialized, more comprehensive in the range of materials they record, or more evaluative in their presentation. The *MLA International Bibliography* is the benchmark for the *Guide to Serial Bibliographies*, however, and the lengthy discussion of its features below should make clear not only its strengths but also the importance and usefulness of other bibliographies. This chapter also describes several other comprehensive bibliographies, a wide range of current indexes to scholarly and popular periodicals, electronic text and bibliographic services, and indexes to news and current events. It concludes with a list of those indexes that provide, in combination, over two hundred years of access to scholarly, specialized, and popular periodicals and newspapers.

COMPREHENSIVE BIBLIOGRAPHIES

These bibliographies aim to record current publication about all the modern literatures in a wide range of sources. The *MLA International Bibliography* is most comprehensive in these senses. *FRANCIS bulletin signalétique 523. Histoire et science de la littérature* (A2), although limited in the materials it covers, does deal comprehensively with world literature, literary theory, and literary history, and it is slightly more current. Several other bibliographies cover world literatures comprehensively but emphasize national publication and are especially useful for their record of former Soviet Union and Eastern bloc publication. The *Quarterly Check-list of Literary History* (A3) was useful for the years it covered.

A1   *MLA International Bibliography of Books and Articles on the Modern Languages and Literatures.* New York: MLA, 1922– . Annual.

Electronic formats: CD-ROM (SilverPlatter, 1963–) and online (OCLC, 1963–).

A comprehensive, classified bibliography of international books, articles, and dissertations on all modern-language literatures, folklore, and linguistics for 1921– . (See below for fuller description of the *MLA International Bibliography*'s evolution.) Items selected for inclusion must deal with literature, and book reviews (but not review articles), notes, letters to the editor, news, and historical and other articles in the journals indexed are generally omitted unless they have a clear bearing on literary issues. Creative writing is not listed. The clothbound print format consists of a five-volume classified section with an author index (in one physical volume) and a detailed, extensive subject index (in one volume). As of this writing, the five volumes cover the following areas: British and Irish, Commonwealth, English Caribbean, and American literature; European, Asian, African, and Latin American literatures; linguistics; general literature and related topics; and folklore. The electronic formats each include the same core of information (although retrospective coverage varies between them), but each adds unique features or search interfaces.

The *MLA International Bibliography* is easiest and fastest to search in its electronic formats, but regular users should become familiar with the print version, which makes the bibliography's structure evident. The classified arrangement of the two national literature volumes is arranged by distinct literatures. For example, English language is sectioned for British and Irish, American, Commonwealth, English Caribbean, and other literatures; French has sections on French, Occitan, French Canadian, and French Caribbean literatures. Within each literature division there is further division by time period, by form (e.g., bibliography, biography, novel, periodical, poetry, theater), and by individual authors and their works. Users should also realize that because both versions cite only complete articles, chapters, and books, not passages or passing mentions, it is important to browse relevant sections of the printed bibliography to identify broad studies that may have important, unindexed material on a specialized topic.

The subject indexing uses standardized terms, such as African American (rather than Afro-American or Black American) and reception study (rather than reputation study). Each item listed is tagged to indicate not only standard bibliographic information but also language, type of publication, and subjects. The electronic formats add both Boolean capability (multiple subject terms can be searched simultaneously using the functions *and*, *or*, and *not*) and multiple-year cumulation. Further, one can usually print citations or download them to one's own disk. To the virtue of the *MLA International Bibliography*'s comprehensiveness, then, has been added the computer's convenience, speed, and precision.

The bibliography was carried as part of *PMLA* (New York: MLA, 1884–) from 1922 to 1968; it was published in three volumes bound as one from 1969 to 1980: volume 1: general; English, American, medieval and Neo-Latin, and Celtic literatures; and folklore; volume 2: non-English language literatures; and volume 3: linguistics. A fourth volume, published from 1969 to 1972, consisted of the ACTFL bibliography (see D293). The present two-part format and electronic access were introduced in 1981. Breadth and depth of coverage have increased over the years, as shown here:

North American publications predominantly, 1921–55; international publications (mainly from North America, the United Kingdom, the Continent, Latin America), 1956– .

Bibliographic essay format, 1921–25.

Index of critics, 1946–55, 1964– .

Linguistics listed under the general literature section and under major language groups, 1921–66, and as a separate section, 1967– .

Folklore included under general literature during 1926–68 and as a separate section starting in 1969, except for African, modern Greek, and east European folklore, which were listed in the literature sections until 1981.

Number of periodicals covered: 1930—35 titles; 1940—50 titles; 1950—120 titles; 1960—1,060 titles; 1980—2,900 titles; 1993—3,500 titles. (Numbers after 1960 are for periodicals on the master list; not all are actually indexed every year.)

Abstracts of major articles for 1970–75 were provided in *MLA Abstracts*, 6 volumes (New York: MLA, 1972–77).

For coverage of North American scholarship before the *MLA International Bibliography*, see the annual reviews for 1910–49 in *The American Year Book: A Record of Events and Progress* (New York: Appleton, 1911–50) and partially cumulated and indexed in Arnold N. Rzepecki, *Literature and Language Bibliographies from the American Year Book, 1910–19* (Ann Arbor: Pierian, 1970). In addition, other yearbooks regularly included overviews of scholarly publication; see the *Annual Register*, for 1758– , *Appleton's Annual Cyclopaedia*, for 1861–1902, and the *New International Year Book*, for 1898–1965 (see D120 for all three titles). Elsewhere, several bibliographies for Continental literatures began coverage in the nineteenth or early twentieth century (see ch. 4), and the *Annual Bibliography of English Language and Literature* (B1) provided better coverage of more sources than the *MLA International Bibliography* through the 1950s.

A2 *FRANCIS bulletin signalétique.* Vandœuvre-lès-Nancy: Institut de l'Information Scientifique et Technique, 1948– . 4/yr. (Originally titled *Bulletin signalétique.*)

Electronic formats: CD-ROM (Centre National de la Recherche Scientifique, 1984–) and online (Questel, 1984–).

FRANCIS bulletin signalétique 523. Histoire et sciences de la littérature is a classified bibliography of articles from about 600 international periodicals, reports, dissertations, congress and colloquium publications, and Festschriften for 1947– , arranged by literary period. Critic and subject indexes in each issue are cumulated annually. Annotations in French.

This bibliographic series also includes, among others: *519. Philosophie, 520. Sciences de l'education, 521. Sociologie, ethnologie, 522. Sciences du langage, 524. Histoire des sciences et des techniques, 526. Art et archéologie,* and *527. Histoire et sciences des religions.*

(C211) *Novaia literatura po sotsial'nym i gumanitarnym naukam: Literaturovedenie: Bibliograficheskii ukazatel'*

A classified bibliography of international books and articles on the literatures of Russia, the nations formerly part of the USSR, and other nations, for 1953– ; part of its strength is its coverage of publications about world literature in Russia and in the former Soviet republics. (Author has not examined the bibliography.)

(C87) *Beiträge zur Literaturkunde: Bibliographie ausgewählter Zeitungs- und Zeitschriftenbeiträge*

Covers former East German and German socialist publications on world literature for the 1950s– . (Author has not examined the bibliography.)

(C201) *A magyar irodalom és irodalomtudomány bibliográfiája*

A classified bibliography of Hungarian books and articles on Hungarian and world literature and literary history for 1976– .

(C205) *Literatura piękna: Adnotowany rocznik bibliograficzny*

A classified bibliography of Polish books, reviews, and articles on Polish and world literature, arranged by country, for 1956– .

(C206) *Polska bibliografia literacka*

A classified bibliography of Polish books and articles on world literature, ancient and modern, as well as on theater, film, radio, and television, for 1945– .

(C171) *Current Contents of Academic Journals in Japan*

A classified listing of articles (titles transliterated) in Japanese journals dealing with literature, arranged in sections for Western, Japanese, and other literatures, for 1971– .

(D159) *South Atlantic Review*

For 1936–66 (in the second issue of vols. 2–34, 1936–69), a listing of new books and articles by members of the South Atlantic Modern Language Association on English and American literature, comparative literature, modern languages, folklore, and linguistics.

(C86) *Literature, Music, Fine Arts: A Review of German-Language Research Contributions on Literature, Music, and Fine Arts with Bibliographies*

Includes a bibliography of recent German-language books and articles for 1968–91 on international literature.

A3 *Quarterly Check-list of Literary History: An International Index of Current Books, Monographs, Brochures, and Separates.* Darien: Amer. Bibliographic Service, 1958–75. 4/yr.

A checklist of books on English, American, French, and German literary history, arranged alphabetically by author.

A4 *LLINQUA: Language and Literature Index Quarterly.* Aachen, Ger.: CoBRa, 1980.

Indexes articles and book reviews in about 500 international periodicals. The quarterly was intended to be comprehensive in materials recorded and subjects covered, but it lasted only one year.

CURRENT INDEXES

Although computerization has improved the currentness and accessibility of entries in the *MLA International Bibliography* (A1) and *FRANCIS bulletin signalétique* (A2), indexes to current periodicals and collective books are usually more current and often more readily accessible than the classified bibliographies.

Humanities Indexes

A6   *Arts and Humanities Citation Index*. Philadelphia: Inst. for Scientific Information, 1978– . 2/yr.

Electronic formats: CD-ROM (ISI) and online (Dialog, OCLC, 1980–).

For 1976– , an author, citation, and permuted title index to articles, reviews, notes, correspondence, creative writing, and illustrations in about 1,150 international periodicals and some Festschriften and collective volumes. "Source Index" is an author list of current articles; "Permuterm Index" is a permuted keyword-in-title index; "Citation Index" lists all authors, works, and critics cited in footnotes or referred to in texts of articles. The index is particularly useful for interdisciplinary and nontraditional studies because of the extensive list of periodicals and collections covered. Supplemented by *Current Contents: Arts and Humanities* (A7).

A7   *Current Contents: Arts and Humanities*. Philadelphia: Inst. for Scientific Information, 1978– . 26/yr.

Biweekly publication of tables of contents of the books and periodicals received by ISI, with author and title indexing.

A8   *Humanities Index*. New York: Wilson, 1974– . 4/yr., with annual cumulation. (Combined with the *Social Sciences Index*, D455, as the *Social Sciences and Humanities Index*, 1965–74, and as the *International Index*, 1916–65.)

Electronic formats: CD-ROM (Wilson, 1983–) and online (OCLC and Wilson, 1983–).

Comprehensive author and subject index to nearly 400 mainly North American scholarly journals in literature, fine and performing arts, history, and the humanities. It is current, it covers about 120 literary journals and reviews, and it includes creative writing and book reviews as well as criticism.

A9   *British Humanities Index*. London: Library Assn., 1962– . 4/yr., with annual cumulation. (Continues the *Subject Index to Periodicals*, 1916–61.)

Electronic format: CD-ROM (Saur, 1985–).

A comprehensive author and subject index to nearly 300 British and Commonwealth journals in literature, fine and performing arts, history, and the humanities (about one-third of which are literary journals). Covers criticism, creative writing, and book, theater, and film reviews.

A10   *Essay and General Literature Index.* New York: Wilson, 1934– . 2/yr., with annual cumulation.

Electronic formats: CD-ROM (Wilson, 1983–) and online (OCLC and Wilson, 1983–).

An author and subject index to English-language collective volumes on all subjects, with emphasis on literature and the humanities, for 1900– . Cites original as well as reprinted articles.

A11   *Index to Social Sciences and Humanities Proceedings.* Philadelphia: Inst. for Scientific Information, 1979– . 4/yr.

An author and subject index to individual papers in published proceedings on a broad range of subjects, including literature, philology, linguistics, theater, and communication.

General Scholarly Indexes

A15   *Infotrac.* Foster City: Information Access, 1977– . 12 updates/yr.

Electronic format only. CD-ROM and a hardware package provided by producer.

An author and subject index to articles and reviews in about 1,000 periodicals in all fields, most of them scholarly and some containing abstracts. It includes several hundred periodicals in literature and the humanities and uses both hierarchically classified and free-text indexing with some Boolean capability. *Infotrac* is the overall name for a family of related indexes that includes *Academic Index* (for scholarly periodicals), *Magazine Index* (for popular periodicals), *National Newspaper Index* (for US newspapers), *Businesstrac*, and *Legaltrac*.

A16   *Periodical Abstracts.* Ann Arbor: UMI, 1988– . Updated continually.

    Electronic formats only: CD-ROM (UMI) and online (Dialog, 1988– ; OCLC, 1986–).

    An author, title, and subject index to articles and reviews in about 1,600 scholarly English-language periodicals in all fields, including several hundred in literature and the humanities, for 1986– . Citations include brief abstracts. Coverage of literature and the humanities is comparable with that of the *Humanities Index* and *Infotrac.*

A17   *Internationale Bibliographie der Zeitschriftenliteratur aus allen Gebieten des Wissens.* Osnabrück, Ger.: Zeller, 1965– . 12/yr. (Continues the *Internationale Bibliographie der fremdsprachigen Zeitschriftenliteratur* published by Zeller, Leipzig, 1911–64.)

    Electronic format: CD-ROM (Zeller, 1986–   ).

    A comprehensive author and subject index to international periodicals on all subjects for 1911– . Subject headings are in German; the literary topics are not as specific, however, as those in the other humanities and general scholarly indexes.

A18   *Biological and Agricultural Index.* New York: Wilson, 1919– . 12/yr. (Titled *Agricultural Index,* 1919–64.)

    Electronic formats: CD-ROM (Wilson, 1983–) and online (Wilson and OCLC, 1983–).

    A subject index to over 225 English-language periodicals covering agriculture and biology but not medicine; includes a separate section of book reviews.

A19   *Applied Science and Technology Index.* New York: Wilson, 1913– . 12/yr. (Titled *Industrial Arts Index,* 1913–57; in 1958 this index split into the present *Applied Science and Technology Index,* which continues the original numbering, and the *Business Periodicals Index,* D201.)

    Electronic formats: CD-ROM (Wilson, 1983–) and online (Wilson and OCLC, 1983–).

    A subject index to about 400 English-language periodicals in all areas of mathematics, physical sciences, and engineering; includes a separate section of book reviews.

General Interest and Popular Indexes

General interest and popular periodicals contain important records of social and cultural history; carry creative writing and serious, engaged journalism; and provide a contemporary view of a wide range of issues. The *Readers' Guide* (A20) and the *Alternative Press Index* (D10) offer current and historical access to this valuable material.

A20   *The Readers' Guide to Periodical Literature.* New York: Wilson, 1905– . 12/yr., with annual cumulation.

Electronic formats: CD-ROM (Wilson, 1983–) and online (OCLC and Wilson, 1983–).

An author and subject index to about 200 mainly American periodicals in all fields, including literary reviews but few scholarly journals. Coverage for 1890–1922 provided by *Nineteenth-Century Readers' Guide to Periodical Literature*, 2 volumes (New York: Wilson, 1944). See also *Cumulated Magazine Subject Index* (A54).

(D10)   *Alternative Press Index: An Index to Alternative and Radical Publications*

Indexes some 230 English-language periodicals that take an alternative approach to political, cultural, and social issues.

A21   *Access: The Supplementary Index to Periodicals.* Evanston: John Gordon Burke, 1976– . 3/yr. (Also published by Gaylord, Syracuse, 1976–78).

Designed to complement coverage of the *Readers' Guide*; indexes some 120 American periodicals.

A22   *Vertical File Index.* New York: Wilson, 1935– . 11/yr.

A subject and title index to pamphlets on all subjects.

International Indexes

National periodical indexes exist in many countries, but since most are described in the *Guide to Reference Books* (D402), only a few are included here; they are listed at appropriate points in chapters 3 and 4.

TEXT AND BIBLIOGRAPHIC SERVICES

The following are examples of some electronic database services that either provide the full text of publications or operate in combination with commercial document-supply services from which users can purchase copies.

A30   Lexis/Nexis. Dayton: Lexis/Nexis. Continual updating.

      An online service providing full text of hundreds of publications arranged into specialized segments and including newspapers, news services, and newsmagazines; specialized business, financial, government, legal, and international publications; reference books and data compilations in business; and legal and medical resources. Dates and extent of coverage vary from publication to publication. Useful for reviews of books, films, plays, dance, music, and exhibits; for current events; and for legal and financial aspects of literature and the arts.

A31   Dow Jones News/Retrieval. New York: Dow Jones. Continually updated.

      Online, full text of the *Wall Street Journal* and business, finance, and news publications from Dow Jones and other publishers.

A32   CARL UnCover. Denver: CARL Systems. Continual updating.

      An online commercial index and document-delivery service drawing on the combined periodical holdings of Colorado universities (the Colorado Alliance of Research Libraries, or CARL). Tables of contents of newly received periodicals can be searched by author, subject, or title, and photocopies of the articles can be ordered online.

A33   OCLC. Dublin: OCLC. Continual updating.

      OCLC produces two sets of about 70 indexes and databases in all fields, Epic and FirstSearch, each set with slightly different search interfaces. Two databases, *Articlefirst* and *Contentsfirst*, cover the most recent issues of all periodicals in the full set. Records note library holdings.

A34   Dialog. Palo Alto: Dialog. Updating frequency varies by file.

An online bibliographic service consisting of several hundred specialized online indexes and information databases, some with abstracts, all with a similar search, display, and print interface. The database *Onesearch* allows searches in multiple files at one time. Online ordering of copies from commercial services is possible.

(A6) *Arts and Humanities Citation Index* and *Current Contents* (A7)
These volumes and companion volumes for the sciences and social sciences (see D456) cover several thousand periodicals and collective volumes, with current indexing (updated monthly), and are supplemented by the publisher's commercial copy service The Genuine Article.

NEWS AND CURRENT EVENTS

Newspapers, radio, and television provide reviews of books, films, and plays; interviews with writers and others; reports on literary events and topics such as prizes, local celebrations, conferences, and controversies; and current general news of interest to writers and scholars.

Newspaper Indexes

A number of commercially produced newspaper indexes are available in print or in electronic format, among them indexes to the *New York Times, Christian Science Monitor, Washington Post, Chicago Tribune, Los Angeles Times, Wall Street Journal,* London *Times,* and several international newspapers. The newspaper indexes listed below each cover several papers; current indexes listed above cover newsmagazines (see A30–A34); electronic text services provide full text, with indexing.

A40 *Newspaper Abstracts.* Ann Arbor: UMI. Continually updated.
Electronic formats: CD-ROM (UMI, 1985–) and online (Dialog, 1988– , OCLC, 1989–).

Using the same search interface as *Periodical Abstracts* (A16), this index covers 26 United States newspapers for 1988– and includes abstracts of stories cited.

A41   *NewsBank Electronic Index.* New Canaan: NewsBank, 1980– . Continually updated. CD-ROM format only.

        CD-ROM index to selected articles from over 400 United States newspapers, with accompanying full text on microfiche.

(A15) *Infotrac*

        The academic and magazine indexes cover the latest six months of the *New York Times*; the *National Newspaper Index* covers eight papers.

(D215) *Ethnic Newswatch: A Multicultural Database*

        A CD-ROM compilation of the full text of about 100 North American ethnic newspapers, newsletters, and periodicals.

A42   *Black Newspapers Index.* Ann Arbor: UMI, 1977– . 4/yr., with annual cumulation. (Titled *Index to Black Newspapers* and published by Bell and Howell, Wooster, 1977–86.)

        A subject index to about 20 United States African American newspapers.

(C92) *Zeitungs-Index: Verzeichnis wichtiger Aufsätze aus deutschsprachigen Zeitungen*

        A subject index to 20 German-language newspapers and newsmagazines published in Austria, Germany, and Switzerland; includes author and geographic indexes and a systematic subject index. (Author has not examined the index.)

Indexes to Radio and Television Transcripts

A43   *Transcript/Video Index.* Denver: Journal Graphics, 1990– . 4/yr. (Annual through 1992).

        Indexes transcripts of programs carried for 1968– on ABC, CBS, CNN, and PBS (but not NBC). (Author has not examined the index.)

A45   *Broadcast News.* Westport: Research Publications, 1993– .

        Full text on CD-ROM of CNN, ABC, CBS, PBS, and NPR news and public-affairs broadcasts. (Author has not examined the database.)

(A30) Lexis/Nexis

        The transcript file "Script" provides full text of regular network news broadcasts.

HISTORICAL INDEXES

Through a combination of original indexes and later compilations there is now remarkably thorough indexing of the more important scholarly, specialized, and popular periodicals of Great Britain and the United States from the mid-eighteenth century to the present.

A49   *Index to English Literary Periodicals, 1681–1914: A Critical Review*. Indianapolis: Computer Indexed Systems, 1989– . Irregular updates.

     Electronic format: CD-ROM (Computer Indexed Systems, 1989–).

     An author and subject index to periodicals included in the microfilm set *English Literary Periodicals* (Ann Arbor: UMI) that gives bibliographic citations and references to reels. In progress.

A50   *Index to American Periodicals of the 1700s and 1800s*. Indianapolis: Computer Indexed Systems, 1986– . Irregular updates.

     Electronic format: CD-ROM (Computer Indexed Systems, 1986–).

     An author and subject index to American periodicals included in the microfilm set *American Periodical Series* (Ann Arbor: UMI), giving bibliographic citations and references to reels. In progress.

A51   *Poole's Index to Nineteenth-Century Periodical Literature*. 1882–1908. Gloucester: Smith, 1963.

     A subject index to British and North American periodicals of the nineteenth century in all fields, 1802–1907. Supplemented by *Poole's Index Date and Volume Key* (Chicago: Assn. for Coll. and Research Libraries, 1958) and *Cumulative Author Index for* Poole's Index to Periodical Literature, *1802–1906* (Ann Arbor: Pierian, 1971).

A52   *Wellesley Index to Victorian Periodicals, 1824–1900*. 5 vols. Toronto: U of Toronto P, 1966–89.

     Volumes 1–4 print tables of contents (prose items only, not poetry) of over 40 British Victorian periodicals, with added information about authors and subjects supplied. Volume 5 is a cumulated author index.

A53   *Combined Retrospective Index to Journals in History, 1838–1974.*
11 vols. Washington: Carrollton, 1977–78.

A classified subject and author index to nearly 600 British and North American periodicals publishing articles on history.

(A20)   *The Readers' Guide to Periodical Literature*

Indexes popular United States magazines from 1890 to the present.

A54   *Cumulated Magazine Subject Index, 1907–1949.* 2 vols. Boston: Hall, 1968.

A cumulation of the *Annual Magazine Subject Index* (Boston: Faxon, 1907–49), an index to some 350 scholarly North American periodicals (not all of which ran for the full forty-two years).

(A17)   *Internationale Bibliographie der Zeitschriftenliteratur*

Indexes international scholarly periodicals from 1911 to the present.

(A8)   *Humanities Index*

This index; its complement, the *Social Sciences Index*; and its predecessors, the *International Index* and the *Social Sciences and Humanities Index,* cover mainly United States scholarly periodicals in the humanities and social sciences from 1916 to the present.

(A9)   *British Humanities Index*

This index and its predecessor, the *Subject Index to Periodicals,* cover mainly British periodicals from 1916 to the present.

(D300) *The American Humanities Index* and *Index to Little Magazines*

In combination, these indexes cover several hundred American little magazines and literary reviews from 1901 to the present.

A55   *The* Times *Index.* Reading, Eng.: Research Publications Intl. 1977– . Monthly, with annual cumulation.

In combination with earlier indexes, recent compilations, and reprints, provides an index to the *Times* of London for 1785– . The other indexes: *The* Times *Index* (Reading, Eng.: Newspaper Archive Developments, 1972–76), *The Official Index to the* Times (London: Times, 1914–71; partial rpt. Nendeln, Liechtenstein: Kraus, 1968–70), *Palmer's Index to the* Times *Newspaper* for 1790–1941 (Hampton, Eng.: Samuel Palmer, 1868–1943; rpt. Vaduz, Liechtenstein: Kraus, 1965), and *The* Times *(the* Daily Universal Register*) Index* for 1785–90 (5 vols., Reading, Eng.: Newspaper Archive Developments, 1978).

A56   *The* New York Times *Index*. New York: New York Times, 1913– . 4/yr., with annual cumulation.

A subject index to the paper, with supplemental volumes extending coverage back to 1851.

Chapter Three

English, American, and Other English-Language Literatures

The *MLA International Bibliography* (A1) should be used first for most topics in English or American literature, but its coverage is complemented by that of the *Annual Bibliography of English Language and Literature* (*ABELL*; B1) and by the bibliographic surveys in *The Year's Work in English Studies* (*YWES*; B2) and *American Literary Scholarship* (B72). The comprehensive bibliographies listed in chapter 2 offer additional international coverage. In its electronic formats the *MLA International Bibliography* is fairly up-to-date, but some of the indexes cited in chapter 2, especially their electronic formats, cover current publications more thoroughly. The major period bibliographies for the Middle Ages, the Renaissance, the eighteenth century, the Romantic period, and the Victorian age cover the arts, religion and philosophy, history and government, and social conditions as well as literature, thus extending the coverage of the *MLA Bibliography*, *ABELL*, and *YWES*. The major bibliographies for the Continental literatures are similarly useful (see ch. 4). Unfortunately, there are no comparably broad bibliographies for American culture or for the twentieth century, and thus the various bibliographies listed in chapter 5 assume even more importance.

The bibliographies in chapter 5 cover subjects ranging from African American studies to literary theory, medieval studies, and women's studies and including literary genres, related academic disciplines (e.g., art, drama, film, folklore, history, linguistics, and philosophy), comparative studies (comparative literature and the relations between literature and art, psychology, science, and religion), literary themes and topics (e.g., the Don Juan theme,

Arthurian studies, and American regionalism), and such professional concerns as composition and rhetoric.

The many author bibliographies for English and American writers are described in chapter 6.

GENERAL BIBLIOGRAPHIES

In addition to those general bibliographies covering all the English-language literatures, this section includes four lists of books received that collectively offer an extensive bibliography of current book publication.

Bibliographies

(A1) *MLA International Bibliography*
    See chapter 2 for a description of coverage and features, including its electronic formats. English-language literatures are covered in volume 1, which is subdivided for English, Irish, Scottish, and Welsh literature, Commonwealth (i.e., English Canadian, Australian, New Zealand) literature, American literature, and English Caribbean literature. The present degree of comprehensiveness began with the 1969 volume; for earlier years *ABELL* (B1) may provide more listings than the *MLA Bibliography*.

B1   *Annual Bibliography of English Language and Literature.* London: Mod. Humanities Research Assn., 1921– . Annual.
    Electronic format: online through Cambridge University libraries catalog, 1991– .
    An annual, comprehensive, and classified bibliography of international books, reviews, articles, and dissertations on English and American literatures, other English-language literatures, English language, folklore, bibliography, and related historical and cultural studies, for 1920– . Classification categories include broad subject areas (literature, language, folklore, bibliography) and subdivisions for literary periods, genres, individual authors, and various

aspects of language, literature, and folklore studies. American and other English-language writers are included with British writers in the appropriate literary periods. Author, critic, and selective subject indexes.

Once several years behind in its coverage, *ABELL* is now more nearly up-to-date (the volume for 1992 was published in 1994), and an electronic version covering 1991– became available in 1995. This bibliography is very useful and manageable and should be consulted along with the *MLA Bibliography*.

B2   *The Year's Work in English Studies.* Oxford: Blackwell, 1921– . Annual. (Sponsored by the English Assn., with various publishers.)

Selective and evaluative bibliographic essays on the year's international books and articles dealing with English, American, and other English-language literatures and with language for 1919– . Chapters cover the literary periods, Chaucer, Shakespeare, Milton, American literature, the other English-language literatures, literary theory, and reference and bibliography. The essays first discuss general studies and scholarly tools and then turn to the criticism on individual authors. Author, title, and subject index (the last is especially detailed starting with 1947); critic index.

B3   *Studies in English Literature, 1500–1900.* Houston: Rice U, 1961– . 4/yr.

Each issue carries a bibliographic essay on the year's international books (and occasionally articles) in one of four periods: English Renaissance (winter issue), Elizabethan and Jacobean drama (spring), Restoration and eighteenth century (summer), and nineteenth century (autumn).

B4   *Abstracts of English Studies.* Oxford: Blackwell, 1958– . 4/yr. (Formerly published by U of Calgary P, 1981–90, and NCTE, Champaign, 1958–80.)

A classified bibliography of abstracts of international, mainly English-language articles from about 500 periodicals and some monographs on general literary studies; on English, American, and other English-language literatures;

and, to a lesser extent, on world literature. The English and American sections are subdivided into literary periods (with subsections for individual authors) and four categories: particularism and regionalism, bibliography, language, and themes and types. Author, subject, and critic index in each issue.

B5   *Literary Criticism Register: A Monthly Listing of Studies in English and American Literature.* DeLand: Literary Criticism Register, 1983– . 6/yr.

Each issue lists the tables of contents of periodicals, covering some 300 English-language periodicals a year, and cites relevant books listed in *American Book Publishing Record* (New York: Bowker, 1960–); a subject index is in each issue, and indexes are cumulated annually.

B6   *English Studies: A Journal of English Language and Literature.* Lisse, Neth.: Swets en Zeitlinger, 1919– . 6/yr.

Publishes three bibliographic essays each year for 1925– , two reviewing current English-language creative writing and one English-language work in criticism, literary theory, literary history, and biography.

B7   *Dutch Quarterly Review of Anglo-American Letters.* Amsterdam: Rodopi, 1971–91. 4/yr.

The "Survey" section in each issue is a bibliographic essay on recent critical books, comparable in coverage to *Studies in English Literature, 1500–1900* (B3).

B8   *English and American Studies in German: Summaries of Theses and Monographs: A Supplement to* Anglia. Tübingen: Niemeyer, 1969– . Annual. (See B13.)

A list of books and dissertations from the German-speaking countries on linguistics, English and American literature, and the teaching of English, with abstracts (often lengthy) in English. Critic and subject indexes.

B9   *English Studies in Africa: A Journal of the Humanities.* Johannesburg: U of the Witwatersrand, 1958– . 2/yr.

The section "Select Bibliography" is an author list of books and articles by South Africans or published in South Africa on English language and literature (excluding those in *English Studies in Africa*).

B10 *Etudes anglaises: Grande-Bretagne, Etats-Unis.* Paris: Didier, 1937– . 4/yr.

"Présentation de thèse," which began in volume 21, 1968, is an annual list, with summaries, of French dissertations on English and American language and literature.

B11 *Current Research in Britain: The Humanities.* Boston Spa, Eng.: British Library Supply Centre, 1979– . Biennial. (Titled *Research in British Universities, Polytechnics, and Colleges,* 1979–84.)

Lists current British research projects in literature and the humanities by school, field, and name of researcher; includes name, classified, and keyword indexes.

Books Received

B12 *Review of English Studies: A Quarterly Journal of English Literature and the English Language.* Oxford: Clarendon, 1923– . 4/yr. (Vols. 1–15, Sidgwick, London.)

Two issues a year, starting with volume 25 (1949), list international books received, providing an extensive (over 500 books a year) record of publication on English, American, and other English-language literatures and related matters (e.g., history, printing and publishing).

(B6) *English Studies: A Journal of English Language and Literature*

An annual list of books received, starting in volume 1 (1919), is arranged by author within literary periods and includes new writing as well as criticism and scholarship.

(B48) *Philological Quarterly*

Two issues each year, starting in volume 44 (1965), list over 500 international books, arranged in sections for language, English literary periods, American literature, critical and miscellaneous studies, and classical and Continental literatures.

B13 *Anglia: Zeitschrift für englische Philologie.* Tübingen: Niemeyer, 1877– . 4/yr. (in 2 parts).

Each issue lists from 100 to 120 new international books on English and American literature, with a good representation of Continental publishers.

LITERARY PERIODS

Specialized period bibliographies can have several advantages over the more general listings in the *MLA Bibliography* (A1) and *ABELL* (B1). They are often more up-to-date, and they often provide a more extensive and varied list of citations. Their classification scheme or subject indexing can be more detailed and precise. They can give a more accurate picture of relevant scholarship, either through annotations and commentary or through the inclusion of studies on other subjects or other literatures. They can be not only a record of scholarship but also a guide to it.

This section is subdivided by period, and within each subsection the bibliographies are listed in order from most comprehensive to most specialized and from most to least readily available in North American libraries. Of the bibliographies and indexes already listed, only the *MLA International Bibliography* (A1), *ABELL* (B1), and *Year's Work in English Studies* (B2) are repeated. The other general bibliographies should be consulted, however, as should the humanities and general indexes in chapter 2, particularly the *Arts and Humanities Citation Index* (A6), *Humanities Index* (A8), *British Humanities Index* (A9), *Infotrac* (A15), *Periodical Abstracts* (A16), and *Essay and General Literature Index* (A10).

Several of the author bibliographies in chapter 6 offer valuable additional citations for the relevant periods.

Medieval

Only the comprehensive medieval bibliographies and the medieval bibliographies covering specifically English topics are listed here; therefore, see the section for medieval studies as well as the sections for art, history, manuscripts, philosophy, and religion, in chapter 5, and see the section for Chaucer in chapter 6.

(D320) *International Medieval Bibliography*

A comprehensive, classified bibliography for 1965– covering international books and articles on all aspects of medieval Europe and of the Middle East and Christian North Africa, 450–1500. Categories include art, folk studies, language, and literature (subdivided by genre and then country or region).

(D321) *Deutsches Archiv für Erforschung des Mittelalters*

Each issue, starting in the early 1930s, carries a comprehensive, classified, and annotated bibliography of international books and articles covering all aspects of medieval life.

(D322) *Cahiers de civilisation médiévale Xᵉ–XIIᵉ siècles: Bibliographie*

Carries an annual bibliography of international books and articles for 1958– .

(D323) *Medioevo latino: Bolletino bibliografico della cultura europea dal secolo VI al XIV*

A comprehensive, classified, annotated (in Italian) bibliography of international books, articles, and reviews on all aspects of the medieval world for 1980– .

(A1) *MLA International Bibliography*

See the sections for 400–1099 (Old English period), 1100–1499 (Middle English period), and related sections in part 1, volume 1, and see the appropriate sections in volume 2 for the non-English literatures as well as the subject index under the heading "Latin-language literature." Before 1981 see the sections for Old English and Middle English, the Medieval and Neo-Latin literature division, and the medieval subsection under "Literature, General and Comparative" in the general literature division.

(B1) *Annual Bibliography of English Language and Literature*

See the Old English and Middle English sections for general subjects and individual writers.

(B2) *The Year's Work in English Studies*

See chapters on Old English, Middle English, and Chaucer.

(D324) *Envoi: A Review Journal of Medieval Literature*

Each issue consists of a review article on a medieval topic, lengthy book reviews, brief notices of new books, and a list of mainly English-language books received on medieval studies.

B20   *Neuphilologische Mitteilungen: Bulletin de la Société Néophilologique / Bulletin of the Modern Language Society.* Helsinki: Mod. Lang. Soc., 1899– . 4/yr.

Publishes an annual list of international work in progress in Old English (for 1964–85/86), Middle English (for 1963–84/85), and Chaucer studies (for 1968–). The Chaucer list is also carried in *Chaucer Review* (E25).

B21   *Old English Newsletter.* Binghamton: Center for Medieval and Early Renaissance Studies, 1967– . 2/yr.

Publishes two annual bibliographies: "Old English Bibliography," 1969– , a classified bibliography of international books, articles, and dissertations, and "The Year's Work in Old English Studies," 1969– , an evaluative bibliographic essay.

B22   *Anglo-Saxon England.* Cambridge: Cambridge UP, 1971– . Annual.

Carries an extensive, classified bibliography of international books, articles, and significant reviews on all aspects of Anglo-Saxon culture. Has sections on general topics, language, literature, Anglo-Latin and ecclesiastical texts, paleography, history, numismatics, and archaeology; also book reviews. Emphasizes history, archaeology, and Anglo-Saxon culture while the *Old English Newsletter* (B21) emphasizes language and literature.

(D30) *Bibliographical Bulletin of the International Arthurian Society / Bulletin bibliographique de la Société Internationale Arthurienne*

A comprehensive, classified, annotated bibliography of international books and articles on Arthurian matters.

(D327) *Bulletin bibliographique de la Société Rencesvals*

A classified bibliography of international books, reviews, and articles on the medieval romance for 1958– .

(D328) *Olifant: A Publication of the Société Rencesvals, American-Canadian Branch*

Carries a quarterly checklist of books, reviews, North American dissertations, and articles on the medieval romance for 1966– .

B23   *Medieval English Theatre.* Lancaster, Eng.: Lancaster U, 1979– . Annual (vols. 1–12, 2/yr.).

Most issues include a list of books received and reports of recent productions of medieval plays.

(B36) *Research Opportunities in Renaissance Drama*

Lists current research projects in medieval drama for 1956–84 in volumes 1–22, 1956–85, and many issues include bibliographies on figures and subjects of medieval drama. Also reviews recent international productions of English medieval plays in volumes 10, 11, and 13– (1967–).

(E100) *The Yearbook of Langland Studies*

The "Annual Bibliography" lists new international books, articles, dissertations, and book reviews covering medieval alliterative poetry as well as Langland studies.

(D330) *Medieval Feminist Newsletter*

Each issue carries a bibliography of relevant international books and articles.

B24 *Speculum: A Journal of Medieval Studies.* Cambridge: Medieval Acad. of America, 1926– . 4/yr.

"Bibliography of Editions and Translations in Progress of Medieval Texts," in volumes 48– (1973–), is an annual subject list of mainly North American and British projects. A classified list of American periodical literature on medieval studies appears in most issues from 1934 to 1972.

B25 *The Year's Work in Medievalism.* Holland: Hope Coll.; Rochester: Boydell and Brewer. Projected annual.

Renaissance and Seventeenth Century

The major Renaissance bibliography—the *Bibliographie internationale de l'humanisme et de la Renaissance* (D432), listed in chapter 5 along with other general Renaissance studies bibliographies—is a comprehensive compilation of international studies on all Renaissance literature and Renaissance subjects. *Renaissance Quarterly* (D433) has a less comprehensive but still valuable list of current books on the Renaissance, and the *MLA International Bibliography* (A1) covers literary studies, although its coverage is spread over two volumes and, in English literature, over two sections. In addition to the other English literary bibliographies included here, see the bibliographies for the Continental literatures in chapter 4 for full coverage of this period. Several subject bibliographies listed in chapter 5 should be of use, especially those for art, history, libraries, philosophy, printing, religion, and science. Author bibliographies for Shakespeare, Cervantes, Racine, and Luther are also useful because of their broad coverage (see ch. 6).

(D432) *Bibliographie internationale de l'humanisme et de la Renaissance*

A comprehensive, classified bibliography of international books and articles on all aspects of the European and Latin American Renaissance—history, religion and philosophy, the arts, literature and language, science and technology, and individuals—for 1965– . Critic index.

(A1)   *MLA International Bibliography*

See subsections 1500–99 and 1600–99 for English literature in volume 1, and see comparable sections in volume 2 for French, Italian (1400–99), German, Scandinavian, and Spanish literature as well as the subject index under such terms as *Siglo de oro*. In addition there is a section for the Renaissance under "Literary Movements" in volume 4. Comprehensive coverage of the period dates from the 1969 bibliography; before 1969 the major Renaissance literary bibliography appeared in *Studies in Philology* (B31).

B31   *Studies in Philology*. Chapel Hill: U of North Carolina P, 1906– . 5/yr.

Volumes 14–66 (1917–69) include an annual, international, comprehensive, and classified bibliography of books and articles on Renaissance literature for 1917–68.

(D433) *Renaissance Quarterly*

The list "Books Received" in each issue records about 200 to 300 international books dealing with the Renaissance each year; in issues from 1952 to 1980 this feature is titled "Renaissance Books" and is an extensive, classified list of new international books drawn from entries in national bibliographies. The section "Reports on Scholarship," which appears irregularly throughout volumes

16–21 (1963–68), contains review articles of current work on a wide range of Renaissance topics.

(B1)   *Annual Bibliography of English Language and Literature*

See chapters on sixteenth- and seventeenth-century literature.

(B2)   *The Year's Work in English Studies*

See chapters on the earlier sixteenth century, Shakespeare, English drama 1550–1660 (excluding Shakespeare), the later sixteenth century (excluding drama), the earlier seventeenth century (excluding drama), and Milton.

(B3)   *Studies in English Literature, 1550–1900*

See the sections "Recent Studies in the English Renaissance" (winter) and "Recent Studies in Elizabeth and Jacobean Drama" (spring).

B33   *Seventeenth-Century News.* College Station: Texas A&M U, 1941– . 4/yr. (Vols. 1–42, Pennsylvania State U, University Park.)

Each issue carries abstracts of recent articles and dissertations on Milton, Donne, Jonson, Dryden, and other seventeenth-century English and American authors and literary subjects. A separate section provides similar coverage for Neo-Latin studies.

B34   *English Literary Renaissance.* Amherst: U of Massachusetts, 1971– . 3/yr.

Each issue carries a bibliographic article on an English Renaissance figure, listing editions and studies on general issues, special topics, and individual works.

B35   Manuscripta: *A Journal for Manuscript Research.* Saint Louis: Saint Louis U, 1957– . 3/yr.

The annual section "A Review of [the year's] Contributions to English Renaissance Textual Studies," in volumes 7–28 (1963–84), covers work for 1962–83 on relevant texts, excluding Shakespeare's.

B36   *Research Opportunities in Renaissance Drama.* Lawrence: U of Kansas, 1956– . Annual. (Titled *Opportunities for Research in Renaissance Drama,* 1956–64.)

The section "Current Projects" lists dissertations, books, and articles in progress in Renaissance and medieval drama, chiefly but not exclusively in English, through volume 27 (1985). Continues to publish bibliographies on figures and subjects in Renaissance and medieval drama, which along with critical articles are cited in Christopher J. Thaiss, "An Index to Volumes I–XVI of *Research Opportunities in Renaissance Drama*," *Research Opportunities in Renaissance Drama* 17 (1974): 34–44; and Maureen Godman, "An Index to Volumes XVII–XXX of *Research Opportunities in Renaissance Drama*," *Research Opportunities in Renaissance Drama* 31 (1992): 105–14.

"Productions of Renaissance Drama," in volumes 15/16 (1974–), reviews recent international productions of English Renaissance plays, and "Productions of Medieval Drama," in volumes 10, 11, and 13– (1967–), does the same for English medieval plays.

B37 Cahiers Elisabéthains: *Late Medieval and Renaissance English Studies*. Montpellier: Centre d'Etudes et de Recherches Elisabéthaines du l'Université Paul Valéry, 1972– . 2/yr.

Each issue reviews recent productions (mainly in Great Britain) of Renaissance Elizabethan and Stuart plays.

B38 *Shakespearean Research and Opportunities*. New York: City U of New York, 1965–74. Irregular.

A classified, comprehensive, and annotated bibliography of international books, articles, and dissertations on a great variety of Elizabethan and Renaissance intellectual issues, such as education, ethics, law, medicine, the arts, and theology. Issues of the bibliography have been collected in W. R. Elton and Giselle Neuschloss, *Shakespeare's World: Renaissance Intellectual Contexts: A Selective, Annotated Guide, 1966–71* (New York: Garland, 1979).

B40 *Elizabethan Bibliographies Supplements*. London: Nether, 1967–71. Irregular.

Each of the 18 issues is a bibliography of editions and studies for individual Elizabethan writers published from the 1930s to the late 1960s. Subject, format, and coverage vary from volume to volume. The issues supplement S. A. Tannenbaum and D. R. Tannenbaum, *Elizabethan Bibliographies* (10 vols., 1937–50; rpt. Port Washington: Kennikat, 1967).

Restoration and Eighteenth Century

The major bibliography of this period—*The Eighteenth Century: A Current Bibliography* (B42)—covers English, Continental, Latin American, and other literatures and includes nonliterary subjects. The *MLA International Bibliography* (A1), *ABELL* (B1), and *The Year's Work in English Studies* (B2) divide their coverage by century, so one must use both the seventeenth- and the eighteenth-century sections. *The Year's Work in Modern Language Studies* (C1) covers Continental literatures. The *Johnsonian News Letter* (B44), the *Scriblerian and the Kit-Cats* (B45), and *Restoration* (B46) provide good coverage of individual authors and of relevant genres and topics. See also the sections in chapter 5 for art, history, libraries, journalism, periodicals, philosophy, printing, religion, science, and women's studies; the author listings in chapter 6; and appropriate sections of chapter 4.

B42   *The Eighteenth Century: A Current Bibliography.* New York: AMS, 1979– . Annual.

    An annual, annotated, and classified bibliography of international books and articles on all aspects of eighteenth-century life in Europe, Great Britain (including the Restoration period), North and South America, and Asia for 1925– . Covers history, society, economics, philosophy, science, religion, and fine arts as well as literature, printing, bibliography, and individual authors. The authors covered include several not primarily associated with literature, such as Hume, Kant, and Leibnitz. Each entry is annotated, and the annotations for books are lengthy and evaluative. The bibliography for 1975 was published at Philadelphia by the American Society for Eighteenth-Century Studies, 1978; bibliographies for 1925–74 appear in volumes 5–54 (1926–75) of *Philological Quarterly* (B48).

    The bibliographies for 1925–69 are collected in Ronald S. Crane and others, *English Literature, 1660–1800: A Bibliography of Modern Studies*, 6 volumes (Princeton: Princeton UP, 1950–72).

(A1)   *MLA International Bibliography*
See the subsections for 1600–99 and 1700–99 under both English and American literature and also under the relevant literatures in volume 2; before 1981 see the sections for the seventeenth and eighteenth centuries.

(B1)   *Annual Bibliography of English Language and Literature*
See the sections for the seventeenth and eighteenth centuries.

(B2)   *The Year's Work in English Studies*
See the chapters for the Restoration and the eighteenth century and for American literature.

(B3)   *Studies in English Literature, 1500–1900*
See "Recent Studies in Restoration and Eighteenth Century" in the summer issue.

B44   *Johnsonian News Letter.* Chicago: U of Chicago, 1940– . 4/yr. (nominally; usually in two physical issues). (Vols. 1–49, Columbia U, New York.)

Each issue includes an extensive classified bibliography of 250 to 300 recent English-language books and articles on eighteenth-century English and American literature, with sections for genres, contexts (e.g., printing and publishing; political, social, and economic history; philosophy and theology; women's studies), and individual authors. Before the combined volumes 45.3–4 and 46.1 (1985–86), this bibliography was a less elaborate list of recent work.

B45   *Scriblerian and the Kit-Cats.* Philadelphia: Temple U, 1969– . 2/yr. (Titled *Scriblerian: A Newsjournal Devoted to Pope and Swift and Their Circle*, 1969–71.)

Each issue consists of annotated lists of international books and articles on Pope, Swift, Dryden, the Kit-Cats, Defoe, Fielding, Richardson, Sterne, Smollett, and related figures and subjects. Items are arranged under "Foreign Reviews" and "Recent Studies." A subject and critic index, published every fifth year (for 1968–83), is in effect a bibliography of studies of Restoration and early-eighteenth-century English literature.

B46   *Restoration: Studies in English Literary Culture, 1660–1700.* Knoxville: U of Tennessee, 1977– . 2/yr.

The section "Some Current Publications" in each issue is an annotated list of books, articles, and dissertations on English and American Restoration figures. Items are listed under subject authors, general literature (with subdivisions for anthologies, editions, compilations, bibliographies, etc.), and general issues (history, philosophy, politics, religion, science, pedagogy, and other arts). Each issue also lists abstracts of recent papers.

B47 *Restoration and Eighteenth Century Theatre Research.* Chicago: Loyola U, 1962– . 2/yr. (Publication lapsed after vol. 16, 1977, and resumed with ns vol. 1, in 1986.)

"Restoration and Eighteenth Century Theatre Research Bibliography" in volumes 1–16 (1962–77) and "Selective Bibliography" in ns 4–6 (1989–91) are annual, classified, and annotated bibliographies of international books, articles, and dissertations for 1961–77 and 1986–90, arranged by subject (e.g., acting, sentimentalism, and names of playwrights and actors). Bibliographies for 1961–67 have been cumulated in Carl J. Stratman, editor, *Restoration and Eighteenth Century Theatre Research Bibliography, 1961–1968* (Troy: Whitston, 1969) and in Carl J. Stratman, David G. Spencer, and Mary Elizabeth Devine, editors, *Restoration and Eighteenth Century Theatre Research: A Bibliographical Guide, 1900–1968* (Carbondale: Southern Illinois UP, 1971).

B48 *Philological Quarterly.* Iowa City: U of Iowa, 1922– . 4/yr.

Volumes 55–59 (1976–80) each include four to six review articles that cover international books and articles in Augustan and eighteenth-century studies.

Romantic

There are two exemplary bibliographies for the Romantic period: *The Romantic Movement: A Selective and Critical Bibliography* (B51) and the annual compilation in the *Keats-Shelley Journal* (B52). They are comprehensive, covering Continental Romanticism, the arts, politics, science, and society as well as literature, and they have thorough subject classification or subject indexing. Coverage of the period in the *MLA International Bibliography* (A1) and *ABELL* (B1) and in *The Year's Work in English Studies* (B2) is comprehensive but less conveniently arranged: there is no separate section for the Romantic period and the Romantics and pre-Romantics are put in separate sections (Blake, for example, is listed as an eighteenth-century writer in these publications). Pre-Romantics and certain Romantic writers are also covered in *The Eighteenth Century: A Current Bibliography* (B42). Several of the Romantics have individual author bibliographies (see ch. 6). See chapter 5 for subject bibliographies and chapter 4 for bibliographies of the Continental literatures.

B51   *The Romantic Movement: A Selective and Critical Bibliography.* West Cornwall: Locust Hill, 1980– . Annual. (Vols. for 1979–86 published by Garland, New York, 1980–87.)

An annotated bibliography for 1936– providing an extensive selection of international books, reviews, articles, and dissertations that comprehensively cover all aspects of the movement in England, France, Germany, Italy, and Spain. Arranged in sections for the countries and then for individual authors; for studies on the social, intellectual, political, scientific, and artistic environment; and for bibliographies. The bibliographies for 1964–78 are in volumes 3–17 of *English Language Notes* (Boulder: U of Colorado, 1963–79), for 1949–63 in volumes, 29–43 of *Philological Quarterly* (1950–64, B48), and for 1936–48 in volumes 4–16 of *ELH: A Journal of English Literary History* (Baltimore: Johns Hopkins UP, 1937–49).

The Romantic bibliography has been collected in A. C. Elkins, Jr., and L. J. Forstner, editors, *The Romantic Movement Bibliography, 1936–1970*, 7 volumes (Ann Arbor: Pierian, 1973).

B52   *Keats-Shelley Journal: Keats, Shelley, Byron, Hunt, and Their Circles.* New York: Keats-Shelley Assn. of America, 1952– . Annual.

Includes an annual bibliography of international editions and studies (books, reviews, articles) of the younger

English Romantics—Keats, Shelley, Byron, Hunt, Hazlitt, and their circles—and of Romanticism in general. Most entries have a one-sentence annotation. There are author, critic, and subject indexes.

The bibliographies for 1950–74 have been collected (but not cumulated) in David B. Green and Edwin G. Wilson, editors, *Keats, Shelley, Byron, Hunt, and Their Circles: A Bibliography: July 1, 1950–June 30, 1962* (Lincoln: U of Nebraska P, 1964) and in Robert A. Hartley, editor, *Keats, Shelley, Byron, Hunt, and Their Circles: A Bibliography: July 1, 1962–December 31, 1974* (Lincoln: U of Nebraska P, 1978).

(A1)   *MLA International Bibliography*

See the sections for 1700–99 and 1800–99 under English and American literature in volume 1 and under the Continental literatures in volume 2; also see the section on Romanticism under "Literary Movements" in volume 4 as well as the subject index under such headings as "Romantic period." Before 1981 see the sections for the eighteenth and nineteenth centuries.

(B1)   *Annual Bibliography of English Language and Literature*

See the sections on eighteenth- and nineteenth-century English literature.

(B2)   *The Year's Work in English Studies*

See the chapters on the eighteenth and nineteenth centuries.

(B3)   *Studies in English Literature, 1500–1900*

See "Recent Studies in the Nineteenth Century" in the autumn issue.

Victorian and Transition

In addition to the very comprehensive "Victorian Bibliography" in *Victorian Studies* (B54) and the *Annual Bibliography of Victorian Studies* (B55) which cover the arts, history, government, religion, philosophy, and other aspects of nineteenth-century British culture, there are several valuable, specialized bibliographies on poetry, prose, periodicals, theater, and transition figures, as well as the *MLA International Bibliography* (A1), *ABELL* (B1), and *The Year's Work in English Studies* (B2). Several of the subject bibliographies in chapter 5 are important, and author bibliographies are listed in chapter 6. See also the sections on American and other English-language literatures in this chapter.

B54   *Victorian Studies*. Bloomington: Indiana U, 1957– . 4/yr.

"Victorian Bibliography" is an annual, classified bibliography for 1932– that provides, in addition to bibliography and studies on individual authors, an extensive selection of international books, reviews, articles, and dissertations that comprehensively cover most aspects of the Victorian period in England, including the arts, economics, education, history, literature, religion, science, and sociology. The bibliography for 1932–56 appears in volumes 30–54 of *Modern Philology* (Chicago: U of Chicago, 1933–57).

Cumulated in Richard C. Tobias, editor, *Bibliographies of Studies in Victorian Literature for the Ten Years 1975–1984* (New York: AMS, 1991); Ronald E. Freeman, editor, *Bibliographies of Studies in Victorian Literature for the Ten Years 1965–1974* (New York: AMS, 1981); Robert C. Slack, editor, *Bibliographies of Studies in Victorian Literature for the Ten Years 1955–1964* (Urbana: U of Illinois P, 1967); Austin Wright, editor, *Bibliographies of Studies in Victorian Literature for the Ten Years 1945–1954* (Urbana: U of Illinois P, 1956); and William D. Templeman, editor, *Bibliographies of Studies in Victorian Literature for the Thirteen Years 1932–1944* (Urbana: U of Illinois P, 1945).

B55   *Annual Bibliography of Victorian Studies*. Edmonton: LITIR Database, 1981– . Annual.

An annual bibliography of international books, reviews, articles, and dissertations for 1976– that comprehensively covers the arts, philosophy and religion, the social sciences, history, and science and technology, as well as the literature, of 1830–1914. There are subject, title, and book-reviewer indexes. Cumulated in Brahma Chaudhari, editor, *A Cumulative Bibliography of Victorian Studies, 1985–1989* (Edmonton: LITIR, 1990), *A Cumulative Bibliography of Victorian Studies,*

1970–1984, 2 volumes (Edmonton: LITIR, 1988), and *A Cumulated Index to Reviews of Books on Victorian Studies, 1975–1989* (Edmonton: LITIR, 1990).

(A1)   *MLA International Bibliography*

See the section for 1800–99 under English and American literature in volume 1 and under appropriate other literatures in volume 2. For material that specifically mentions Victorian literature, see the subject index under "Victorian period."

(B1)   *Annual Bibliography of English Language and Literature*

See the section on nineteenth-century English literature.

(B2)   *The Year's Work in English Studies*

See the chapter on nineteenth-century English literature; a separate chapter covers nineteenth-century American literature.

(B3)   *Studies in English Literature, 1500–1900*

See "Recent Studies in the Nineteenth Century" in the autumn issue.

B56   *Victorian Newsletter.* Bowling Green: Western Kentucky U, 1952– . 2/yr. (Formerly published by New York U, New York.)

"Recent Publications: A Selected List," in each issue, 1952–78, lists books and articles on individual English authors, criticism and literary history, and bibliography; "Books Received," 1979– , provides an extensive list of relevant new publications.

B57   *Victorian Poetry: A Critical Journal of Victorian Literature.* Morgantown: West Virginia U, 1963– . 4/yr.

"Guide to the Year's Work in Victorian Poetry" is an annual bibliographic essay, 1962– , covering the year's international books and articles on poetry and, frequently, prose. Sections, written by different scholars, deal with general issues and individual authors.

B58   *Victorian Periodicals Review.* Toronto: Research Soc. for Victorian Periodicals, 1968– . 4/yr. (Titled *Victorian Periodicals Newsletter*, 1968–78.)

"Victorian Periodicals [year]: An Annotated Bibliography," in volumes 6– (1973–), is an annual compilation of

North American and British books and articles on Victorian periodicals for 1971– . Critic and subject index.

B59   *Nineteenth Century Theatre.* Amherst: U of Massachusetts, 1973– . 2/yr. (Vols. 1–14 titled *Nineteenth Century Theatre Research* and published by the U of Arizona, Tucson.)

An annotated list of books received appears in each issue, volumes 15– . "Nineteenth-Century Theatre Research: A Bibliography," which was published annually in volumes 1–10 (1973–82), lists international books, articles, and dissertations about subjects such as acting, audience, Australian theater, and persons for 1972–81. A newsletter that supplements volumes 1–10 lists works in progress and items overlooked in the annual listing. Critic index.

B60   *English Literature in Transition, 1880–1920.* Tempe: Arizona State U, 1957– . 4/yr.

"Bibliography, News, and Notes," in volumes 1–18 (1957–75), is an annual bibliography of international books, reviews, and articles on transition period writers for 1956–74; it contains annotations for articles and long reviews. Since 1975 the journal has published bibliographical articles on individual transition figures.

(D385) *Prose Studies: History, Theory, Criticism*

The journal published a bibliography of prose studies for 1977–78 covering Victorian nonfiction prose.

Twentieth Century

The current indexes described in chapter 2 are especially helpful for twentieth-century and contemporary literature, as are the specialized bibliographies for transition and modernist literature listed here. See also sections in chapter 5 on the literary genres and on such subjects as the alternative press, censorship, children's literature, comparative literature, creative writing, film, little magazines, periodicals, science fiction, and women's studies. Author bibliographies are listed in chapter 6.

(A1)   *MLA International Bibliography*

See the section for 1900–99 under English, American, and other English-language literatures; there are also sections for modernism and postmodernism under "Literary Movements" in volume 4.

(B1) *Annual Bibliography of English Language and Literature*

The chapter on the twentieth century covers English, American, and other English-language literatures.

(B2) *The Year's Work in English Studies*

One chapter covers British twentieth-century literature; separate chapters cover American and other English-language literatures.

(B60) *English Literature in Transition, 1880–1920*

Volumes 1–18 provide an annual bibliography of transition figures for 1956–74.

B65 *Journal of Modern Literature.* Philadelphia: Temple U, 1970– . 4/yr.

Carries an annual, classified bibliography providing an extensive selection of international, mainly English-language scholarship on modern (1885–1950) and contemporary world writers for 1970– , emphasizing British and American figures. Lists books, articles, dissertations, symposia and special numbers, and miscellaneous information (such as library holdings, conferences, and important sales). Categories include bibliography, literary history, themes and movements, comparison studies, criticism, film as literature, and individual writers. Author and critic index.

B66 *Twentieth Century Literature: A Scholarly and Critical Journal.* Hempstead: Hofstra UP, 1955– . 4/yr.

Most issues through volume 27, number 2 (1981), include an annotated bibliography of international, mainly English-language articles on twentieth-century world writers. Items are listed by subject (such as American fiction, criticism, and Marxism) and by subject author. The bibliographies for 1954–70 have been augmented and cumulated in David Pownall, *Articles on Twentieth Century Literature: An Annotated Bibliography*, 7 volumes (New York: Kraus, 1973–82).

(D177) *Modern Drama*

Carries an annual bibliography for 1959– of studies on international twentieth-century world drama and dramatists.

B67   *Contemporary Literary Criticism: Excerpts from Criticism of the Works of Today's Novelists, Poets, Playwrights, and Other Creative Writers.* Detroit: Gale, 1973– . Irregular, now usually 5/yr.

Selective excerpts from English-language books, articles, and reviews on literary figures who are living or who died after 1959, mainly covering English and American writers but also including writers from other countries and and writers who worked in other languages. Unlike the *MLA International Bibliography* (A1) and *ABELL* (B1), the periodical indexes, and *Essay and General Literature Index* (A10), *CLC* includes passages as well as chapters and articles and also selects from significant reviews; thus, it often has criticism not cited in other bibliographies. Cumulative author and critic indexes in each volume and a separate index of titles.

AMERICAN LITERATURE

The current indexes listed in chapter 2 cover American literature; one should use them as well as the *MLA International Bibliography* (A1) and *ABELL* (B1) and relevant period bibliographies. Many of the subject bibliographies listed in chapter 5 are essential. See, for example, the literary genres and the sections for African American studies, American studies, children's literature, ethnic studies, film, journalism, little magazines, periodicals, regionalism, science fiction, and women's studies. *The Year's Work in English Studies* (B2) offers a corrective—or at least a stimulating alternative—to Americans' view of their own literature, and it, along with *American Literary Scholarship* (B72), not only reviews and evaluates the year's criticism but also comments on such matters as the state of editions, manuscripts, archives, and bibliography. Most of the major, and numerous minor, authors have author bibliographies (ch. 6).

(A1)   *MLA International Bibliography*

The American literature section of volume 1 is subdivided into 1500–99, 1600–99, 1700–99, 1800–99, and

1900–99, and each section lists scholarship on genres and individual authors.

B71 *American Literature: A Journal of Literary History, Criticism, and Bibliography*. Durham: Duke UP, 1929– . 4/yr.

"Articles on American Literature Appearing in Current Periodicals," a selective list of articles on major authors and general issues, appeared in each issue from volume 1, number 3, through volume 53, number 4 (1929–82), and was succeeded by an abbreviated bibliography, "A Select, Annotated List of Current Articles on American Literature," from volume 54, number 1, through volume 62, number 4 (1982–90). Dissertations and other projects were listed separately as "Works in Progress" through volume 51, number 2 (1979).

The bibliographic lists are cumulated and augmented in Lewis Leary and John Auchard, *Articles on American Literature, 1968–1975* (Durham: Duke UP, 1979); Lewis Leary, Carolyn Bartholet, and Catherine Roth, *Articles on American Literature, 1950–1967* (Durham: Duke UP, 1970); and Lewis Leary, *Articles on American Literature, 1900–1950* (Durham: Duke UP, 1954).

(B1) *Annual Bibliography of English Language and Literature*

Books, reviews, articles, and dissertations on American authors are included in the appropriate literary century along with those on British and other English-language writers.

B72 *American Literary Scholarship: An Annual*. Durham: Duke UP, 1965– . Annual.

Evaluative bibliographic essays on the year's work in American literature for 1963– . The annual is arranged in two parts, the first containing chapters on individual major authors, the second containing chapters on periods, genres, and related subjects (folklore, 1963–74; African American literature, 1975–88; foreign scholarship, 1974– ; and themes, topics, and criticism, 1966–). The chapters on individual authors comment on editions, bibliographical materials, biographical studies, and criticism (books and articles); the other chapters note general studies, and the chapter on themes, topics, and criticism is a particularly useful survey of trends in American literary theory. No subject index; author and critic indexes.

(B2) *The Year's Work in English Studies*

Studies on American literature are surveyed in two chapters (one chapter in vols. 35–48).

(D16) *American Quarterly*

Volumes 7–25 (1955–73) include an annual list of articles on American studies, 1954–72.

(B33) *Seventeenth-Century News*

"Americana Abstracts" is a list of abstracts of current articles on seventeenth-century American literature.

(B42) *The Eighteenth Century: A Current Bibliography*

Includes books and articles on American literature and individual authors of the eighteenth century.

B73 *Studies in the American Renaissance.* Charlottesville: UP of Virginia, 1978– . Annual. (Vols. numbered 1977– ; first 5 vols. published by Twayne, Boston.)

The section "Books Received" for 1976– in volumes 1977– (published 1978–) lists English-language books on the transcendentalists and on the literature, history, and culture of New England and the mid-nineteenth-century United States.

B74 *American Renaissance Literary Report.* Hartford: Transcendental, 1987– . Annual.

Most of the annual volumes include checklists that update standard bibliographies of the major transcendentalist figures.

B75 *Legacy: A Journal of American Women Writers.* Amherst: U of Massachusetts, 1984– . 2/yr. (Subtitled *A Journal of Nineteenth-Century American Women Writers*, issues 2.2 through 8.1.)

The "Legacy Bookshelf" in each issue is a classified list of current books, articles, and dissertations on American women writers (restricted to nineteenth-century American women writers through issue 8.1); there are sections for studies of individual writers, general literature, and diaries and journals, and there is a list of current dissertations.

(B65) *Journal of Modern Literature*

The annual bibliography on modern (1885–1950) and contemporary writers includes Americans.

(B66) *Twentieth Century Literature: A Scholarly and Critical Journal*

The quarterly bibliography for 1954–80 included studies on twentieth-century American authors.

(D177) *Modern Drama*

The annual bibliography for 1959– includes twentieth-century American dramatists.

(B67) *Contemporary Literary Criticism: Excerpts from the Criticism of the Works of Today's Novelists, Poets, Playwrights, and Other Creative Writers*

Coverage includes studies of contemporary American authors.

B76 *American Literature Abstracts: A Review of Current Scholarship in the Field of American Literature*. San Jose: California State Coll., 1967–72. 2/yr.

A compilation of abstracts of articles on American literature, arranged by period and then by subject author. A separate section in each issue summarizes major reviews of 5 to 10 recent books.

OTHER ENGLISH-LANGUAGE LITERATURES

The other English-language literatures include those of Africa, Australia and New Zealand, the Caribbean, Canada, India, Ireland, Malta, Scotland, Southeast Asia, and Wales. They are covered in the major comprehensive bibliographies such as the *MLA International Bibliography* (A1) but also in numerous specialized bibliographies, especially the *Journal of Commonwealth Literature* (B80) and *The Year's Work in English Studies* (B2). See also the appropriate bibliographies in the sections for African, French Caribbean and Latin American, and Asian literatures in chapter 4.

New creative writing is indexed in the general periodical indexes (ch. 2) and the *Index to Commonwealth Little Magazines* (D301); in the literary bibliographies and periodical indexes of Australia, Canada, New Zealand, and South Africa; in *Callaloo* (D1); and in the annual bibliography in the *Journal of Commonwealth Literature* (B80). In addition, the general periodical indexes in chapter 2 include Canadian and Australian little magazines in their coverage and several of the indexes of specific literatures listed below also include new writing.

General

(A1)   *MLA International Bibliography*
      Coverage is comprehensive but distributed throughout the volumes. Studies of Irish, Scottish, and Welsh literature are included in the section for British and Irish literatures in volume 1; the Commonwealth section in this volume contains studies on Australian, Canadian, and New Zealand literature; and listings in the English Caribbean section include those for each English-speaking Caribbean country.
      The English literatures of Africa and Asia are listed in volume 2. Within the Asian literature section are subsections for India, Pakistan, Sri Lanka, the Philippines, Singapore, Papua New Guinea, Malaysia, and Indonesia, and in the African section are subsections for Ghana, Kenya, Liberia, Nigeria, and South Africa. English-language literature from countries that are not English-speaking can be found by using the subject index under the heading "English-language literature." French Caribbean, French Canadian, and Latin American literatures are also covered in volume 2.

(B1)   *Annual Bibliography of English Language and Literature*
      English-language writers from all countries are included in the century-by-century coverage.

B80   *Journal of Commonwealth Literature.* Oxford: Zell, 1965– . 3/yr.

The "Annual Bibliography of Commonwealth Literature" for 1964– is a classified bibliography of international creative writing, belles lettres, and critical books and articles on individual authors and on the literature of various other English-language countries.

(B2)　*The Year's Work in English Studies*

Starting with volume 63 (1983, for 1982), the annual devotes a separate chapter to new literatures in English; earlier volumes include selective coverage of these literatures with coverage of English writers.

(D301)　*Index to Commonwealth Little Magazines*

Indexes 15 British, Australian, Canadian, and Tanzanian little magazines; coverage includes critical and bibliographical articles and book reviews as well as new writing.

(B65)　*Journal of Modern Literature*

The annual bibliography for 1970– includes studies on modern (1885–1950) and contemporary English-language writers.

(B66)　*Twentieth Century Literature: A Scholarly and Critical Journal*

A quarterly bibliography for 1954–80 includes coverage of twentieth-century English-language writers.

(D177)　*Modern Drama*

The annual bibliography for 1959– includes coverage of twentieth-century English-language dramatists.

(B67)　*Contemporary Literary Criticism: Excerpts from Criticism of the Works of Today's Novelists, Poets, Playwrights, and Other Creative Writers*

Coverage emphasizes contemporary English-language writers.

Africa

(D1)　*Callaloo: A Journal of Afro-American and African Arts and Letters*

"Studies in African Literatures and Oratures: An Annual Annotated Bibliography," in volumes 9– (1987–), is a classified bibliography of international books, articles, and dissertations (from *Dissertation Abstracts International*) on all

African literatures for 1985– and includes new writing as well as criticism and scholarship.

B83   *Index to South African Periodicals / Repertorium van Suid-Afrikaanse tydskrifartikels.* Johannesburg: Public Library, 1940– . Annual.

Electronic format: online (SABINET [South African Library Network System], 1986–).

An author and subject index to about 500 periodicals in all fields.

(D185) *South African Theatre Journal: SATJ*

"A Bibliography of South African Theatre" is a biennial list for 1987– . (Author has not examined the bibliography.)

Australia

B85   *Australian Literary Studies.* Saint Lucia: U of Queensland P, 1963– . 2/yr.

The "Annual Bibliography of Studies on Australian Literature" for 1963– , in volumes 2– (1964–), lists international books and articles on Australian literary figures, works, and subjects and on Australian culture in general. North American studies have generally been excluded since coverage started in *Antipodes* (B86). The author entries, but not the general entries, are cumulated in *The ALS Guide to Australian Writers: A Bibliography, 1963–1990,* edited by Martin Duwell and others (Saint Lucia: U of Queensland P, 1992).

Also lists new books by contemporary writers, with reviews.

B86   *Antipodes: A North American Journal of Australian Literature.* Austin: Harry Ransom Center, U of Texas, 1987– . 2/yr.

The "Bibliography of Australian Literature and Criticism Published in North America," in volumes 3– (1989–), lists works by Australian writers, with reviews, along with critical books and articles published in North America on Australian writers and on literature in general for 1989– .

B87   *Pinpointer: A Current Guide to Popular Periodicals.* Adelaide: Libraries Board of South Austral., 1963– . 6/yr.

Author and subject index to general-interest Australian periodicals, although with relatively little coverage of literature.

B88   *Index to Australian Book Reviews*. Adelaide: Libraries Board of South Austral., 1965–81. 4/yr.

Indexes book reviews carried in Australian journals of books by Australians, published in Australia, or of Australian interest, with an emphasis on books in literature, humanities, and social sciences.

Canada

For French-language literature of Quebec, see the section on French and Francophone literature in chapter 4.

B90   *Canadian Book Review Annual*. Toronto: Simon, 1975– . Annual.

Brief evaluative reviews of Canadian English-language books are listed in five classes: reference, humanities and fine arts, literature, social sciences, and science and technology. Literature covered includes novels, short stories, poetry, drama, criticism, folklore, mythology, and children's literature. Humanities includes language, linguistics and philosophy, theater, cinema, and radio and television. Author, title, and subject indexes.

B91   *University of Toronto Quarterly*. Toronto: U of Toronto, 1932– . 4/yr.

"Letters in Canada" is an annual, evaluative bibliographic essay surveying the year's fiction, poetry, drama, and belles lettres for 1935– . Covers both French and English writing and includes a section on work in other languages. Author index to the books surveyed.

B92   *Canadian Literary Periodicals Index*. Teeswater, ON: Reference, 1994– . Annual.

Electronic format: CD-ROM (Reference, 1984–87, 1992–). Includes all indexing here and in *Canadian Literature Index* (B93).

An author and subject index for 1992– to 95 Canadian literary periodicals and the literary articles in the Toronto

Globe and Mail. Continues coverage of the *Canadian Literature Index* (B93).

B93   *Canadian Literature Index*. Toronto: ECW, 1985–88. 4/yr.

Provides an index to primary and secondary literature for 1984–87 by author and subject in about 100 international periodicals, including the major Canadian titles. Continues coverage in *The Annotated Bibliography of Canada's Major Authors* (Downsview, ON: ECW, 1979– ; irregular, 8 vols. to date), each volume of which provides an extensive primary and secondary bibliography of Canada's French- and English-language authors through 1978.

(D85)   *Canadian Review of Comparative Literature / Revue canadienne de littérature comparée*

"Preliminary Bibliography of Comparative Canadian Literature (English-Canadian and French-Canadian)," an annual classified list in volumes 3–14 (1976–87), covers books, articles, and dissertations on relations between French Canadian and English Canadian literatures for 1976–86. The first bibliography was retrospective; subsequent ones cover each year's work in the field. Cumulated in Antoine Sirois et al., *Bibliography of Studies in Comparative Canadian Literature / Bibliographie d'etudes de littérature canadienne comparée, 1930–1987* (Sherbrooke, PQ: Université de Sherbrooke, 1989). One "Supplementary Bibliography of Comparative Canadian Literature" has appeared in the journal since this cumulation.

B94   *Journal of Canadian Fiction*. Guelph, ON: Journal of Canadian Fiction, 1972– . 4/yr.

Includes "Canadian Literature: An Annotated Bibliography / Littérature canadienne: Une bibliographie avec commentaire," an annual, classified list of international (but mainly Canadian) books, reviews, articles, and dissertations on all aspects of Canadian literature for 1972–75.

B95   *Canadian Literature*. Vancouver: U of British Columbia, 1959– . 4/yr.

Numbers 7–48 (1960–71) include "Canadian Literature," an annual list of the year's critical and creative writing by and about Canadians in French and English for

1959–70, an important period in the history of Canadian literature.

B96 *Canadian Poetry: Studies, Documents, Reviews.* London, ON: Canadian Poetry, 1977– . 2/yr.

Numbers 2–20 include "The Year's Work in Canadian Poetry Studies," an annotated list of international books and articles on Canadian poetry and poets for 1976–86.

(D199) *Canada On Stage*

Surveys the year's theater work in Canada for 1974– , including a record of professional and not-for-profit production arranged by province and then by company or theater.

(D219) *Yearbook of German-American Studies*

The annual bibliography includes German Canadian studies.

(C44) *Italica*

Includes an annual bibliography of Italian American and Italian Canadian studies.

B97 *Canadian Periodical Index / Index de périodiques canadienne.* Toronto: Globe and Mail, 1938– . 12/yr. (Formerly titled *Canadian Index to Periodicals and Documentary Films,* 1948–63, and *Canadian Periodical Index,* 1938–47, and published by Canadian Library Assn., Ottawa, through 1985.)

Electronic formats: CD-ROM and online (Globe and Mail, 1977–).

An author and subject index to some 400 general-interest Canadian periodicals.

B98 *Canadian Essay and General Literature Index.* Toronto: U of Toronto P, 1975–79. Annual.

Provides an index to Festschriften and collective volumes published in Canada on all subjects. An additional year of coverage for 1971–72 is provided by *Canadian Essays and Collections Index, 1971–1972* (Ottawa: Canadian Library Assn., 1976).

Caribbean Islands

See also bibliographies for French- and Spanish-language literatures listed in chapter 4.

(A1)   *MLA International Bibliography*
    Coverage is distributed throughout the volumes: English Caribbean literature is listed in volume 1, French Caribbean literature (French Guyana, Guadelupe, Haiti, and Martinique) is listed with French literature in volume 2, and Spanish American literature (Costa Rica, Cuba, Dominican Republic, El Salvador, Guatemala, Nicaragua, and Panama) is also in volume 2.

(C1)   *The Year's Work in Modern Language Studies*
    Covers French- and Spanish-language Caribbean literatures starting in 1988.

(D1)   *Callaloo: A Journal of Afro-American and African Arts and Letters*
    "Studies in Caribbean and South American Literature: An Annual Annotated Bibliography," in volumes 9– (1987–), is a classified bibliography of international books, articles, and dissertations for 1985– ; it is arranged by language area and then within each area by new original writing, interviews, general studies, genres, and individual authors.

(D52) *Journal of Caribbean Studies*
    See the language and literature section of the classified bibliography "Caribbean Studies: Recent Publications" in most issues.

(C62) *Handbook of Latin American Studies*
    Studies on the English-speaking Caribbean, including literature, are listed in the humanities volumes, which appear in alternate years.

India

(C151) *Indian Literary Index*
    Indexes creative writing and critical articles in Indian periodicals. (Author has not examined the index.)

(C152) *Indian Literature: Sahitya Akademi's Literary Bi-monthly*
    "Annual Surveys" for 1981– , in volumes 25– (1982–), are 10-page essays on new writing in about 20 Indian languages and regions.

(C154) *Guide to Indian Periodical Literature*
    Author and subject index to Indian periodicals in the humanities and social sciences. Book reviews are indexed.

Ireland

B101   *Irish University Review: A Journal of Irish Studies.* Dublin: Irish University Review, 1970– . 2/yr.

"IASAIL Bibliography Bulletin" for 1970– , produced by the International Association for the Study of Anglo-Irish Literature, is an extensive list of international books, articles, dissertations, and reviews on Irish literature in English, with a section on general studies and one on specific writers, including current new writing (with reviews cited).

B102   *Etudes irlandaises: Revue française d'histoire, civilisation et littérature de l'Irlande.* Sainghin en Melantois, Fr.: Etudes Irlandaises, 1972– . 2/yr. (The earlier volumes published annually by the Centre d'Etudes et de Recherches Irlandaises, Lille.)

"Irish Literature in English: The Year's Work" is an annual, international list of books and articles about Irish literature in English, including current creative writing, for 1975– . Accompanied by a separate bibliography of studies on Irish history, politics, and institutions.

(C1)   *The Year's Work in Modern Language Studies*

Provides coverage on Celtic literatures (Breton, Cornish, Irish, Manx, Scottish Gaelic, and Welsh) in the volumes for 1930–36 and 1974– .

B103   *Handlist of Work in Progress.* Dublin: Royal Irish Acad., 1969– . Annual, with some gaps.

A classified list of international work in progress on Irish and Anglo-Irish literature and language.

B104   *Books Ireland: A Monthly Review.* Dublin: Addis, 1976– . 10/yr.

A book review journal. (Author has not examined the journal.)

New Zealand

B110   *INNZ: Index New Zealand: Subject Index to Current New Zealand Literature.* Wellington: Natl. Library of New

Zealand, 1941– . Annual. (Titled *Index to New Zealand Periodicals*, 1941–86.)

Electronic format: online (Kiwinet, 1987–).

General index to New Zealand periodicals and other publications. (Author has not examined the index.)

Scotland

B113 *Annual Bibliography of Scottish Literature.* Glasgow: Glasgow U Library, 1970– . Annual. (Published for 1970– as a supplement to the *Bibliotheck*, Stirling.)

An extensive, classified bibliography of international books, reviews, and articles arranged under headings for general studies, individual authors, and ballads and folk literature for 1969– . Author and critic indexes.

B114 *Scottish Literary Journal: A Review of Studies in Scottish Languages and Literature.* Aberdeen: Assn. for Scottish Lit. Studies, 1974– . 2/yr. (Continues *Scottish Literary News*, 1970–74.)

"The Year's Work in Scottish Literary and Linguistic Studies" is an annual bibliographic essay reviewing selected items for 1969– listed in the *Annual Bibliography of Scottish Literature.*

The journal also carried the checklist "Current Scottish Prose and Verse" through 1979 (supplement 13, 1980). Subsequently most supplements (now 2/yr.) publish extensive reviews of new fiction and poetry, providing a record of new Scottish writing.

B115 *Studies in Scottish Literature.* Columbia: U of South Carolina, 1963– . Annual. (Vols. 1–12 published 4/yr.; vols. 1–2 published by Texas Tech U, Lubbock.)

"Scottish Poetry," in volumes 6– (1968–), is a biennial bibliographic essay on new books by Scottish poets for 1968– . "Scottish Fiction," in volumes 14–18 (1979–83), is a biennial bibliographic essay on Scottish fiction for 1975–81.

(C1) *The Year's Work in Modern Language Studies*

Provides annual coverage on Celtic literatures (Breton,

Cornish, Irish, Manx, Scottish Gaelic, and Welsh) in the volumes for 1930–36 and 1974– .

Wales

(C1)   *The Year's Work in Modern Language Studies*
    Provides annual coverage on Celtic literatures (Breton, Cornish, Irish, Manx, Scottish Gaelic, and Welsh) in the volumes for 1930–36 and 1974– .

(D56) *Bibliography of Wales: A Register of Publications Relating to Wales and the Celtic Peoples*
    An extensive, classified bibliography of international books, articles, and pamphlets on all aspects of current and historic Celtic life. Author and subject index.

Chapter Four
Non-English Literatures

This chapter describes bibliographies devoted to literatures other than English; it is divided among Romance, French, Italian, Spanish and Portuguese (including Latin American), German and Netherlands, Modern Greek, Asian (Near and Middle Eastern, south and east Asian), African, and eastern European literatures; it opens with a brief section of more comprehensive bibliographies. Bibliographies that cover all the world's literatures are listed in chapter 2, along with current indexes to English-language periodicals. For most North American students and scholars the *MLA International Bibliography* (A1) and the general humanities indexes provide comprehensive, convenient, and accessible coverage of a wide range of scholarly publications. *FRANCIS bulletin signalétique 523. Histoire et sciences de la littérature* (A2) is similarly comprehensive, convenient, and accessible for Europeans; records European scholarship; and, like the *MLA Bibliography* and several of the indexes, is computerized.

General periodical indexes and trade and national bibliographies for individual countries are very important; they usually list new writing along with critical studies. They are not included here, however, because they are fully described in the *Guide to Reference Books* (D402).

For studies of language-teaching issues and methodologies, see "Language, Linguistics, and Language Teaching" in chapter 5. Other relevant subjects, such as drama, folklore, history, literary theory, philosophy, religion, and science, are also covered in chapter 5. Chapter 6 lists author bibliographies.

MODERN INTERNATIONAL LITERATURES

(A1) *MLA International Bibliography*

The *MLA Bibliography* covers all modern literatures, recording international books, articles, and dissertations and arranging in sections for European, Asian, African, and Latin American literatures.

C1 *The Year's Work in Modern Language Studies.* London: Modern Humanities Research Assn., 1931– . Annual.

An evaluative survey of the year's international books and articles on modern European non-English languages and literatures for 1930– . There are major chapters for medieval and Neo-Latin, Romance (including South American), Germanic (including Netherlandic and Scandinavian), Celtic, and Slavonic literatures; each chapter has subsections for language studies and for specific literatures and literary periods. Within the last subsection are further subdivisions for genres and individual writers. Not every volume, however, has complete coverage of all the languages and literatures listed. The subject indexing, an outstanding feature since volume 30 (1968) includes headings for such subjects as fables, the Fall, fascism, the Faust theme, the Federal Bureau of Investigation, feminism, and folklore. Author and critic indexes.

C2 *Modern Language Journal.* Madison: U of Wisconsin P, 1916– . 4/yr.

"Doctoral Degrees Granted in Foreign Languages in the United States" is a classified list of dissertations for 1925– , arranged by the literature or language covered and including author, title, school, and dissertation director.

C3 *PAIS International in Print.* New York: Public Affairs Information Service, 1971– . 4/yr. (Titled *Foreign Language Index*, 1971–84, and *PAIS Foreign Language Index*, 1985–90.)

Electronic formats: CD-ROM (SilverPlatter, 1972–) and online (Dialog and OCLC, 1972–).

A subject index to periodicals, collections and proceedings, monographs, and government and international-organization publications concerning the social sciences, economics and business, and international and governmental affairs in French, German, Italian, Portuguese, and Spanish, as well as English. Although *PAIS International* does not index topics in the humanities and literature, it does index foreign language studies on individual countries and in area and cultural studies. Author index.

GENERAL ROMANCE-LANGUAGE LITERATURE

(A1)   *MLA International Bibliography*
       Covers studies in all the Romance-language literatures.
C5   *Romanische Bibliographie / Bibliographie romane / Romance Bibliography.* Tübingen: Niemeyer, 1965– . Annual.
       A comprehensive, classified bibliography that lists international books, articles, and reviews on linguistics and literature of all the Romance languages, including non-European ones (e.g., Canadian and Louisianan French and Cape Verdean Portuguese). The bibliography has three parts: part 1 has author, subject, and book review indexes for parts 1, 2, and 3; part 2 covers linguistics; part 3 covers literature and contains sections for bibliographic and general studies and then for studies arranged by nation, subdivided for individual authors and subjects. Coverage dates from 1875, starting with the bibliography's predecessor, *Zeitschrift für romanische Philologie. Supplementheft* (Tübingen: Niemeyer, 1878–1964).
C6   *KLRG: Kritisches Lexikon der romanischen Gegenwartsliteraturen.* Tübingen: Narr, 1984– . Annual.
       A loose-leaf service that records international books and articles about twentieth-century French, French Canadian, Italian, Latin American, Portuguese, and Spanish writers and includes writing by these authors.
C7   *Revue des langues romanes.* Montpellier: Centre d'Etudes Occitanes de l'Université, 1870– . 2/yr.
       "Bibliographie des études romanes en Amérique du Nord," in volumes 78–83 (1968–79), is a classified checklist of North American scholarship (chiefly books) on the

Romance languages and literatures for 1968–78, arranged by country and literary period.

C8   *Romania: Revue consacrée à l'étude des langues et des littératures romanes.* Paris: Centre National de la Recherche Scientifique, 1872– . 4/yr.

Most issues list contents, along with annotations, of international periodicals publishing on the Romance languages and literatures.

C9   *Romanistisches Jahrbuch.* Berlin: Gruyter, 1947– . Annual.

Lists current academic publications and dissertations on Romance languages and literatures written at German (West German before reunification) and Austrian universities, for 1945– .

C10   *Revue de linguistique romane.* Strasbourg: Société de Linguistique Romane, 1925– . 2/yr.

"Chronique bibliographique," 1950–83, is a classified list of reviews of recent international books on Romance linguistics.

FRENCH AND FRANCOPHONE LITERATURES

French literary studies are served by several excellent general bibliographies that are listed here in order of their availability and comprehensiveness. The *MLA International Bibliography* (A1) and the *Bibliographie der französischen Literaturwissenschaft* (C15) are similar in coverage, but the former provides better access to North American journals and books and is more readily usable in the United States. In contrast, the latter not only lists more French publications but also is more varied and thorough in listing studies of subjects related to French literature, such as film and French culture. See the list of general Romance bibliographies in the previous section, especially the *Romanische Bibliographie* (C5) and *The Year's Work in Modern Language Studies* (C1). Other important bibliographies are the bimonthly *Revue d'histoire littéraire de la France* (C17) and

FRANCIS bulletin signalétique 523. Histoire et sciences de la littérature (A2). These general bibliographies also include francophone literature.

Bibliographies of dissertations on French literature and linguistics are included here in the first section. There is a second section for literary periods and a third for francophone literatures. The subject bibliographies in chapter 5 for the literary genres and for art, comparative literature, film, linguistics, literary theory, music, periodicals, printing, and women's studies should be useful. Author bibliographies are listed in chapter 6. Also see the listings under general literary bibliographies and humanities periodical indexes in chapter 2. For additional periodical indexes and for national bibliography see the *Guide to Reference Books* (D402).

For language teaching see the linguistics section in chapter 5, as well as the regular reviews in *French Review* (C19).

General Bibliographies

(A1)   *MLA International Bibliography*
         Studies are divided by period into sections (400–1499, 1500–99, 1600–99, etc.), within which are subdivisions for genres and individual authors. Separate sections follow for Occitan studies and French literatures of Canada and the Caribbean; the French literatures of Africa are covered in the African section. See also under "Literary Movements" in volume 4.

C15   *Bibliographie der französischen Literaturwissenschaft.* Frankfurt: Klostermann, 1960– . Annual.
         A comprehensive, classified bibliography of international books, reviews, articles, and dissertations on French literature and related subjects for 1956– , with critic, author, and subject indexes. French-language items predominate, and editorial matter is in French. Sections include generalities (e.g., culture and civilization, structuralism, cinema, stylistics and rhetoric), literary periods (with subdivisions for such subjects as *chanson de geste, Encyclopédie,*

and *surrealisme et dada*), French-language literatures outside France, and individual authors.

(A2)   *FRANCIS bulletin signalétique 523. Histoire et sciences de la littérature*

Coverage of French literature and French publications is especially good.

(C5)   *Romanische Bibliographie / Bibliographie romane / Romance Bibliography*

Provides comprehensive coverage of international scholarship on French literature.

C16   *Studi francesi: Cultura e civiltà letteraria della francia.* Turin: Rosenberg, 1957– . 2/yr.

"Rassegna bibliografica" in each issue contains summary reviews (often lengthy) of international books and articles for 1955– on French literature and language, arranged by literary period (medieval to the present), language and linguistics, and general studies.

C17   *Revue d'histoire littéraire de la France.* Paris: Société d'Histoire Littéraire de la France, 1894– . 6/yr. (Suspended 1940–46.)

Each bimonthly issue since 1894 has carried a list of current scholarship, arranged by century (sixteenth to twentieth) and then by subject and subject author. Covers books, articles, pamphlets, and dissertations about literature and literary history. The lists for 1963– are available separately from the publisher. No index; no annual cumulation, but see the next entry for information about the 1949–63 cumulations.

C18   *Bibliographie de la littérature française du Moyen age à nos jours.* Paris: Colin, 1967–81. Annual. (Supersedes *Bibliographie de la littérature française moderne [XVI–XXe siècles]*, 1964–66; *Bibliographie littéraire*, 1953–63; and *Revue d'histoire littéra-ture de la France*, 1949–51.)

A comprehensive, classified bibliography of international books, articles, and dissertations, for 1948–80. It is arranged by bibliographies, generalities, and periods or centuries, and within the last grouping are subsections for general studies, themes, and individual writers.

There are indexes for authors, subjects, and principal themes.

Coverage from 1949 to 1963 duplicated that in the *Revue d'histoire littéraire de la France*, but then coverage separated and became more extensive here.

(C1)   *The Year's Work in Modern Language Studies*

The annual bibliographic essay reviews international scholarship, scholarly tools, and new editions as well as criticism and is subdivided for language studies, studies on the literary periods, and Provençal studies.

C19   *French Review.* Champaign: Amer. Assn. of Teachers of French, 1927– . 4/yr.

Most issues include an extensive section of reviews of international books that is divided into sections for literary history and criticism; technology in teaching and research; linguistics; civilization; film; French-language creative writing; and textbooks, CAI software, and methodology.

"Dissertations in Progress," 1963– , is an annual list of current North American dissertations, arranged by subject.

C20   *Bulletin analytique de linguistique française.* Paris: Didier, 1970– . 6/yr.

A bimonthly, classified bibliography of international books, articles, and dissertations on French linguistics, with brief annotations in French. Bimonthly author index is cumulated annually.

C21   *Bulletin critique du livre français.* Paris: Bulletin Critique du Livre Français, 1946– . 11/yr.

A monthly list of brief reviews of French books in all subjects, including translations into French. The literature section includes criticism and creative writing. Author and title indexes are in each issue and are cumulated annually.

C22   *Point de repère: Index analytique d'articles de périodiques de langue française.* Montreal: Bibliothèque Nationale du Québec, 1966– . Annual. (Titled *Index analytique*, published by Presses de l'Université Laval, Quebec, 1966–72, and *Periodex*, published by Centrale des Bibliothéques, Montreal, 1972–83.)

Electronic format: online as *Repère* (Services Documentaires Multimedia, 1972–).

Provides an author and subject index for 1966– to about 90 French-language periodicals published in France and Quebec; covers philosophy, religion, cinema, social criticism, and intellectual history but excludes literature and literary criticism.

C23   *French Periodical Index: Repertoriex.* Morgantown: Ponchie, 1976– . Annual. (Vols. 1–5 published by Faxon, Boston.)

A general periodical index covering 1973– . Volumes 1–5 index 10 French-language periodicals, and a 1988 volume expands coverage to about 50 and covers 1979–87. Relevant sections are on film, literature, books, libraries, publishing, and theater.

C24   *Current Research in French Studies at Universities and Polytechnics in the United Kingdom and Ireland.* Bath: Soc. for French Studies, 1969– . Annual. (Place of publication varies; coverage of Ireland added after 1988.)

A classified list of United Kingdom and Irish theses and research in progress, arranged in sections for literary periods, linguistics, and francophone studies. The critic index has an elaborate code indicating the researcher's institution, the nature of the research, and whether the research has been completed or abandoned.

(D182) *Revue d'histoire du théâtre*

An annual bibliography for the mid-1940s to 1980 of international books and articles on most aspects of the international theater, except stagecraft; especially useful for French theater.

(D188) *L'annuel du théâtre*

"Revue des livres" is a classified bibliography of the year's French books about international theater along with new plays and translations.

(D200) *Année du théâtre [year]*

A survey of the theatrical season in France for 1992– , with a calendar of productions, cast and crew information, and brief articles about principal people, plays, and productions.

Literary Periods

See also the general bibliographies listed above and the general period bibliographies listed in chapter 3. Author bibliographies are listed in chapter 6, subject bibliographies in chapter 5.

MEDIEVAL

(D320) *International Medieval Bibliography*
A comprehensive, classified bibliography for years 1965– covering international books and articles on all aspects of medieval Europe and of the Middle East and Christian North Africa, 450–1500. Categories include art, folk studies, language, and literature (subdivided by genre and then by country or region).

(D321) *Deutsches Archiv für Erforschung des Mittelalters*
Each issue carries a comprehensive, classified, and annotated bibliography of international books and articles from the early 1930s covering all aspects of medieval life.

(D322) *Cahiers de civilisation médiévale Xᵉ–XIIIᵉ siècles: Bibliographie*
Carries an annual bibliography of international books and articles for 1958– .

(D323) *Medioevo latino: Bolletino bibliografico della cultura europea dal secolo VI al XIV*
A comprehensive classified, annotated (in Italian) bibliography of international books, articles, and reviews on all aspects of the medieval world, 1980– .

(C30) *TENSO: Bulletin of the Société Guilhem IX*
The annual bibliography on Occitan language and literature includes significant coverage of the medieval period.

RENAISSANCE

(D432) *Bibliographie internationale de l'humanisme et de la Renaissance*
A comprehensive, classified bibliography for 1965– covering international books and articles on all aspects of the European and Latin American Renaissance.

(B31) *Studies in Philology*
Includes an annual, international, comprehensive, and classified bibliography of books and articles on Renaissance

literature for 1917–68, with coverage of Continental literatures added in 1939.

(D433) *Renaissance Quarterly*

"Books Received" in each issue records about 200–300 international books a year dealing with the Renaissance; for 1952–80 this list, titled "Renaissance Books," is an extensive, classified list of new international books drawn from entries in national bibliographies.

C25 *French 17: An Annual Descriptive Bibliography of French Seventeenth-Century Studies.* Fort Collins: Colorado State U, 1953– . Annual.

Published for the Division on Seventeenth-Century French Literature of the Modern Language Association, this comprehensive, classified bibliography contains brief annotations and lists international books, reviews, and articles in five sections: "Bibliography and Linguistics," "Artistic, Political, and Social Background," "Philosophy, Science, and Religion," "Literary History and Criticism," and "Authors and Personages"; a sixth section lists work in progress.

C26 *Papers on Seventeenth Century French Literature.* Tübingen: U of Tübingen, 1973– . 2/yr.

Carries an annual list of North American dissertations and continues coverage formerly in *Œuvres et critiques* (D296).

(D296) *Œuvres et critiques: Revue internationale d'étude de la réception critique des œuvres littéraires de langue française*

"North American Research in Progress on Seventeenth Century French Literature" lists dissertation topics by subject and research projects by critic (the latter has a subject index), and "North American Doctoral Theses on Seventeenth Century French Literature Completed" lists items by genre or subject author, both for 1973–77.

"North American Publications on French Seventeenth-Century Literature," 1973–75, culls studies from *French 17* (C25) and arranges them by subject author.

ENLIGHTENMENT

See also *Annales de la Société Jean-Jacques Rousseau* (E149).

(B42) *The Eighteenth Century: A Current Bibliography*

An annual, annotated, and classified bibliography of international books and articles for 1925– on all aspects of eighteenth-century life in Europe, Great Britain (including the Restoration period), North and South America, and Asia. Coverage of French literature began with the 1970 bibliography.

(E46) *Recherches sur Diderot et sur l'*Encyclopédie

Each issue for 1986– lists new European books, articles, and dissertations dealing with Diderot, the *Encyclopédie*, and the *Encyclopédistes*.

ROMANTICISM AND NINETEENTH CENTURY

(B51) *The Romantic Movement: A Selective and Critical Bibliography*

An annual, annotated bibliography for 1936–providing an extensive selection of international books, reviews, articles, and dissertations that comprehensively cover all aspects of the movement in England, France, Germany, Italy, and Spain. Arranged in sections for the countries and then for individual authors; for studies on the social, intellectual, political, scientific, and artistic environment; and for bibliographies.

C27 *French VI Bibliography: Critical and Biographical References for the Study of Nineteenth Century French Literature.* New York: French Inst. and MLA, 1955–69. Annual.

A classified bibliography for 1954–67 of international books, reviews, articles, and dissertations. Subject index.

(E215) *Les cahiers naturalistes. Bulletin*

The annual bibliography lists work on naturalism in general and Zola specifically.

TWENTIETH CENTURY

See also the next section for francophone literatures and relevant sections of chapter 5, such as film and literary theory.

C28   *French XX Bibliography*. New York: French Inst. and MLA, 1949– . Annual. (Formerly *French VII Bibliography: Critical and Biographical References for the Study of Contemporary French Literature*, Stechert, New York, 1949–58.)

A comprehensive, classified, international bibliography of books, articles, and newspaper stories (chosen selectively) for 1940– . Arranged in three parts: part 1 covers general aspects, bibliographies, literary genres, aesthetics, themes, literary history, philosophy, religion, surrealism, symbolism, and theater; part 2 covers individual authors and lists editions and studies; part 3 covers cinema.

(B65) *Journal of Modern Literature*

Carries an annual, classified bibliography of international, mainly English-language scholarship on modern (1885–1950) and contemporary world writers for 1970– .

(B66) *Twentieth Century Literature: A Scholarly and Critical Journal*

Most issues for 1955–1981 include an annotated bibliography of international, mainly English-language articles on twentieth-century world writers and literary subjects.

(D177) *Modern Drama*

Carries an annual bibliography for 1959– of studies on international twentieth-century world drama and dramatists.

C29   *La revue des lettres modernes: Histoire des idées et des littératures*. Paris: Minard, 1954– . Irregular.

An extensive critical series on twentieth-century French writing, with subseries devoted to a number of individual authors. During the 1960s and early 1970s nearly every issue (made up of several numbers) carried a bibliography of editions, books, and articles, and since 1983 the review carries *Les carnets bibliographiques de la* Revue des lettres modernes, an irregular series of bibliographies of recent criticism on single authors. These writers have subseries: Apollinaire, Barbey d'Aurevilly, Bernanos, Bloy, Camus, Céline, Claudel, Cocteau, Flaubert, Gide, Giono, Gracq, Hugo, Jacob, Jouve, Joyce, Malraux, Mauriac, Péguy, Perse, Proust, Ramuz, Rimbaud, Suarès, Valéry, and Verne.

Occitan Literature and the Francophone Literatures of Africa, Canada, and the Caribbean

See also the sections for Canadian literature in chapter 3 and those for Latin American and African literatures in this chapter, below.

(C1)   *The Year's Work in Modern Language Studies*

Has included a chapter on Occitan or Provençal studies in every volume and starting with volume 50 (1989) has chapters for French African and Caribbean literature and for Canadian literature, both for 1988– .

C30   *TENSO: Bulletin of the Société Guilhem IX.* Louisville: Société Guilhem, 1985– .

Each volume carries an annual bibliography of studies on Occitan literature and language for 1985– .

(C28)   *French XX Bibliography*

French African literatures are included in the section on francophone literary history, and studies on individual African authors are included in part 2.

C31   *Livres et auteurs québecois: Revue critique de l'année littéraire.* Québec: Presses de l'Université Laval, 1966–82. Annual. (Titled *Cahiers bibliographique des lettres québecoises,* 1966–69.)

Each volume lists new books in several categories, notably fiction, poetry, drama, literary criticism, literary essays, children's literature, linguistics, history and geography, and philosophy and theology, along with theses and dissertations at Quebec universities and articles on Quebecois literature and culture in Canadian periodicals.

C32   *Revue d'histoire littéraire du Québec et du Canada français.* Montreal: Bellarmin, 1980–87.

"Bibliographie de la critique," in most issues, lists new books and articles on Quebecois literature and culture; the list of books covers 1978–85 and the list of articles 1974–84.

C33   *Etudes françaises.* Montreal: Presses de l'Université Montréal, 1965– . 3/yr.

"Bibliographie des lettres canadiennes-françaises" for 1964–66 was an annual listing of studies on French Canadian literature.

C34   *Bulletin bibliographique de la Société des Ecrivains Canadiens.* Montreal: Société des Ecrivains Canadiens, 1941–58. Annual.

An author list of mainly French-language books in all fields for 1937–57.

(C62)   *Handbook of Latin American Studies*
Includes studies of French Caribbean literature.

ITALIAN LITERATURE

After the *MLA International Bibliography* (A1), the major Italian bibliography is carried in *La rassegna della letteratura italiana* (C40), which is international in coverage but puts special emphasis on Italian scholarship. Two new bibliographies that have just started may prove to be important; they are *Bibliografia generale della lingua e della letteratura italiana* (C42) and *Letteratura italiana. Aggiornomento bibliografico* (C43). There are two lists of North American studies (in *Italica*, C44, and *Revue des langues romanes*, C7) and one of British studies (in *Italian Studies*, C47). *The Year's Work in Modern Language Studies* (C1) provides comprehensive bibliographic essays on the year's international scholarship, as does *Lettere italiane* (C46) from an Italian point of view.

The major period bibliographies in chapter 3 that are important for students of Italian literature are included below. Author bibliographies are listed in chapter 6, subject bibliographies in chapter 5 (see, among others, the sections for the literary genres and for art, comparative literature, film, history, linguistics, literary theory, and music), and general humanities periodical indexes in chapter 2. For additional periodical indexes and for national bibliographies, see *Guide to Reference Books* (D402).

For language teaching, see the section for linguistics in chapter 5; see also *Italica*.

General Bibliographies

(A1)　*MLA International Bibliography*
International books, articles, and dissertations on Italian literature are arranged by period in sections (400–1399, 1400–99, 1500–99, etc.), within which are subsections for genres and authors. See also under literary movements in volume 4.

C40　*La rassegna della letteratura italiana.* Florence: Sansoni, 1893– . 3/yr. (usually in two issues). Suspended 1949–52.

Each issue carries a classified, comprehensive, and annotated bibliography of international books, articles, and reviews on Italian literature. Arranged by literary period (trecento, quattrocento, cinquecento, settecento, etc.) and including a section of Dante studies. Annotations are in Italian and are often extensive.

C41　*Rivista di studi italiani.* Toronto: U of Toronto, 1983– . 2/yr.

"Rassegna bibliografica" in each issue is an extensive, classified list of international books, articles, and book reviews on Italian literature for 1982– , including some coverage of cultural studies; it is arranged by century with a section for Dante studies and with the twentieth century subdivided for *critica, narrativa, poesia, teatro, linguistica,* and occasionally *varia* or *cinema.* Some 500 periodicals are scanned.

C42　*Bibliografia generale della lingua e della letteratura italiana.* Rome: Salerno, 1991– . Annual.

Electronic format: CD-ROM (Salerno, 1994–).

An annual, classified bibliography of international books, articles, and reviews on Italian language and literature, arranged by period and with a subject index. In two volumes, the second of which contains author, publisher, and subject indexes. (Author has not examined the bibliography.)

C43　*Letteratura italiana. Aggiornamento bibliografico.* Trieste: Alcione, 1991– . 2/yr.

A classified bibliography of international books and articles on Italian literature, with indexes of subjects, authors, and publishers. (Author has not examined the bibliography.)

(C5)　*Romanische Bibliographie / Bibliographie romane / Romance Bibliography*

Part 3, subdivided by nation, lists international books and articles on Italian literature and individual writers.

C44　*Italica.* New Brunswick: Amer. Assn. of Teachers of Italian, 1924– . 4/yr.

A quarterly "Bibliography of Italian Studies in North America" for 1923– lists books, reviews, articles, and bibliographies on general, pedagogical, and Italian American studies, with studies of Italian literature arranged by century. Items listed have been published in North America or abroad by North American scholars; subjects covered include comparative literature, translations, art, music, philosophy, history, film, and sociology (if relevant to literary issues).

C45　*Studi e problemi di critica testuale.* Bologna: Risparmio, 1970– . 2/yr.

"American Bibliography" in each issue is a checklist of articles in North American journals and of North American reviews of books on Italian literature, film, theater, and arts. In addition there is an annotated bibliography of Italian books and articles on literature and philology in general.

(C1)　*The Year's Work in Modern Language Studies*

Italian language and literature studies are covered in a single chapter, which is subdivided by literary periods.

C46　*Lettere italiane.* Florence: Olschki, 1949– . 4/yr.

The quarterly "Rassegna," a bibliographic essay, reviews recent criticism on Italian writers and literary subjects.

C47　*Italian Studies: An Annual Review.* Leeds: Soc. for Italian Studies, 1937– . Annual. (Place of publication has varied.)

"Works of Italian Interest Published in Great Britain" for 1937–82, in volumes 1–38 (1937–83), is a classified, selective bibliography of books and articles published in Great Britain on Italian studies in general. Note the sections on language and on literature and philosophy; the latter lists criticism, new translations, and studies on comparative literature, especially those linking Italy and Great Britain.

Literary Periods

Except for coverage provided by the general Italian literature bibliographies just described, there seem to be no specialized period bibliographies of Italian literature. The following, however, do provide useful coverage.

MEDIEVAL

(D320) *International Medieval Bibliography*
    A comprehensive, classified bibliography for years 1965– covering international books and articles on all aspects of medieval Europe and of the Middle East and Christian North Africa, 450–1500. Categories include art, folk studies, language, and literature (subdivided by genre and then by country or region).

(D321) *Deutsches Archiv für Erforschung des Mittelalters*
    Each issue carries a comprehensive, classified, and annotated bibliography of international books and articles from the early 1930s covering all aspects of medieval life.

(D322) *Cahiers de civilisation médiévale Xᵉ–XIIᵉ siècles: Bibliographie*
    Carries an annual bibliography of international books and articles for 1958– .

(D323) *Medioevo latino: Bolletino bibliografico della cultura europea dal secolo VI al XIV*
    A comprehensive classified, annotated (in Italian) bibliography of international books, articles, and reviews on all aspects of the medieval world, 1980– .

RENAISSANCE

(D432) *Bibliographie internationale de l'humanisme et de la Renaissance*

A comprehensive, classified bibliography for 1965– covering international books and articles on all aspects of the European and Latin American Renaissance.

(B31) *Studies in Philology*

Volumes 14–66 (1917–69) include an annual, international, comprehensive, and classified bibliography of books and articles on Renaissance literature for 1917–68, with coverage of Continental literatures added in 1939.

(D433) *Renaissance Quarterly*

"Books Received" in each issue records about 200–300 international books a year dealing with the Renaissance; for 1952–80 this list, titled "Renaissance Books," is an extensive, classified list of new international books drawn from entries in national bibliographies.

EIGHTEENTH CENTURY

(B42) *The Eighteenth Century: A Current Bibliography*

An annual, annotated, and classified bibliography of international books and articles on all aspects of eighteenth-century life in Europe, Great Britain (including the Restoration period), North and South America, and Asia for 1925– . Coverage of eighteenth-century Italian culture began with the 1970 bibliography.

ROMANTICISM

(B51) *The Romantic Movement: A Selective and Critical Bibliography*

An annual, annotated bibliography for 1936– providing an extensive selection of international books, reviews, articles, and dissertations that comprehensively cover all aspects of the movement in England, France, Germany, Italy, and Spain. Coverage of studies on Italian literature has been spotty; see bibliographies for 1936–42, 1953–72, 1976, 1978, and following.

TWENTIETH CENTURY

(B65) *Journal of Modern Literature*

Carries an annual, classified bibliography of international, mainly English-language scholarship on modern (1885–1950) and contemporary world writers for 1970– .

(B66)   *Twentieth Century Literature: A Scholarly and Critical Journal*
Most issues for 1955–1981 include an annotated bibliography of international, mainly English-language articles on twentieth-century world writers and literary subjects.

(D177) *Modern Drama*
Carries an annual bibliography for 1959– of studies on international twentieth-century world drama and dramatists.

SPANISH AND PORTUGUESE LITERATURES

The *MLA International Bibliography* (A1), *Nueva revista de filología hispánica* (C51), *Revista de filología española* (C52), and the *Romanische Bibliographie* (C5) cover both peninsular and Latin American Spanish and Portuguese writing. Other Latin American bibliographies are listed under "Latin American Literature" below. Among the useful subject bibliographies in chapter 5 are those for the literary genres and for African American studies, American studies, art, comparative literature, the Don Juan theme, ethnic studies, film, history, linguistics, philosophy, printing, and religion. Author bibliographies are listed in chapter 6, and current indexes in chapter 2. See the *Guide to Reference Books* (D402) for additional periodical indexes and national bibliographies.

For language teaching see the bibliographies listed under linguistics in chapter 5 and reviews in *Hispania* (C55).

General Bibliographies

(A1)   *MLA International Bibliography*
Contains sections for Spanish and Portuguese literatures (including Catalan and Galician) and for Latin American literatures (with sections for individual countries), which are arranged by period (400–1499, 1500–99, 1600–99, etc.) and within which are subsections for genres and authors. Spanish language and literature and Spanish American literature have been covered from the beginning of

the bibliography, Portuguese (including Brazilian) literature was added in 1928, and Brazilian literature and language gained a separate section in 1938. See also under "Literary Movements" in volume 4.

C51 *Nueva revista de filología hispánica.* Mexico City: Colegio de México, 1947– . 2/yr.

Continuing coverage formerly in *Revista de filología hispánica* (Buenos Aires: Universidad Nacional, 1939–46, for 1937–46), each issue carries a comprehensive, classified bibliography of international books, reviews, articles, and dissertations on Spanish and Latin American language and literature, including new writing by and material about writers of Brazil, the Caribbean, Mexico, and Central and South America. Arranged in broad sections for general studies (including related historical studies), linguistics, and literature, the last subdivided for general studies, literary theory, and comparative literature and then for literature of Spain and Latin America, which is further subdivided for genre studies and then for author studies organized by period. Latin American coverage started with volume 34, 1985.

C52 *Revista de filología española.* Madrid: Consejo Superior de Investigaciones Científicas, Instituto de Filología, 1914– . 4/yr.

Carries an annual, classified bibliography of international books, reviews, and articles on Spanish linguistics and Spanish and Spanish American literature for 1913– .

(C5) *Romanische Bibliographie / Bibliographie romane / Romance Bibliography*

Coverage includes all the Portuguese and Spanish-language literatures, including those of Latin America.

C53 *Revista de literatura.* Madrid: Consejo Superior de Investigaciones Científicas, Instituto de Filología, 1952– . 2/yr.

"Información bibliográfica," starting in number 6 (1954), is a comprehensive bibliography of international books and articles on Spanish peninsular literature, arranged by period, genre, and author. The bibliography is usually annual but sometimes biannual. Numbers 9–18 (1956–60) also include bibliographies of Spanish books and articles about French, German, Italian, and English literature.

C54   *Journal of Hispanic Philology.* Tallahassee: Florida State U, 1976– . 3/yr.

Starting with volume 7 (1981), the journal lists contents of newly published Festschriften and other collections on Spanish and Latin American language and literatures, and usually one issue a year has an extensive list of new international books received.

(C1)   *The Year's Work in Modern Language Studies*

Contains separate bibliographic essays on current, international books and articles on Spanish, Catalan, Portuguese, and Latin American language and literature.

C55   *Hispania: A Journal Devoted to the Interests of the Teaching of Spanish and Portuguese.* Washington: American Assn. of Teachers of Spanish and Portuguese, 1918– . 5/yr. (Place of publication varies.)

Extensive book reviews in most issues, arranged for peninsular and Latin American literatures and for linguistics, pedagogy, and sometimes Spanish-language creative writing.

"Dissertations in the Hispanic Languages and Literatures," 1935– , is an annual author list of North American dissertations completed or in progress. "Research Tools in Progress," a subsection of "Professional News" in each issue 1978–81, contains reports on bibliographies, on editions, on concordances, and on other scholarly tools for language and literature study.

C56   *Revista de dialectología y tradiciones populares.* Madrid: Consejo Superior de Investigaciones Científicas, Instituto de Filología, 1944– . 4/yr.

Carries an annual, classified bibliography of international books and articles, 1948– , on linguistics and dialectology and on folklore, music, and religion, chiefly in Spain and Spanish-speaking America.

C57   *Revista hispánica moderna.* New York: Hispanic Inst., Columbia U, 1934–69.

"Bibliografía hispánica" for 1947–54, in volumes 14–21

(1948–55), lists books and articles on Spanish, Portuguese, and Latin American literature.

C58   *Boletim internacional de bibliografia luso-brasileira.* Lisbon: Fundaçao Calouste Gulbenkian, 1960–73. 4/yr.

"Registo bibliografico" lists new books and articles published in or about Portugal and Brazil. The literature section is further subdivided for creative writing and literary studies.

Latin American Literatures

Several of the bibliographies in the previous section cover Latin American literature, both Spanish and Portuguese. See also sections in chapter 3 on English Caribbean literature and above on francophone Caribbean literature.

C60   *HAPI: Hispanic American Periodicals Index.* Los Angeles: U of California, Los Angeles, Latin American Center, 1977– . Annual.

Electronic formats: CD-ROM and online (RLIN, 1970–).

An author and subject index to over 240 international scholarly periodicals of Latin American interest, 1970– . Covers the humanities and social sciences and includes creative writing, criticism, and reviews of books, plays, and films. Continues coverage provided by the *Index to Latin American Periodical Literature, 1929–1960* and its supplements for 1961–65 and 1966–70 (Boston: Hall, 1962, 1968, 1980).

C61   *Chasqui: Revista de literatura latinoamericana.* Williamsburg: Coll. of William and Mary, 1971– . 3/yr.

Each issue through volume 14, number 1 (1984), includes a list of current criticism and essays on Latin American literature and, selectively, of contemporary creative writing.

C62   *Handbook of Latin American Studies.* Gainesville: U of Florida P, 1936– . Annual.

Electronic format: online (RLIN, 1983–).

A selective and annotated bibliography of Latin American and international publications in literature and the humanities (art, history, language, music, and philosophy) and in the social sciences. Humanities and social sciences studies were combined in each annual for volumes 1–26, but now appear in alternate years, humanities and literature in the even-numbered volumes and social sciences in the odd-numbered volumes. Brazilian, Spanish American, and French West Indian literatures are covered, and creative writing is listed as well as criticism; all items are annotated.

C63   *Bibliographic Guide to Latin American Studies.* Boston: Hall, 1979– . Annual.

An international, comprehensive bibliography of books, serials, and other separate publications cataloged by the Library of Congress and the New York Public Library for 1978– . Items are arranged by author, title, and subject.

C64   *Revista interamericana de bibliografía / Inter-American Review of Bibliography.* Washington: Organization of Amer. States, 1951– . 4/yr.

Each issue carries a selective, classified list of international books (through 1983), articles (1979–), dissertations (1979–), and work in progress (1982–) on Latin American subjects acquired by the Organization of American States and by various libraries. See the sections on language, literature, art, music and dance, philosophy and psychology, and religion.

C65   *A Guide to Reviews of Books from and about Hispanic America / Guía a las reseñas de libros de y sobre Hispanoamérica.* Ponce, PR: AMM, 1965– . Irregular. (Formerly published in Río Piedras, Puerto Rico, in 1965 for 1960–64 and in 1973 for 1965; in Detroit by Blaine Etheridge, 1972–78 for 1972–76; and in New York by Garland, 1987 for 1983.)

An annotated index to international reviews. Arranged by author, with title and subject indexes.

C66   *Latin American Theatre Review.* Lawrence: U of Kansas, 1967– . 2/yr.

"Recent Publications, Materials Received and Current Bibliography" for 1967– , in volumes 1– (1967–), is a checklist of international books, articles, and unpublished papers on Latin American theater, largely from Latin America but also from other countries; the list includes plays as well as criticism and scholarship.

(D1) *Callaloo: A Journal of Afro-American and African Arts and Letters*

"Studies in Caribbean and South American Literature: An Annual Annotated Bibliography" for 1985– , in 1987– , is a classified bibliography of international books, articles, and dissertations; arranged by language area and then within each by new original writing, interviews, general studies, genres, and individual authors.

C67 *Caribbean Studies*. Río Piedras: U of Puerto Rico, 1961– . 4/yr.

"Current Bibliography" lists books and articles published in or about the Caribbean nations. Two issues a year are devoted to the island nations and two to the circum-Caribbean nations.

C68 *Cuban Studies*. Pittsburgh: U of Pittsburgh P, 1970– . Annual. (Titled *Cuban Studies Newsletter*, 1970, and vols. 1–15 published 2/yr.)

Carries an annual bibliography of international books, pamphlets, articles, and dissertations on all aspects of Cuba, classified with a section on language and literature.

C69 *Latin American Indian Literatures Journal: A Review of American Indian Texts and Studies*. McKeesport: Pennsylvania State U, 1985– . 2/yr. (Vols. 1–4 published by Geneva Coll., Beaver Falls.)

Most issues carry separate checklists of international books on Latin American Indian languages, literatures, and religion and myth.

(C57) *Revista hispánica moderna*

"Bibliografía hispanoamericana" for 1934–46 and 1955–66, in volumes 1–13 and 22–33, lists books and articles about Latin American literature. "Bibliografía hispánica" for 1947–54, in volumes 14–21 (1948–55), lists books and articles on Spanish, Portuguese, and Latin American literature.

Literary Periods

The only exclusively Spanish period bibliography is that carried in the *Bulletin of the* Comediantes (C71), but the major period bibliographies include studies of Spanish and Portuguese literature.

MEDIEVAL

(D320) *International Medieval Bibliography*
A comprehensive, classified bibliography for 1965– covering international books and articles on all aspects of medieval Europe and of the Middle East and Christian North Africa, 450–1500. Categories include art, folk studies, language, and literature (subdivided by genre and then by country or region).

(D321) *Deutsches Archiv für Erforschung des Mittelalters*
Each issue carries a comprehensive, classified, and annotated bibliography of international books and articles from the early 1930s covering all aspects of medieval life.

(D322) *Cahiers de civilisation médiévale X^e–XIIe siécles: Bibliographie*
Carries an annual bibliography of international books and articles for 1958– .

(D323) *Medioevo latino: Bolletino bibliografico della cultura europea dal secolo VI al XIV*
A comprehensive classified, annotated (in Italian) bibliography of international books, articles, and reviews on all aspects of the medieval world, 1980– .

RENAISSANCE

(D432) *Bibliographie internationale de l'humanisme et de la Renaissance*
A comprehensive, classified bibliography for 1965– of international books and articles on all aspects of the European and Latin American Renaissance.

(B31) *Studies in Philology*
Includes an annual, international, comprehensive, and classified bibliography of books and articles on Renaissance literature for 1917–68, with coverage of Continental literatures added in 1939.

(D433) *Renaissance Quarterly*
"Books Received" in each issue records about 200–300 international books a year dealing with the Renaissance; for 1952–80 this list, titled "Renaissance Books," is an extensive, classified list of new international books drawn from entries in national bibliographies.

C71　*Bulletin of the* Comediantes. Los Angeles: U of Southern California, 1948– . 2/yr.
"Bibliography of Publications on the *Comedia*" is an annual, international bibliography of books, articles, dissertations, and reviews on Spanish drama and dramatists of the golden age. First issued as a supplement to the 1950 volume and covering only non–North American items, the bibliography includes North American publications beginning with volume 26 (1974).

EIGHTEENTH CENTURY

(B42)　*The Eighteenth Century: A Current Bibliography*
An annual, annotated, and classified bibliography of international books and articles on all aspects of eighteenth-century life in Europe, Great Britain (including the Restoration period), North and South America, and Asia for 1925– . Coverage of Continental literatures began with the 1970 bibliography.

ROMANTICISM

(B51)　*The Romantic Movement: A Selective and Critical Bibliography*
An annual, annotated bibliography for 1936– providing an extensive selection of international books, reviews, articles, and dissertations that comprehensively cover all aspects of the movement in England, France, Germany, Italy, and Spain. Covers Spanish literature, 1936– . Formerly covered Spanish American literature, 1955–58; Portuguese literature, 1947–69; and Brazilian literature, 1946–69.

TWENTIETH CENTURY

(B65) *Journal of Modern Literature*
Carries an annual, classified bibliography of international, mainly English-language scholarship on modern (1885–1950) and contemporary world writers for 1970– .

(B66) *Twentieth Century Literature: A Scholarly and Critical Journal*
Most issues for 1955–1981 include an annotated bibliography of international, mainly English-language articles on twentieth-century world writers and literary subjects.

(D177) *Modern Drama*
Carries an annual bibliography for 1959– covering studies on international twentieth-century world drama and dramatists.

GERMAN AND NETHERLANDS LITERATURES

Although the *Bibliographie der deutschen Sprach- und Literaturwissenschaft* (C81) provides the most comprehensive coverage, both the *MLA International Bibliography* (A1) and *The Year's Work in Modern Language Studies* (C1) list items more likely to be available in North American libraries. German literary studies are included in the major period bibliographies listed in chapter 3. Author bibliographies are listed in chapter 6. Special subject coverage is described in chapter 5 (see especially the sections on the literary genres and on art, children's literature, comparative literature, film, folklore, linguistics and language, and music.) General humanities periodical indexes are listed in chapter 2.

For language teaching see the bibliographies listed under linguistics in chapter 5 and reviews in *German Quarterly* (D220).

General Bibliographies

(A1) *MLA International Bibliography*
International books, articles, and North American dissertations are arranged by period into sections (400–1499, 1500–99, 1600–99, etc.), within which are subsections for

genres and authors. See also under "Literary Movements" in volume 4.

C81 *Bibliographie der deutschen Sprach- und Literaturwissenschaft.* Frankfurt: Klostermann, 1957– . Annual.

The most comprehensive German bibliography. Provides classified coverage of international books, reviews, articles, dissertations, current new writing, and new editions of older works, 1945– . The literature part of the bibliography is arranged by period (medieval period, sixteenth–eighteenth centuries, *Goethezeit*, Romantic period, 1830–80, 1880–1914, 1914–45, and 1945–), with additional sections on literary history and theory. Each section has appropriate subdivisions, including ones for individual authors. Critic and author index and subject index (subjects include, e.g., *Amerika, Melancholie, Metaphor, Politik,* and *Strukturalismus*).

Although not directly related to the following, this bibliography continues coverage that had been continuous for over a century:

Jahresbericht für deutsche Sprache und Literatur. Berlin: Akademie, 1960, 1966. Annual. For 1940–50.

Jahresbericht über die wissenschaftlichen Erscheinungen auf dem Gebiete der neuren deutschen Literatur. Berlin: Gruyter, 1924–39, 1956. Annual. For 1921–36 and 1937–39.

Jahresbericht für neue deutsche Literaturgeschichte. Stuttgart: Behrs, 1890–1916, 1919. Annual. For 1892–1915.

Jahresbericht über die Erscheinungen auf dem Gebiete der germanischen Philologie. Berlin: German Philological Soc., 1879–1939.

Germania: Vierteljahrsschrift für deutsche Altertumskunde. Vienna: Gerold, 1856–92. 4/yr. Carried the annual "Bibliographische Übersicht der Erscheinungen auf dem Gebiete der germanischen Philologie" for 1862–88.

C82 *Germanistik: Internationales Referatenorgan mit bibliographischen Hinweisen.* Tübingen: Niemeyer, 1960– . 4/yr.

An extensive, classified bibliography of international

books, articles, and dissertations, with annotations in German. The sections include collections and general works, language and linguistics, general literary studies, literary studies by period, folk literature, and theater. Annual author and critic index and a list of editions in progress or newly published.

(C1)   *The Year's Work in Modern Language Studies*

The bibliographic essay on German literature has sections on medieval, sixteenth- and seventeenth-century, classical, Romantic, mid-nineteenth-century, and modern literatures. Author and critic index.

C83   *Monatshefte.* Madison: U of Wisconsin P, 1900– . 4/yr.

Carries an annual list of North American dissertations in German studies, listed in the section "Personalia."

C84   *Jahrbuch für internationale Germanistik. Reihe 3. Germanistische Dissertationen in Kurzfassung.* Bern: Lang, 1975– . Annual.

Lists international dissertations on German language, literature, folklore, and related topics, with an extensive summary of each.

(D166) *Deutsche Bibliographie: Hochschulschriften-Verzeichnis* and *Deutsche Bibliographie: Dissertationen und Habilitationsschriften*

Include dissertations and other academic writing in German universities.

C85   *Deutsche Literatur.* Stuttgart: Reclam, 1982– . Annual.

Each volume contains an overview of the year's German writing, a literary calendar, and a long section of reviews of new books including reviews reprinted from other publications. Author and title index.

C86   *Literature, Music, Fine Arts: A Review of German-Language Research Contributions on Literature, Music, and Fine Arts with Bibliographies.* Section 3 of *German Studies: German-Language Research Contributions: A Current Survey in English.* Tübingen: Inst. for Scientific Cooperation, 1968–91. 2/yr.

Consists of extensive reviews of new German-language books on literature (predominantly Germanic) and a bibliography of recent German-language books and articles on international literature.

C87   *Beiträge zur Literaturkunde: Bibliographie ausgewählter Zei-
       tungs- und Zeitschriftenbeiträge.* Leipzig: Bibliographisches
       Institut, 1952– . 2/yr. (Vol. 1 published as Supplement 3
       of *Der Bibliothekar: Zeitschrift für das Bibliothekswesen,* Volk,
       Berlin, 1946–90.)
          A classified, international bibliography for 1945– of for-
       mer East German and German-language socialist books,
       reviews, and articles on world literature. (Author has not
       examined the bibliography.)

C88   *Referatendienst zur Literaturwissenschaft.* Berlin: Förderungs-
       gesellschaft Wissenschaftliche Neuvorhaben, 1969– . 4/yr.
       (Titled *Referatendienst zur germanistischen Literaturwis-
       senschaft,* 1969–70).
          A selective, classified collection of book reviews and ab-
       stracts of articles, with emphasis on former East German
       and German socialist publications.

C89   *Internationale germanistische Bibliographie: IGB.* Munich:
       Saur, 1981–82. Annual.
          A comprehensive classified bibliography of interna-
       tional books, articles, dissertations, microforms, reviews,
       and some unpublished materials dealing with German-
       language linguistics and literature.

(D219) *Yearbook of German-American Studies*
          The "Annual Bibliography of German-Americana: Arti-
       cles, Books, and Dissertations" for 1979– continues earlier
       compilations in *German Quarterly* and *American German Re-
       view* and their cumulations.

(D220) *German Quarterly*
          Each issue has an extensive list of reviews of new books
       about German-language literature and teaching. "Bibliog-
       raphy Americana Germanica" for 1967–69, in volumes
       41–43 (1968–70), continues coverage previously carried
       for 1941–66 in *American German Review* (Philadelphia:
       Natl. Carl Schurz Foundation) volumes 8–33 (1941/42–
       66/67) and for 1933–40 in *JEGP* (C90) volumes 34–40
       (1935–41).

C90   *JEGP: Journal of English and Germanic Philology.* Urbana: U
       of Illinois, 1897– . 4/yr.

"Anglo-German Literary Bibliography" for 1933–69, in volumes 34–69 (1935–70), lists international books and articles; after 1940 this bibliography focused on Anglo-German literary relations and left biographical and historical subjects to the bibliography in *American German Review* (see D220).

C91   *Maske und Kothurn: Internationale Beiträge zur Theaterwissenschaft.* Vienna: Böhlau, 1955– . 4/yr.

Carries an annual bibliography of German books and articles on international theater, but with emphasis on German theater and German productions of non-German drama.

(D179) *Theater [year]: Jahrbuch der Zeitschrift* Theater heute

"Die deutschsprachige Theaterliteratur," for 1975– , is a classified list of new German-language books and dissertations on all aspects of international theater, including history, stagecraft, individual playwrights and performers, musical theater, and opera. Most volumes also carry a calendar of German theater productions of the year.

C92   *Zeitungs-Index: Verzeichnis wichtiger Aufsätze aus deutschsprachigen Zeitungen.* Munich: Saur, 1974– . 4/yr.

Electronic format: CD-ROM (Bowker).

An author, subject, and geographic index to twenty German-language newspapers and newsmagazines published in Austria, Germany, and Switzerland. (Author has not examined the index.)

(E151) *Modern Austrian Literature: Journal of the International Arthur Schnitzler Research Foundation*

Carries an annual list of North American dissertations on Austrian literature for 1977– starting in volume 11 (1978).

C93   *Plattdeutsche Bibliographie.* Bremen: Institut für Niederdeutsche Sprache, 1974– . 2/yr.

A bibliography of new writing in and about the Low German dialect and its literature. (Author has not examined the bibliography.)

C94   *Bibliographie zur deutschsprachigen Schweizerliteratur.* BSL. Bern: Schweizerische Landesbibliothek, 1976– . Annual.

(Vols. 1–3 titled *Bibliographie zur deutschsprachigen Schweizer-literatur, schweizerdeutschen Dialektologie und Namenkunde.*)
A bibliography of studies on Swiss literature and language. (Author has not examined the bibliography.)

Literary Periods

See also the general bibliographies just listed, subject bibliographies in chapter 5, and author bibliographies in chapter 6.

MEDIEVAL

(D320) *International Medieval Bibliography*
A comprehensive, classified bibliography for years 1965– covering international books and articles on all aspects of medieval Europe and of the Middle East and Christian North Africa, 450–1500. Categories include art, folk studies, language, and literature (subdivided by genre and then by country or region).

(D321) *Deutsches Archiv für Erforschung des Mittelalters*
Each issue carries a comprehensive, classified, and annotated bibliography of international books and articles from the early 1930s covering all aspects of medieval life.

(D322) *Cahiers de civilisation médiévale Xᵉ–XIIᵉ siècles: Bibliographie*
Carries an annual bibliography of international books and articles for 1958– .

(D323) *Medioevo latino: Bolletino bibliografico della cultura europea dal secolo VI al XIV*
A comprehensive, classified, annotated (in Italian) bibliography of international books, articles, and reviews on all aspects of the medieval world, 1980– .

RENAISSANCE

(D432) *Bibliographie internationale de l'humanisme et de la Renaissance*
A comprehensive, classified bibliography for 1965– covering international books and articles on all aspects of the European and Latin American Renaissance.

(B31) *Studies in Philology*
Includes an annual, international, comprehensive, and classified bibliography of books and articles on Renaissance literature for 1917–68, with coverage of Continental literatures added in 1939.

(D433) *Renaissance Quarterly*
"Books Received" in each issue records about 200–300 international books a year dealing with the Renaissance; for 1952–80 this list, titled "Renaissance Books," is an extensive, classified list of new international books drawn from entries in national bibliographies.

C95 *Wolfenbütteler Barock-Nachrichten.* Wiesbaden: Harrassowitz, 1974– . 3/yr. (Formerly published by Hauswedell, Hamburg, 4/yr.)
Most issues include an extensive, classified bibliography of international books, reviews, articles, and German dissertations on German baroque culture. Subdivided for texts and general studies, individual authors, and book reviews.

(E109) *Luther Jahrbuch*
The "Lutherbibliographie" for 1927– is an annual, comprehensive bibliography of international books and articles on Luther and aspects of the Reformation.

EIGHTEENTH CENTURY

See also Goethe and Lessing in chapter 6.

(B42) *The Eighteenth Century: A Current Bibliography*
An annual, annotated, and classified bibliography of international books and articles on all aspects of eighteenth-century life in Europe, Great Britain (including the Restoration period), North and South America, and Asia for 1925– . Coverage of German literature began with the 1970 bibliography.

C96 *Internationale Bibliographie zur deutschen Klassik, 1750–1850.* Weimar: Nationale Forschungs- und Gedenkstätten der klassischen deutschen Literatur, 1964– . Annual. (Formerly 2/yr.)

A classified bibliography of international books, reviews, and articles. Covers cultural background, aesthetic and literary theory, and authors. Occasional annotations; critic and subject index.

ROMANTICISM

(B51) *The Romantic Movement: A Selective and Critical Bibliography*
An annual, annotated bibliography for 1936– providing an extensive selection of international books, reviews, articles, and dissertations that comprehensively cover all aspects of the movement in England, France, Germany, Italy, and Spain. Arranged in sections for the countries and then for individual authors; for the social, intellectual, political, scientific, and artistic environment; and for bibliographies.

TWENTIETH CENTURY

C97 *KLG: Kritisches Lexikon der deutschsprachigen Gegenwartsliteratur*. Munich: Text und Kritik, 1978– . Annual.
A loose-leaf service offering critical introductions to contemporary writers followed by primary and secondary bibliographies, the former classified by genre and the latter arranged chronologically.

C98 *Basis: Jahrbuch für deutsche Gegenwartsliteratur*. Frankfurt: Athenäum, 1970– . Annual.
"Bibliographische Hinweise zur Sekundärliteratur" for 1971–72, in volumes 3–4 (1972–73), is a classified bibliography of mainly German-language books and articles on post-1945 German-language literature, with sections for countries, genres, and individual authors.

(B65) *Journal of Modern Literature*
Carries an annual, classified bibliography of international, mainly English-language scholarship on modern (1885–1950) and contemporary world writers for 1970– .

(B66) *Twentieth Century Literature: A Scholarly and Critical Journal*
Most issues for 1955–81 carried an annotated bibliography of international, mainly English-language articles on twentieth-century world writers and literary subjects.

(D177) *Modern Drama*

Carries an annual bibliography for 1959– covering studies on international twentieth-century world drama and dramatists.

Netherlands Literature

See coverage in the *MLA International Bibliography* (A1), *The Year's Work in Modern Language Studies* (C1), period bibliographies, and relevant subject bibliographies in chapter 5, especially those for the Renaissance, art, history, printing, and the literary genres.

C101   *Dutch Studies: An Annual Review of the Language, Literature, and Life of the Low Countries.* The Hague: Nijhoff-Wolters, 1974– . Annual.

"Publications on Dutch Language and Literature in Languages Other Than Dutch" covers international books and articles on authors and on Dutch language and literature in general.

C102   *Bibliografie van de Nederlandse taal- en literatuurwetenschap.* The Hague: Stichting Bibliographia Nederlandica, 1970– . Annual.

Electronic format: online (Nederlands Centrum voor Bibliotheekautomatisering Pica, 1940–45, 1960–).

A classified bibliography of international books and articles on Dutch language and literature. Subject and critic indexes.

C103   *Nijhoff's index op Nederlandse en Vlaamse periodiken.* The Hague: Nijhoff, 1910–71. 12/yr.

A subject index to Netherlands periodicals in all fields. Creative writing indexed by author.

SCANDINAVIAN AND OLD NORSE LITERATURES

Scholarship in the Scandinavian literatures is covered in the *MLA International Bibliography* (A1) and *The Year's Work in Modern Language Studies* (C1), in *Scandinavian Studies* (C105), and in national literary yearbooks. Specialized subject bibliographies are listed in chapter 5 (see especially children's literature, drama, film, folklore, linguistics and language, and the literary genres). General literary bibliographies and humanities periodical indexes are listed in chapter 2. Author bibliographies are in chapter 6.

The *MLA International Bibliography* is the only bibliography covering Baltic and Finnish literatures, both of which are included in the section for Northern European literature.

For language teaching, see the bibliographies listed under linguistics in chapter 5.

Scandinavian Literatures

(A1)   *MLA International Bibliography*
       Coverage of studies on Scandinavian literature is divided into sections for national languages: Old Norse, Danish, Finnish, Icelandic, Norwegian, and Swedish. Each national section is further subdivided for century, genres, and authors.

(C1)   *The Year's Work in Modern Language Studies*
       Separate chapters are devoted to Danish, Norwegian, and Swedish literatures.

C105   *Scandinavian Studies*. Provo: Soc. for the Advancement of Scandinavian Study, 1911– . 4/yr. (Publisher and place have varied.)
       "American Scandinavian Bibliography" for 1947–72, in volumes 20–45 (1948–73), and "Scandinavia in English: A Bibliography of Books, Articles, and Book Reviews," in volume 47, number 4 (1975), provide coverage of studies in the social sciences and humanities. Relevant subject categories include folklore and mythology, language, literature (subdivided by nation and including film and philosophy), theater and drama, and children's books.

C106   *Acta philologica scandinavica / Tidsskrift for nordisk sprogforskning / Journal of Scandinavian Philology*. Copenhagen: Munksgaard, 1926– . 2/yr.
       "Bibliography of Scandinavian Philology" for 1925– is

a classified, annotated bibliography mainly of Scandinavian books, articles, and dissertations on Scandinavian names, language, and philological aspects of literary texts. Supplemented since volume 29 (1970) by "Bulletin of Scandinavian Philology," a list of current books and articles without summary annotations. The bibliography is considerably behind schedule.

(B65) *Journal of Modern Literature*

Carries an annual, classified bibliography of international, mainly English-language scholarship on modern (1885–1950) and contemporary world writers for 1970– .

(B66) *Twentieth Century Literature: A Scholarly and Critical Journal*

Most issues for 1955–81 carried an annotated bibliography of international, mainly English-language articles on twentieth-century world writers and literary subjects.

(D177) *Modern Drama*

Carries an annual bibliography for 1959– covering studies on international twentieth-century world drama and dramatists.

C107 Dania Polyglotta: *Literature on Denmark in Languages Other Than Danish and Books of Danish Interest Published Abroad.* Copenhagen: Bibliothekscentralen, 1946– . Annual. (Subtitle in French, 1946–60.)

An annual bibliography for 1945– , continuing coverage in Dania Polyglotta: *Répertoire bibliographique des ouvrages, etudes, articles, etc. en langues étrangères parus en Danemark de 1901 à 1944,* 3 volumes (Copenhagen: Bibliothèque Royale, 1948–51).

C108 *Dansk tidsskrift-index.* Copenhagen: Bibliotekscentralen, 1916– . Annual.

A classified bibliography for 1885– of articles in about 360 Danish periodicals on all subjects. Author and subject indexes.

C109 *Norsk litterær årbok.* Oslo: Norske Samlaget, 1966– . Annual.

"Bibliografi til norsk litteraturforskning" for 1965– is a classified list mainly of Norwegian books and articles on Norwegian literature. Some entries are annotated in Norwegian.

C110   *Norsk tidsskriftindex.* Oslo: Steenske, 1918–65. Annual.
        A classified bibliography of articles in about 250 Norwegian periodicals on all subjects.

C111   *Samlaren: Tidskrift för svensk litteraturvetenskaplig forskning.* Uppsala: Litteraturvetenskapliga, Uppsala U, 1880– . Annual.
        "Svensk litteraturhistorisk bibliografi," 1880– , is a classified bibliography mainly of Swedish books and articles on Swedish literature, including religious and folk literatures, with brief descriptive annotations in Swedish. Published separately 1881–1928.

C112   *Svenska tidskriftsartiklar.* Lund: Bibliotekstjänst, 1953– . 12/yr.
        A classified index to about 400 Swedish periodicals covering all subjects. Coverage extended to 1940 by *Svenska tidskriftsartiklar 1940–1945* (Borås: Hogskolar i Borås, 1985). Author index.

Old Norse Literature

See also the medieval studies bibliographies listed in chapter 5.

C115   *Bibliography of Old Norse and Icelandic Studies.* Copenhagen: Royal Library, 1964– . Annual.
        A bibliography of international books, reviews, and articles for 1963– covering medieval Icelandic and Norwegian language, literature, and culture. Items listed by author, or title if anonymous. Subject index.

(A1)   *MLA International Bibliography*
        See the section for Scandinavian literature.

(C1)   *The Year's Work in Modern Language Studies*
        See the section on Norwegian literature.

(C82)   *Germanistik: Internationales Referatenorgan mit bibliographischen Hinweisen*
        Lists current studies in the sections "Nordische Altertumskunde" and "Altnordische Literaturgeschichte."

MODERN GREEK LITERATURE

(A1)   *MLA International Bibliography*
       Studies on modern Greek have been listed for 1968– .

C121   *Bibliographia neoellénikés philologias.* Athens: U of Athens, 1959– . Annual. (Titled *Bibliographikon deltion neoellénikés philologias,* 1959–65.)

       A classified bibliography of international books, reviews, and articles on modern Greek literature, philology, and culture. Critic index.

C122   *Bulletin signalétique de bibliographie hellénique.* Athens: Institut Français d'Athenènes, 1947–78. Annual. (Titled *Bulletin analytique de bibliographie hellénique,* 1947–73.)

       An extensive, classified bibliography for 1940– of international books, articles on all aspects of modern Greece, including literature, language, and the arts. Abstracts and author index.

C123   *Bibliographical Bulletin of the Greek Language / Deltion vivliographias tés hellénikés glóssés.* Athens: U of Athens, 1974– . Annual.

       An international, classified bibliography for 1973– of books, reviews, and articles on ancient, Byzantine, and modern Greek language. It emphasizes linguistics more than it does philology. Author index.

ASIAN LITERATURES

The most general coverage of English-language literary scholarship is provided by the *MLA International Bibliography* (A1). Other bibliographies either limit coverage to individual literatures or include scholarship on nonliterary subjects. See the general periodical indexes listed in chapter 2 and see chapter 5 for subject bibliographies.

For language teaching see the bibliographies listed under linguistics in chapter 5.

The arrangement here follows that of the *MLA International*

Bibliography, and items are listed in order of their comprehensiveness and general availability in North American libraries.

General Bibliographies

(A1) *MLA International Bibliography*
Coverage of the Asian literatures began in 1956; items were listed under the general section through 1968 and then given a separate section, 1969– . The general Asian section is followed by the geographically based subdivisions of east Asian, south Asian, southeast Asian, and west Asian literatures, with each further subdivided by country. Central Asian literature is classified with the literatures of east Europe and Siberia.

C125 *Asien Bibliographie.* Bad Wildungen, Ger.: Asien Bucherei, 1949–86. 4/yr. (Absorbed *Bibliographia asiatica*, Asien Bucherei, Bad Wildungen, Ger. 1953–77.)
An international, classified list of articles on all aspects of near and east Asia, with items arranged by region and then by country. No index.

(B65) *Journal of Modern Literature*
Carries an annual, classified bibliography of international, mainly English-language scholarship on modern (1885–1950) and contemporary world writers for 1970– , with an emphasis on British and American figures.

(B66) *Twentieth Century Literature: A Scholarly and Critical Journal*
Most issues for 1955–81 include an annotated bibliography of international, mainly English-language articles on twentieth-century world writers and literary subjects.

(D177) *Modern Drama*
Carries an annual bibliography of studies on international twentieth-century world drama and dramatists for 1959– .

Near and Middle Eastern Literatures

C131 *Journal of Arabic Literature.* Leiden, Neth.: Brill, 1970– . 2/yr. (Annual for vols. 1–18.)

"Recent Publications," in volumes 4– (1973–), lists international books by and about Arabic writers, with brief annotations.

"Bibliographie littéraire tunisienne," appearing in alternate years (approximately) for 1972– , lists books on Tunisian literature.

"Annual Bibliography of Works on Arabic Literature Published in the Soviet Union," covering 1973–80, is in volumes 1–14.

C132 *Quarterly Index Islamicus: Current Books, Articles and Papers on Islamic Studies.* London: Saur, 1977– . 4/yr. (Vols. 1–15, Mansell, London.)

An extensive, classified, bibliography of international books, articles, and papers for 1906– . Supplements the *Index Islamicus* and its five-year supplements (London: Heffer, 1958–67; Mansell, 1972–).

C133 *Middle East Journal.* Washington: Middle East Inst., 1947– . 4/yr.

"Bibliography of Periodical Literature" in each issue is an international, classified list of articles on all aspects of the Middle East since the rise of Islam. Includes North Africa, Muslim Spain, and Israel. See the section on language, literature, and the arts. Cumulated in Peter M. Rossi and Wayne E. White, editors, *Articles on the Middle East, 1947–1971: A Cumulation of the Bibliographies from the* Middle East Journal, 4 volumes (Ann Arbor: Pierian, 1980).

C134 *Revue des études islamiques.* Paris: Geuthner, 1927– . 2/yr.

"Abstracta islamica," an annual supplement, is an international classified list of books, reviews, and articles. See the sections for languages, literatures, and folklore. Critic index.

C135 *The Middle East Abstracts and Index.* Tucson: Aristarchus, 1978– . Annual. (Vols. 1–10 published by Northumberland, Pittsburgh and then Seattle, 4/yr.)

A classified bibliography of international publications on Near East affairs, with English abstracts and a subject index.

C136 *Muslim World Book Review.* Leicester: Islamic Foundation, 1981– . 4/yr.

Reviews new international books.

C137   *Bibliography of Modern Hebrew Literature in Translation.* Tel
Aviv: Inst. for the Translation of Hebrew Lit., 1979– .
2/yr.

Lists book and periodical translations for 1972– into
English in issue number 1 and into other languages in
number 2. Continues Yahai Goell, *Bibliography of Modern
Hebrew Literature in English Translation* (Jerusalem: Israel
Universities, 1968) and *Bibliography of Modern Hebrew Litera-
ture in Translation* (Tel Aviv: Inst. for the Translation of
Hebrew Lit., 1975).

C138   *Abstracta iranica.* Paris: Institut Française de Recherche en
Iran, 1978– . Annual, as a supplement to *Studia iranica*
(Louvain, Belg.: Peeters, 1972–).

Lists international books and articles on Iran, Afghani-
stan, and all areas relevant to Iranian culture and includes
sections on linguistics, ancient and modern Persian literature, and Kurdish literature.

C139   *Turkologischer Anzeiger / Turkology Annual.* Vienna: Oriental-
istisches Institut der Universität Wien, 1975– . Annual.
(Vols. 1–2 published in *Wiener Zeitschrift für die Kunde des
Morgenlands.*)

An extensive, classified bibliography of international
books and articles on Turkish culture, with extensive sections on literature, theater, folk literature, and language.

South and East Asian Literatures

GENERAL

C145   *Bibliography of Asian Studies.* Ann Arbor: Assn. for Asian
Studies, 1969– . Annual. Continues coverage in *Journal of
Asian Studies*, 1959–69, *Far Eastern Quarterly*, 1941–56, and
Bulletin of Far Eastern Bibliography, 1936–40.)

A classified list of international books and articles on all
subjects for 1941– , arranged first by country and then by
subject (e.g., literature). Critic index. Partially cumulated
as *Cumulative Bibliography of Asian Studies, 1942–1965*, 4
volumes (Boston: Hall, 1969–70).

C146   *Annual Review of English Books on Asia.* Salt Lake City: Brigham Young UP, 1974– . Annual.

A catalog of books published in North America and Great Britain and acquired by the Harold B. Lee Library at Brigham Young University. Books are listed by country and then by subject, form (for example, bibliography and directory), and author.

C147   *Doctoral Dissertations on Asia: An Annotated Bibliographical Journal of Current International Research.* Ann Arbor: Assn. for Asian Studies, 1975– . 2/yr.

A classified bibliography of international dissertations on all aspects of Asia, arranged by region and then country. It continues coverage formerly in Frank J. Shulman, editor, *Doctoral Dissertations on China, 1971–1975: A Bibliography of Studies of Western Languages* (Seattle: U of Washington P, 1978), and Leonard H. Gordon and Frank J. Shulman, editors, *Doctoral Dissertations on China: A Bibliography of Studies in Western Languages, 1945–1970* (Seattle: Assn. for Asian Studies, 1972).

(B1)   *Annual Bibliography of English Language and Literature*

Covers English-language writers of India and other Asian countries.

(B80)   *Journal of Commonwealth Literature*

"Annual Bibliography of Commonwealth Literature," an international, classified bibliography of books and articles for 1964– , covers studies on the literature of India, Pakistan, Sri Lanka, Singapore, and Malaysia and lists new creative writing.

C148   *Books and Articles on Oriental Subjects Published in Japan during [year].* Tokyo: Inst. of Eastern Culture, 1954– . Annual.

An author list of books and a classified bibliography of Japanese articles, with major sections on Korean and Chinese language and literature. Critic index.

C149   *Quarterly Check-list of Oriental Studies.* Darien: Amer. Bibliographic Service, 1959–78. 4/yr.

An international author list of books, with an annual author, translator, and editor index. Continues *Quarterly*

Check-list of Oriental Art and Archeology and *Quarterly Check-list of Oriental Religions* (both Darien: Amer. Bibliographic Service, 1958–59).

INDIAN LITERATURE

C151   *Indian Literary Index.* New Delhi: Sahitya Akademi, 1988– . 2/yr.

Indexes creative writing and critical articles in Indian periodicals. (Author has not reviewed the index.)

C152   *Indian Literature: Sahitya Akademi's Literary Bi-monthly.* New Delhi: Sahitya Akademi, 1981– . 2/yr.

The journal's annual surveys (in English; title varies) for 1981– in volumes 25– (1982–) are 10-page essays on new writing in about 20 Indian languages and regions.

C153   *Index Indo-Asiaticus.* Calcutta: Centre for Asian Documentation, 1978– . 4/yr.

Lists contents of Indian journals and of North American and European journals with articles on Indian culture.

C154   *Guide to Indian Periodical Literature.* Gurgaon: Indian Documentation Service, 1964– . 4/yr.

Author and subject index to Indian periodicals in the humanities and social sciences. Indexes book reviews.

CHINESE LITERATURE

C159   *Chinese Literature: Essays, Articles and Reviews.* Madison: U of Wisconsin, 1978– . 2/yr.

"Recent Publications on Chinese Literature," a review article, covers current scholarship in specific countries.

C160   *Modern Chinese Literature.* Boulder: U of Colorado, 1984– . 2/yr.

"Doctoral Dissertations in Western Languages on Modern Chinese Literature," covering 1980– , is in three installments in volumes 1 (1984), 4 (1987), and 7 (1993).

C161   *Pao k'an tzu liao so yin.* Beijing: Chung-Kuo Jen Min Ta Hsueh Shu Pao Tzu Liao She, 1980– . Annual. (Titled *Fu yin pao k'an tzu liao so yin,* 1980–82.)

An index to Chinese periodicals and newspapers in the humanities and social sciences.

C162   *Ch'uan kuo pao k'an so yin. Che she pan.* Shanghai: Shang-
        hai T'u Shu Kuan, 1973– . 12/yr.
        An index to Chinese periodicals and newspapers in the
        humanities and social sciences.
C163   *Index to Chinese Periodical Literature.* Taipei: Natl. Central
        Library, 1970– . Frequency varies.
        Classified subject arrangement with author index.
C164   *Classified Index to Chinese Periodicals.* Taipei: Natl. Taiwan
        U Library, 1960– .
        Covers mainly Taiwanese periodicals since 1945.
C165   *Bibliography Quarterly.* Taipei: Student Book, 1966– . 4/yr.
        Each issue carries an index to scholarly books and articles
        in literature, history, and philosophy.
C166   *Publishing and Research Semimonthly.* Taipei: Ch'eng-wen,
        1977– . 24/yr.
        Each issue carries a classified subject index to current
        articles in Taiwan periodicals and newspapers.
C167   *China aktuell.* Hamburg: Institut für Asienkunde, 1972– .
        12/yr.
        "Articles on China" is a selective, classified list of articles
        that mainly covers public affairs but includes five or ten
        items an issue on culture, literature, and the arts.
C168   *Tamkang Review: A Quarterly of Comparative Studies between
        Chinese and Foreign Literatures.* Taipei: Tamkang U, 1970– .
        4/yr.
        "Chinese English Comparative Literature Bibliography"
        has appeared twice, listing studies for 1978– in volume 12,
        number 4 (1982), and volume 17, number 4 (1987), and
        continuing John J. Deeney, "Comparative Literature and
        China: A Bibliographical Review of Materials in English,"
        China and the West: Comparative Literature Studies, edited by
        William Tay, Ying-hsiung Chou, and Heh-hsiang Yüan
        (Hong Kong: Chinese UP, 1980, 287–301).

JAPANESE LITERATURE

C171   *Current Contents of Academic Journals in Japan.* Tokyo: Cen-
        ter for Academic Publications, 1973– . Annual.
        A classified listing of articles (titles transliterated) in

Japanese journals for 1971– dealing with literature, arranged in three sections for Western, Japanese, and other literatures. Listed about 560 articles in 1990.

C172   *Zasshi kiji sakuin: Jinbun-shakai-hen.* Tokyo: Natl. Diet Library, 1948– . 12/yr.

An index to Japanese periodicals covering the humanities and social sciences. Cumulated for 1955–74: *Zasshi kiji sakuin: Jinbun-shakai-hen. Ruiseki sakuin ban* (Tokyo: Natl. Diet Library, 1977).

C173   *Journal of the Association of Teachers of Japanese.* Middlebury: Middlebury Coll., 1957– . 2/yr.

Publishes biennially abstracts of dissertations and theses on Japanese literature, language, and linguistics, drawing mainly from *Dissertation Abstracts International* (D154) but including some additional items.

C174   *Shukan dokushojin.* Tokyo: Dokushojin, 1958– . 52/yr.

Weekly index of book reviews in Japan. (Author has not examined the index.)

C175   *Bibliography of the Humanistic Studies and Social Relations.* Tokyo: Assn. for Science Documents Educ., Tokyo Inst. of Tech., 1955–63.

A classified bibliography of Japanese books and articles for 1952–61, with a section for language and literature, further divided for Japanese, English and American, German, French, Chinese, and other languages and literatures.

KOREAN LITERATURE

C177   *Asiatic Research Bulletin.* Seoul: Asiatic Research Center, 1957– . 4/yr.

Includes a classified list of Korean books and articles on all aspects of Korea.

C178   *Chonggi kanhaengmul kisa saegin / Korean Periodicals Index.* Seoul: Natl. Assembly Library, 1969– . Annual.

An author and subject index to Korean periodicals, with cumulations extending coverage back to 1910.

AFRICAN LITERATURES

There are as yet no specialized bibliographies for individual African national literatures, but there are several general bibliographies. In addition to the titles listed in this section, one should consult appropriate subject bibliographies listed in chap-. ter 5, such as those on African American studies and on folk-lore, and the humanities periodical indexes listed in chapter 2.

For language teaching, see the bibliographies listed under linguistics in chapter 5.

(A1) *MLA International Bibliography*

Coverage of black African literatures began in 1965 and is now arranged by region and then by country. In 1969–80 the African section was divided topically (general, bibliography, folklore, and literature) and then further subdivided for the major language groups of Arabic, English, French, Portuguese, and Swahili.

(B80) *Journal of Commonwealth Literature*

The annual bibliography for 1964– covers Africa in general, southern and western African nations, and South Africa (since vol. 10, 1975). Lists creative writing as well as literary studies.

(D1) *Callaloo: A Journal of Afro-American and African Arts and Letters*

"Studies in African Literatures and Oratures: An Annual Annotated Bibliography," is a selective, classified bibliography of international books, articles, and dissertations for 1985– and of primary works for 1986– . *Callaloo*'s similar Caribbean bibliography may also contain items of interest.

(B1) *Annual Bibliography of English Language and Literature*

Coverage includes all writers in English. Items are arranged by century, and there is an author and critic index.

(C15) *Bibliographie der französischen Literaturwissenschaft*

Studies on individual French-language authors are included in the two chapters on twentieth-century literature, and studies on African French-language literature and film in general are included in the chapter "La littérature française hors de France."

(C28)   *French XX Bibliography*
    French African literatures are included in the section
    on francophone literary history and studies on individual
    African authors are included in part 2.

C181   *International African Bibliography*. London: Mansell, 1971– .
    4/yr.
    A comprehensive, classified bibliography of interna-
    tional books and articles for 1971– , continuing coverage
    for 1928–70 in *Africa: Journal of the International African
    Institute* (London: Oxford UP, 1929–70), emphasizing so-
    cial sciences, social and public policy, humanities, and tech-
    nology. Items are now arranged by region, then nation,
    and then subject (see the sections for language and litera-
    ture) but earlier were arranged by subject and then nation.
    Author and detailed subject indexes are cumulated annu-
    ally. The articles for 1948–71 are also abstracted in *African
    Abstracts: Quarterly Review of Articles in Current Periodicals*
    (London: Intl. African Inst., 1950–72; 4/yr.).
    Cumulated for 1929–72 in Ruth Jones, editor, *Cumula-
    tive Bibliography of African Studies*, 5 volumes (Boston: Hall,
    1973) and for 1973–78 in J. D. Pearson, editor, *International
    African Bibliography, 1973–1978: Books, Articles, and Papers
    in African Studies* (London: Mansell, 1982).

C182   *A Current Bibliography on African Affairs*. Farmingdale: Bay-
    wood, 1962– . 4/yr.
    A selective, classified, international bibliography of
    books and articles on various aspects of African affairs. See
    sections for literature, linguistics, plays and drama, mass
    communication, and folktales.

C183   *African Bibliography*. Edinburgh: Edinburgh UP, 1985– .
    Annual. (Published by Manchester UP, Manchester,
    1985–90.)
    A classified bibliography for 1984– covering interna-
    tional books and articles on all aspects of Africa, containing
    entries arranged by country and then subject (e.g., lan-
    guage, literature, media) and a detailed subject index.

C184   *Quarterly Index to Periodical Literature, Eastern and Southern
    Africa*. Nairobi: Library of Congress Office, 1991– . 4/yr.

A classified index to articles in eastern and southern African periodicals, with author, subject, and geographic indexes. Includes literature; language; and art, music, and drama.

(B83) *Index to South African Periodicals / Repertorium van Suid-Afrikaanse tydskrifartikels*

An author and subject index to about 500 periodicals in all subjects.

C185 *Research in African Literatures.* Bloomington: Indiana UP, 1970– . 3/yr. (Vols. 1–20 published by U of Texas P, Austin.)

Recent North American dissertations on African literature were listed at least once a year through volume 17 (1986) and most issues through volume 20 (1989) include a section of bibliographic articles.

C186 *Africana Journal: A Bibliographic and Review Quarterly.* New York: Africana, 1970–83. 4/yr. (Formerly *Africana Library Journal*, 1970–73.)

Each issue includes a classified bibliography of international books on all aspects of Africa. Items arranged by subject and then by region or country. See the sections on children's literature, folklore, languages, linguistics and literature, and literary criticism. Critic and subject indexes.

C187 *Journal des Africanistes.* Paris: Société des Africanistes, 1931– . 2/yr. (Titled *Journal de la Société des Africanistes*, 1931–75.)

Includes an annual, classified bibliography for 1931–74 covering mainly French-language books and articles on all aspects and areas of Africa. See sections on linguistics, arts, and literature.

EAST EUROPEAN LITERATURES

These literatures are particularly well served by bibliographies of current scholarship, although in North America access to both the bibliographies and the studies is not so easy as it is for other literatures. Besides the items listed here, one should

consult the major period bibliographies (see ch. 3), the appropriate subject bibliographies in chapter 5 (see, e.g., art, drama,
folklore, history, Jewish studies, medieval studies, philosophy,
religion, and Renaissance), the author bibliographies in chapter
6, and the humanities periodical indexes in chapter 2.

For language teaching, see the bibliographies listed under
linguistics in chapter 5.

General Bibliographies

(A1)   *MLA International Bibliography*
       The section "Literatures of East Europe, Central Asia,
and Siberia" covers most of the former Soviet literatures,
mainly Russian. Limited coverage in the general studies
section began in 1929. In 1950 a separate section for east
European literatures was added, and the present detailed
coverage began with the 1967 bibliography. Folklore studies were included in the literature section through 1980.
       The Baltic literatures are listed under northern Euro-
pean literature, and Czech, Slovak, Hungarian, and Polish
literatures under central European; Balkan literature includes Albanian, Bulgarian, Croatian, Romanian, Slov-
enian, Yugoslavian and former Yugoslavian, and Greek
literatures.

(C1)   *The Year's Work in Modern Language Studies*
       Covers international studies of Czech, Slovak, Polish,
Russian, Belorussian, Ukrainian, and Serbo-Croatian language and literature.

C191   *American Bibliography of Slavic and East European Studies for
[year]*. Columbus: American Assn. for Advancement of
Slavic Studies, 1957– . Annual.
       A classified bibliography of North American books, arti-
cles, and dissertations on all areas of Slavic and east European studies. Chapters on language and linguistics and
on literature are subdivided by national language. Book
reviews are listed separately. Writer and critic indexes.

C192   *Soviet, East European, and Slavonic Studies in Britain*. Glasgow: U of Glasgow, 1971– . Annual.

A classified bibliography of books, reviews, articles, and newspaper stories published in Great Britain. Items are arranged by country and then subject, with headings under Russian literature for individual authors. Editions and translations are listed if published in Great Britain. Critic index.

C193 *Bibliographic Guide to Soviet and East European Studies.* Boston: Hall, 1978– . Annual.

A bibliography of international books, serials, and other separate publications cataloged by the Library of Congress and the New York Public Library, 1978– . Items arranged by author, title, and subject.

C194 *New Contents Slavistics / Inhaltsverzeichnisse slavistischen Zeitschriften: Contents of Current Periodicals in the Field of Slavic Linguistics, Literature, and Folklore.* Munich: Sagner, 1976– . 4/yr. (Vols. for 1976–79 titled *Inhaltsverzeichnisse slavistische Zeitschriften: ISZ* and published by Bayerische Staatsbibliothek, Munich.)

Reprints the contents pages of some 340 international periodicals, along with yearbooks, collections, and conference proceedings. No index.

C195 *Slavic Review: American Quarterly of Soviet and East European Studies.* Urbana: Amer. Assn. for the Advancement of Slavic Studies, 1941– . 4/yr.

"Doctoral Dissertations on Russia, the Soviet Union, and Eastern Europe Accepted by American, Canadian, and British Universities," for 1960– , is an annual listing in volumes 23– (1964–).

C196 *Revue slavistique / Rocznik slawistyczny.* Warsaw: Ossolineum, 1908– . Annual.

Through volume 49 (1973) the review includes an international, comprehensive, classified bibliography of books, reviews, and articles on all Slavic languages and literatures, 1908–72. *Revue slavistique* now regularly publishes bibliographies on a variety of subjects. Critic index; editorial matter in French and Polish.

(D177) *Modern Drama*

Carries an annual, international bibliography of books and articles on twentieth-century dramatists.

Individual Countries

HUNGARY

C201 A magyar irodalom és irodalomtudomány bibliográfiája. Budapest: Országos Széchényi Könyvtár, 1979– . Annual.

A classified bibliography of Hungarian books and articles on Hungarian and world literature and literary history for 1976– . Continues coverage for 1945–65 in *A magyar irodalom bibliográfiája* (Budapest: Muvelt, 1950–78) and coverage extended by *A magyar irodalom és irodalomtudomány bibliográfiája 1971–1975*, 2 volumes (Budapest: Országos Széchényi Könyvtár, 1989).

C202 *Irodalomtörténeti közlemények*. Budapest: Akadémiai Kiadó, 1891– . 4/yr.

Since 1962, has carried an annual list of books and articles on Hungarian literary history.

POLAND

C205 *Literatura piękna: Adnotowany rocznik bibliograficzny*. Warsaw: Stowarzyszenie Bibliotekarzy Polskich, 1956–86. Annual.

A classified bibliography of Polish books, reviews, and articles on Polish and world literature, arranged by country. Lists translations into Polish. Abstracts and critic and subject indexes.

C206 *Polska bibliografia literacka*. Warsaw: Państwowe Wydawnictwo Naukowe, 1958–83. Annual.

Classified bibliography of Polish books and articles on world literature, ancient and modern, as well as theater, film, radio, and television for 1946–82. Author and subject indexes.

RUSSIA

C211 *Novaia literatura po sotsial'nym i gumanitarnym naukam: Literaturovedenie: Bibliograficheskii ukazatel'*. Moscow: Institut Nauchnoi Informatsii po Obshchestvennym Naukam, Rossiiskaia Akademiia Nauk, 1993– . 12/yr.

A classified bibliography of international books and articles on the literatures of Russia, the nations formerly part of the Soviet Union, and other nations for 1953– .

Combines and continues coverage of Soviet publications formerly listed in *Novaia sovetskaia literatura po obshchestvennym naukam: Literaturovedenie*, 1976–92 (titled *Novaia otechestvennaia literatura po obshchestvennym naukam* in 1992), and *Novaia sovetskaia literatura po literaturovedenie*, 1954–75, and of international publications formerly in *Novaia inostrannaia literatura po obshchestevennym naukam. Literaturovedenie*, 1976–92, and *Novaia inostrannaia literatura po literaturovedeniiu*, 1954–91. (Author has not examined the bibliography.)

C212 *Sotsial'nye i gumanitarnye nauki. Seria 7, literaturovedenie: Otechestvennaia literatura.* Moscow: Institut Nauchnoi Informatsii po Obshchestvennym Naukam, Rossiiskaia Akademiia Nauk, 1993– . 4/yr.

A journal of abstracts of recent articles on Russian and world literature.

C213 *Sovetskaia khudozhestvennaia literatura i kritika.* Moscow: Sovetskii Pisatel', 1952– . 2/yr.

A classified bibliography for 1938– of current Russian (formerly Soviet) creative writing and criticism (books, reviews, and articles). Author, critic, and title index and an index to Russian-language translations of other former Soviet writing. Continues coverage provided by *Khudozhestvennaia literatura, russkaia i perevodnaia: Bibliografia*, 6 volumes (Moscow: Gosudarstvennaia Izdatel'stvo Khudozhestvennai Literatury, 1926–59).

C214 *Sovetskoe literaturovedenie i kritika: Russkaia sovetskaia literatura.* Moscow: Nauka, 1966–79. Irregular.

A classified bibliography of Russian-language books, reviews, and articles on Soviet literature. Author and subject indexes.

Chapter Five
Subjects

I his chapter lists bibliographies for subjects not covered in the chapters on national literatures. They range from the literary (genres, themes and topics, cross-national subjects) to comparative and area studies (classical, medieval, women's), the fine and performing arts, related fields (art, film, folklore, history, religion), and related professional work (composition, journalism, language teaching)—anything, in short, that would be needed by, or of use to, literary scholars and teachers. Although English and American literature subjects and sources are emphasized, there are many bibliographies here for study and teaching in the other languages and literatures. In most of the categories the list of bibliographies is selective, but the selections, individually or as groups, are intended to be comprehensive, to cover a wide range of formats and publishing sources, to be accessible in North American libraries, to be relevant to literary study or professional work, and to express historical, philosophical, or humanistic interests. The categories are listed alphabetically, and they contain some cross-references; the index gives further subject access.

African American Studies

See also under American studies, ethnic and minority studies, and regionalism, below, as well as the American literature section of chapter 3.

D1   *Callaloo: A Journal of Afro-American and African Arts and Letters*. Charlottesville: UP of Virginia, 1976– . 4/yr.

"Studies in African-American Literature: An Annual

Annotated Bibliography," beginning with volume 7 (1984), covers mainly United States books, articles, and dissertations for 1983– ; it includes new primary works and interviews, as well as criticism on individual writers and relevant genres, such as slave narratives. *Callaloo* publishes similar bibliographies for African literatures and Caribbean and South American literatures. See the sections on Latin American literature and on African literature in chapter 4.

D2   *CLA Journal: A Quarterly.* Baltimore: Coll. Lang. Assn., 1957– . 4/yr.

The annual listing "Publications by CLA Members" for 1982– appears beginning with volume 28 (1984). The "Annual Bibliography of Afro-American Literature, [year], with Selected Bibliographies of African and Caribbean Literature," volumes 20–21 (1976–77), lists creative writing and scholarly books and articles about African American literature for 1975–76.

D3   *African American Review.* Terre Haute: Indiana State U, 1967– . 4/yr. (Vols. 1–10, 1967–76, titled *Negro American Literature Forum*; vols. 11–25, 1977–91, titled *Black American Literature Forum.*)

"Current Bibliography," in volumes 22–25 (1989–91), lists new North American books by and about African Americans in all subjects, including new poetry and fiction.

D4   *Obsidian II: Black Literature in Review.* Raleigh: North Carolina State U, 1975– . 2/yr. (Continues *Obsidian: Black Literature in Review*, vol. 1–8, 1975–82.)

"Studies in Afro-American Literature: An Annual Annotated Bibliography" for 1974–76 is comparable to the listing in the *CLA Journal* (D2) but also includes annotations.

(A1)   *MLA International Bibliography*

Studies on African American literature in general are listed under "Afro-American" in all the American literature sections for 1970–80; starting in 1981 African American literature is included with American literature. Users should also search the subject index and the electronic versions under the heading "African American."

D5   *Index to Black Periodicals.* Boston: Hall, 1950– . Annual.
      (Title varies.)

    An author, subject, and title index to about 35 scholarly
and popular African American periodicals covering African American life in general and African American studies,
including headings for literary genres and literary studies.

D6   *Bibliographic Guide to Black Studies.* Boston: Hall, 1976– .
      Annual.

    An author, subject, and title list to international books
for 1975– cataloged by the Library of Congress and the
New York Public Library. Updates the *Dictionary Catalog of
the Schomburg Collection of Negro Literature and History,* 9
volumes (Boston: Hall, 1962; first supplement, 2 vols.,
1967; second supplement, 4 vols., 1972).

(A42) *Black Newspapers Index*

    A subject index to some 20 current African American
newspapers in the United States.

(D215) *Ethnic Newswatch: A Multicultural Database*

    A full-text compilation on CD-ROM of some 90 United
States ethnic and minority newspapers and periodicals, including African American titles, for 1991– .

African Studies

See the sections for African literature in chapters 3 and 4.

Alternative Press

In the alternative press editorial emphasis is on politics, culture,
and social sciences more than on art, literature, and the humanities issues dealt with by little magazines and small presses. For
the latter, see the section on little magazines and small presses,
below. See also the sections on African American studies, ethnic
and minority studies, gay and lesbian studies, journalism and
mass communication, and women's studies.

D10   *Alternative Press Index.* Baltimore: Alternative Press Center,
      1969– . 4/yr.

A subject index to about 230 international English-language periodicals and newspapers. Also indexes creative writing (excluding poetry after 1988) and reviews of books, plays, films, television, and recordings.

D11 *Left Index: A Quarterly Index to Periodicals on the Left.* Santa Cruz: Left Index, 1982– . 4/yr.

An author and subject index to about 80 periodicals that have a "Marxist, radical or left perspective and contain lengthy, critical analytical material" (preface), with a separate listing of book reviews.

American Studies

Researchers must consult specialized bibliographies in the various areas of American studies because there is no regular, comprehensive bibliography of American studies. See also, therefore, the sections in this chapter on African American studies, art, ethnic and minority studies, folklore, history, humor, journalism and mass communication, linguistics and language, popular culture, regionalism, and women's studies, as well as the American literature section in chapter 3.

D15 *Prospects: An Annual of American Cultural Studies.* Cambridge: Cambridge UP, 1975– . Annual. (Vols. 1–9 published by Burt Franklin, New York.)

Volumes 10 and 11 (both 1987) include a separate, classified, annotated bibliography of books and articles for 1984 and 1985, which continued and expanded to periodicals the coverage of Jack Salzman, editor, *American Studies: An Annotated Bibliography*, 3 volumes (Cambridge: Cambridge UP, 1986), and was in turn continued by Jack Salzman, editor, *American Studies: An Annotated Bibliography, 1984–1988* (Cambridge: Cambridge UP, 1990), though this volume was limited to books. The bibliography contains sections for anthropology, art, biography, folklore, history, literature, music, political science, religion, science and technology. Author and title indexes.

D16   *American Quarterly*. Baltimore: Johns Hopkins UP, 1949– .
       4/yr. (Vols. 1–2 published by U of Minnesota P, Minne-
       apolis; vols. 3–39 published by U of Pennsylvania, Phil-
       adelphia.)
       "Doctoral Dissertations in American Studies," in volume
       38– (1986–), lists current American dissertations in prog-
       ress. Earlier coverage was provided by "American Studies
       Dissertations," in volumes 8–26 (1956–74).
       "American Studies Research in Progress," an annual sec-
       tion in volumes 27–37 (1975–85), lists books and disserta-
       tions in progress or recently completed.
       "Articles in American Studies" an annual, selective, clas-
       sified bibliography for 1954–72, in volumes 7–25
       (1955–73), lists articles that deal with a relation between
       two or more aspects of American culture (and that were
       not published in *American Quarterly*). Partially cumulated
       in Henig Cohen, *Articles in American Studies, 1954–68: A
       Cumulation of the Annual Bibliographies from* American Quar-
       terly, 2 volumes (Ann Arbor: Pierian, 1972).

D17   *Amerikastudien / American Studies*. Stuttgart: Metzlersche,
       1956– . 4/yr. (Titled *Jahrbuch für Amerikastudien*, vols. 1–18,
       1956–73.)
       "Deutsche amerikanistische Veröffentlichungen" is an
       annual classified bibliography of German books and arti-
       cles on American studies for 1945– . Items are listed by
       author under several broad subject headings, such as
       "Sprache und Literatur."

D18   *American Studies Bibliography*. London: Inst. of US Studies,
       U of London, 1974–82. Monthly; cumulated annually.
       Microfiche only.
       A classified bibliography of books, pamphlets, govern-
       ment documents, and conference proceedings with author,
       title, and Dewey decimal classification indexes. (Author has
       not examined the bibliography.)

(D216) *Minorities in America: The Annual Bibliography*
       A classified bibliography of the year's books and articles
       for 1976–78 that continues Wayne Charles Miller, *Compre-
       hensive Bibliography for the Study of American Minorities*, 2
       volumes (University Park: Pennsylvania State UP, 1976).

(D277) *Journalism History*

"Communication History Abstracts" and "Recent Scholarship" together list articles for 1974– on United States communication history.

(D360) *American Periodicals: A Journal of History, Criticism, and Bibliography*

"American Periodicals: A Selected Checklist of Scholarship and Criticism" for 1985– lists books, articles, and dissertations.

(D219) *Yearbook of German-American Studies*

"Annual Bibliography of German-Americana: Articles, Books, and Dissertations" is an extensive author list for 1979– , with subject index, that continues earlier bibliographies and contains about 500 items each year.

(D220) *German Quarterly*

"Bibliography Americana Germanica," 1967–69 (in vols. 41–43, 1968–70), is an annual bibliography of books, articles, and dissertations on German American literary, historical, and cultural relations. Coverage for 1941–66 was carried in *American German Review* (Philadelphia: Natl. Carl Schurz Foundation), volumes 8–33 (1941/42–66/67), and for 1933–40 in *JEGP* (C90), volumes 34–40 (1935–41).

(A1) *MLA International Bibliography*

"Americana Germanica" (title varied) is a subsection under German literature, 1926–80.

(C90) *JEGP: Journal of English and Germanic Philology*

See "Anglo-German Literary Bibliography" for 1933–69, in volumes 34–69 (1935–70); after 1940 this bibliography focused on Anglo-German literary relations and left biographical and historical subjects to the bibliography in *American German Review* (see D220).

(C44) *Italica*

Lists Italian American and Italian Canadian studies for 1975– in volume 52– and before 1975 included these studies in the general section of the bibliography.

(D441) *Journal of American Culture*

See the checklist "Technology in American Culture: Recent Publications" for 1979–80 in volumes 3–4 (1980–81).

Anthropology

See the section on social sciences, sociology, and anthropology.

Archives

See the section on manuscripts and archives.

Art, Aesthetics, Architecture

The bibliographies here cover the fine arts (painting, sculpture, drawing, and prints), interior and landscape design, fashion and costume, folk art, crafts, and the visual elements of film, theater, and dance, as well as aesthetics and architecture. See also the bibliographies in this chapter listed under comparative literature, education (for art education), film, folklore, literary theory, and philosophy, as well as the current indexes described in chapter 2.

D20　*Art Index.* New York: Wilson, 1929– . 4/yr., with annual cumulation.

　　　Electronic formats: CD-ROM and online (OCLC and Wilson, 1984–),

　　　An author and subject index to American and European periodicals that deal with art and aesthetics. Subjects covered include broad areas such as art, architecture, art history, city planning, film, arts and crafts, and interior and landscape design and specific subjects such as art and literature, aesthetics, criticism, Romanticism, concrete poetry, and exhibits of artists' and writers' work.

D21　*BHA: Bibliography of the History of Art.* Vandœuvre-lès-Nancy: Institut de l'Information Scientifique et Technique, Centre National de la Recherche Scientifique; Santa Monica: Getty Trust, 1991– .

　　　Electronic format: online (Dialog, 1973–).

　　　A comprehensive, classified bibliography, including abstracts, of international books, reviews, articles, newspaper stories, Festschriften, proceedings, exhibition catalogs, museum publications, and dissertations in the fields of

postclassical European and post-Columbian American art.
Author and subject index in each issue.

BHA continues two earlier bibliographies, as follows:

RILA: Répertoire internationale de la littérature de l'art / International Repertory of the Literature of Art. Williamstown:
RILA and Getty Trust, 1975–89.

Répertoire d'art et d'archéologie. Paris: Centre National de
la Recherche Scientifique, 1910–89. 5/yr.

D22   *Artbibliographies Modern.* Santa Barbara: ABC-Clio, 1969– .
(Vols. 1–3, 1969–71, titled *LOMA: Literature on Modern Art*
and published by Lund, London.)

Electronic format: online (Dialog, 1974–).

Covers nineteenth- and twentieth-century art (excluding
architecture after 1988).

(A2)   *FRANCIS bulletin signalétique 526. Art et archéologie*

A comprehensive, classified, bibliography of international books, articles, and other publications, 1947– , on
various aspects of art and archaeology, now also accessible
online and on CD-ROM.

(A1)   *MLA International Bibliography*

Since 1981 there has been no classified section for studies
on aesthetics, but see part 2, the subject index. Before 1981
there was a major section for aesthetics within the general
literature division (spelling and placement varied).

See "Aesthetics" in part 1, volume 4, under "General
Literature and Related Topics I."

(D87)   *Yearbook of Comparative and General Literature*

Since 1986, has carried the "Bibliography on the Relations of Literature and Other Arts," an extensive, classified,
and annotated bibliography of international books and articles on the relations between literature and music, visual
art, dance, and film. See main entry for earlier versions of
the bibliography for 1952– .

(D375) *ABHB: Annual Bibliography of the History of the Printed Book
and Libraries*

Includes chapters on book design, printing, bookbinding, and book illustration.

D23   *Journal of Aesthetics and Art Criticism.* Philadelphia: Amer.
Soc. for Aesthetics, 1941– . 4/yr.

"Selective Current Bibliography for Aesthetics and Related Fields" for 1941–72, volumes 1–31 (1941–73), was an annual, international bibliography of books and articles on the philosophy and psychology of art.

(D365) *Philosopher's Index: An International Index to Periodicals and Books*

Indexes books and articles on aesthetics and the philosophy of art.

D24 *Bibliographie zur Symbolik, Ikonographie und Mythologie.* Baden-Baden: Koerner, 1968– . Annual.

An international, extensive author list of books and articles, with annotations in French, German, or English. Subject index.

D25 *Dada/Surrealism.* New York: Queens Coll. P, 1971– . Annual. (No. 1 published by Texas Tech UP, Lubbock.)

Includes a classified bibliography of international books, articles, exhibition catalogs, and dissertations on, as well as new primary writings, translations, and manuscript materials by, dada and surrealist writers and artists and of materials on dadaism and surrealism. Numbers 1–3 include a bibliography for 1971–73, number 10/11 includes a bibliography for 1973–78, and number 13 includes a bibliography for 1978–83.

D26 *Avery Index to Architecture.* Mountain View: RLIN, 1979– . Continually updated; computer file only (also available online from Dialog for 1979–).

An author and subject index to over 1,000 international periodicals in architecture and related fields. The electronic index continues the *Avery Index to Architectural Periodicals* (15 vols., 2nd ed., Boston: Hall, 1973, and supps., 1975–90).

Arthurian Studies

See also the bibliographies listed in this chapter under medieval studies.

D30 *Bibliographical Bulletin of the International Arthurian Society / Bulletin bibliographique de la Société Internationale Arthurienne.*

Madison: A-R, 1948– . Annual. (Vols. 1–26 published by the Société Internationale Arthurienne, Paris.)

A comprehensive, classified, annotated bibliography of international books and articles on Arthurian matters. Items are arranged by country and then by major subjects, if there are sufficient entries. Annotations are written in the language of the item listed. Author and critic index; subject and title index.

(A1) *MLA International Bibliography*

Studies on the Arthurian legends are listed under "Themes and Figures" in part 1, volume 4, and under entries for specific works; see also part 2, the subject index.

(D320) *International Medieval Bibliography*

Use the subject index to find studies of Arthurian matters.

D31 *Modern Language Quarterly*. Seattle: U of Washington, 1940– . 4/yr.

"A Bibliography of Critical Arthurian Literature" for 1936–62, in volumes 1–24 (1940–63), provided comprehensive coverage of international books, articles, and reviews, with occasional brief annotations.

Scholarship for 1922–35 was covered in *A Bibliography of Critical Arthurian Literature* (New York: MLA, 1931 and 1936).

Asian Studies

See the section on Asian literatures in chapter 4.

Autobiography

See the section on biography.

Bibliography, Enumerative: Authors and Subjects

Analytical bibliography is covered in the section on printing, publishing, history of the book, and textual studies. For enumerative bibliography, see also the section on reference books in this chapter, as well as most of the bibliographies listed in chapters 3 and 4. Chapter 6 lists regular, continuing serial bibliographies devoted to single authors.

D35   *Bibliographic Index: A Cumulative Bibliography of Bibliographies.* New York: Wilson, 1937– . 3/yr., with annual cumulation.

Electronic format: online (Wilson, 1984–).

A subject index to bibliographies that consist of 50 or more items and that are published separately or as parts of books or articles. About 2,800 international periodicals (but predominantly in English or in Germanic or Romance languages) are scanned regularly.

D36   *Bibliographische Berichte / Bibliographical Bulletin.* Frankfurt: Klostermann, 1959–88. Annual (frequency varied). (Continues *Bibliographische Beihefte, Neue Bibliographien,* and *Bibliographie,* all supplements to *Zeitschrift für Bibliothekswesen und Bibliographie,* 1955–58, D404.)

Complements *Bibliographic Index* (D35) for 1949–87, especially in coverage of east European publications. A classified list of bibliographies published separately or in books or articles. See, for example, "Philologie / Language and Literature," under which are such subheadings as "Anglistik," "Germanistik," "Skandinavistik." Cumulative indexes.

(B1)   *Annual Bibliography of English Language and Literature*

Through volume 59 for 1984 (1987), the general bibliography section includes bibliographies on themes, subjects, and genres.

D37   *Index to Reviews of Bibliographical Publications: An International Annual.* Troy: Whitston, 1978–91. Annual. (Vols. 1–3 published by Hall, Boston.)

An annual classified bibliography and checklist of bibliographical publications for 1976–85 of international reviews of international bibliographical publications, mainly in literature and including editions of literary texts and materials (such as letters and manuscripts), concordances and indexes, bibliographies, and books on textual and editorial theory. The bibliography for 1976 was carried in *Analytical and Enumerative Bibliography* 1 (1977): 273–437.

D38 *Literary Research.* College Park: U of Maryland, 1976–90. 4/yr. (Vols. 1–10 titled *Literary Research Newsletter*; vols. 1–9 published at State Univ. Coll. of New York, Brockport, and Manhattan Coll., New York.)

"Record of Current Publication" lists international literary reference books, specialized dictionaries and encyclopedias, and, especially, primary and secondary author bibliographies for 1985–90 (the first listing was titled "Update").

(D382) *Proof: The Yearbook of American Bibliographical and Textual Studies*

"The Register of Current Publications" in volumes 1–4, 1971–75, lists editions, subject and author checklists, national bibliographies, and studies, and listed scholarly tools on literature, writing, printing, publishing, bookselling, libraries and collecting, and bibliographic theory and practice.

Biography and Autobiography

The items in the first section list studies of biography and autobiography as literary genres or social and personal phenomena, while those in the second section index biographical information or publications about literary figures.

BIOGRAPHY AS GENRE

D40 *Biography: An Interdisciplinary Quarterly.* Honolulu: U of Hawaii P, 1978– . 4/yr.

"Bibliography of Works about Life-Writing" for 1977– in volumes 1– (omitted from vol. 7, 1984) lists mainly English-language books, articles, and dissertations about biography as a literary form or as a significant cultural phenomenon.

(A1) *MLA International Bibliography*

Studies of autobiography and biography as a genre are listed under "Genres" in part 1, volume 4, and under the various literary period subsections. In the pre-1981 editions see "Biography" under "Themes and Types" in the general literature section. Biographies and autobiographies of literary subjects are listed under the subjects' names in volumes 1 and 2.

(B1)   *Annual Bibliography of English Language and Literature*
See the section "Biography and Autobiography" within the literary periods for studies of biography as a genre.

(B6)   *English Studies: A Journal of English Language and Literature*
See the annual review article "Current Literature II: Criticism and Biography."

(B2)   *The Year's Work in English Studies*
The subject index has had entries for autobiography and biography since volume 57 (1976).

(C1)   *The Year's Work in Modern Language Studies*
Since volume 34 (1972), the index has included references to works of autobiography and biography.

(C15)   *Bibliographie der französischen Literaturwissenschaft*
Autobiography and biography are included in the subsection "Genres et formes de la prose" in section 1, "Généralités," starting with volume 2 (1961; in vol. 1, 1960, under "Prose"); both terms are also index entries.

(C28)   *French XX Bibliography*
Volumes 38– (1986–) include the section "Autobiography as Genre."

(C81)   *Bibliographie der deutschen Sprach- und Literaturwissenschaft*
Autobiography and biography are included within "Weitere Formen" in the subsection "Gattungen und Formen" in the chapter "Deutsche Literaturgeschichte," and both subjects are index entries.

(D121) *Dictionary of Literary Biography Yearbook*
The *Yearbook* has included a review article covering the year's English-language biographies of literary figures since the third volume, 1983.

(B44)   *Johnsonian News Letter*
The regular checklists include a section that lists biographies of eighteenth-century figures, new editions of eighteenth-century autobiographies, and studies on biographical topics.

INDEXES TO CURRENT BIOGRAPHICAL
INFORMATION AND PUBLICATIONS

See also the current indexes listed in chapter 2.

D42   *Biography Index: A Cumulative Index to Biographical Material in Books and Magazines.* New York: Wilson, 1946– . 4/yr.

Electronic formats: CD-ROM (Wilson, 1984–) and online (OCLC and Wilson, 1984–).

A name index to biographical information on people living or dead published in international books and articles. Presence of portraits is noted. Contains an index to such professional and occupational categories as painters, parachutists, peasants, and poets.

D43   *Biography and Genealogy Master Index.* Detroit: Gale, 1981– . Annual, with five-year cumulations.

Electronic formats: CD-ROM (Gale, 1980–) and online (Dialog, 1980–); these databases include the base set and all subsequent volumes.

An annual index to about 100 biographical dictionaries, including some serials, such as *The Writers Directory* (Chicago: St. James, 1973–), some retrospective compilations, and other standard reference books. Continues *Biography and Genealogy Master Index*, second edition, 8 volumes (Detroit: Gale, 1981), an index to 350 retrospective biographical dictionaries.

(D47)   *Book Review Digest*

The subject index to book reviews has included a heading for biographies since 1926.

Book History

See the section on printing, publishing, the history of the book, and textual studies.

Book Reviews

Only general book review indexes are listed here. See also, therefore, the periodical and newspaper indexes in chapter 2, particularly *Infotrac* (A15), *Periodical Abstracts* (A16), and *Newspaper*

Abstracts (A40); the literary and period bibliographies in chapters 3 and 4; and many of the subject bibliographies in this chapter, especially those for the alternative press, children's literature, creative writing, and women's studies.

(B1)   *Annual Bibliography of English Language and Literature*
         Cites reviews of the books it lists.

D45   *Book Review Index*. Detroit: Gale, 1965– . 6/yr., with annual cumulation.

         Electronic formats: CD-ROM (Gale, 1965–) and online (Dialog, 1965–).

         An author and title index to reviews in about 330 predominantly North American periodicals. Reviews cover creative writing and scholarly studies. Title index was added with volume 12, 1976.

D46   *Internationale Bibliographie der Rezensionen / International Bibliography of Book Reviews*. Osnabrück: Dietrich, 1971– . Annual. (Vols. 1–13, 1971–83, published 6/yr.)

         Indexes book reviews from about 1,000 international journals in all fields in three lists: a subject classified list of books reviewed, an author list of books reviewed, and a reviewer list. Entries provide cross-references and explanatory notes about subjects. Continues, after a lapse of more than two decades, part C of the *Internationale Bibliographie der fremdsprachigen Zeitschriftenliteratur* (A17), 1911–44.

D47   *Book Review Digest*. New York: Wilson, 1905– . 12/yr., with annual cumulation.

         Electronic formats: CD-ROM (Wilson, 1983–) and online (OCLC and Wilson, 1983–).

         An author, title, and subject index to book reviews in about 90 North American general-interest periodicals that provides excerpts of some reviews. To be included, a book must have been published or distributed in the United States and must have had two reviews if nonfiction or four if fiction; further, its reviews must have appeared within eighteen months of its publication. The index is most useful for reviews of new writing and of trade books; for scholarly reviews, *Book Review Index* (D45) and appropriate subject bibliographies are preferable.

D48 *Scholarly Book Reviews on CD-ROM.* Bethesda: University Publications of America, 1991– . 4/yr. CD-ROM format only.

Full-text database of book reviews from over 100 mainly English-language scholarly periodicals in the social sciences and humanities, searchable by author, title, reviewer, publishers, source journal, subject terms, and free text. (Author has not examined the database.)

D49 *Index to Book Reviews in the Humanities.* Williamstown: Phillip Thompson, 1960–92. Annual.

An author index to book reviews in humanities and related social sciences published in about 360 international journals.

D50 *Current Book Review Citations.* New York: Wilson, 1976–82. 11/yr., with annual cumulation.

An author and title index to book reviews in about 1,200 North American and British periodicals and in 3 newspapers, for books on all subjects, including creative writing, and from all countries. Coverage of book reviews has reverted to the various specialized Wilson indexes, as follows: *Applied Science and Technology Index* (A19), *Art Index* (D20), *Biology and Agricultural Index* (A18), *General Science Index* (D437), *Humanities Index* (A8), *Library Literature* (D280), *Readers' Guide* (A20), and *Social Sciences Index* (D455).

Business

See the section on economics and business.

Caribbean Studies

For English-, French-, and Spanish-language literature, see the section on other English-language literatures in chapter 3 and the sections on French and francophone literatures and on Spanish and Portuguese literatures in chapter 4.

D52 *Journal of Caribbean Studies.* Lexington: Assn. of Caribbean Studies, 1980– .

"Caribbean Studies: Recent Publications" in most issues is a classified bibliography of international, English-language books and articles about all aspects of the Caribbean. Arranged by subject and then by country.

(C62)   *Handbook of Latin American Studies*

An extensive, annotated bibliography of international books and articles in literature and the humanities (art, history, language, music, and philosophy) and in the social sciences, with coverage of each broad area appearing in alternate years.

Celtic Studies

See also the sections for Arthurian studies and history in this chapter and the sections on Irish and Scottish literature in chapter 3.

(A1)   *MLA International Bibliography*

Celtic literatures are covered in volume 1 in sections for Breton, Cornish, Irish Gaelic, Manx, Scottish Gaelic, and Welsh. See also the subject index under "Celtic literature."

(C1)   *The Year's Work in Modern Language Studies*

Annual coverage of Breton, Cornish, Irish Gaelic, Manx, Scottish Gaelic, and Welsh literatures, 1930–36, 1974– .

D55   *Etudes celtiques.* Paris: Centre National de la Recherche Scientifique, 1936– . Annual.

"Bibliographie" in most issues lists recent international books and articles, with summaries in French.

D56   *Bibliography of Wales: A Register of Publications Relating to Wales and the Celtic Peoples.* Aberystwyth: Natl. Library of Wales, 1910– . Irregular. (Titled *Bibliotheca celtica*, 1909–90; incorporated the *Subject Index to Welsh Periodicals.*)

An extensive, classified bibliography of international books, articles, and pamphlets on all aspects of current and historic Celtic life. Author and subject index.

Censorship

The items listed here emphasize intellectual freedom and censorship of literature and the arts, in contrast to the more political emphasis in the publications of such organizations as Human Rights Watch and Amnesty International. See also the sections in this chapter on the alternative press, children's literature, ethnic and minority studies, gay and lesbian studies, journalism, and libraries.

D60   *Newsletter on Intellectual Freedom.* Chicago: Amer. Library Assn., 1962– . 6/yr.

"Intellectual Freedom Bibliography" in each issue, 1962– , is an author list of mainly United States books and articles about intellectual-freedom issues; most issues also carry book reviews, and many issues before 1962 list recent publications.

In addition the *Newsletter* cites recent censorship actions in the United States, reports on related issues, and summarizes United States court decisions.

D61   *Free Speech Yearbook.* Falls Church: Speech Communication Assn., 1970– . Annual.

Includes a bibliography of current publications on free speech issues, with an emphasis on scholarly journals and law reviews.

D62   *Index on Censorship: The International Magazine for Free Expression.* London: Writers and Scholars Intl., 1972– . 10/yr.

The "Index Index" in each issue is a country-by-country chronicle of censorship activities, including assassinations, torture, and imprisonment, in which writers and journalists figure disproportionately. This index has been indexed in Judi Vernau with Alison Bennett, *An Index to* Index on Censorship: *No. 1 (1972) to No. 100 (1988)* (London: Zell, 1989).

(A1)   *MLA International Bibliography*

Studies on censorship are listed under the heading "Professional Topics" in part 1, volume 4. See also the subject index for studies of censorship of individual literatures or authors.

(D280) *Library Literature: An Index to Library and Information Science*

See the heading for censorship and its cross-references.

(D10)   *Alternative Press Index*

See the heading for censorship and its cross-references.

Children's Literature

See also bibliographies for English, American, and other literatures and see the sections on censorship, education, folklore, and libraries in this chapter.

D65   *Children's Literature Association Quarterly.* Battle Creek: Children's Lit. Assn., 1976– . 4/yr. (Place of publication varies.)

      Publishes an annual, classified, annotated, and extensive bibliography of international books and articles on children's literature for 1982 in volume 8 (1983) and then for 1986– . Sections cover topics (canon, criticism, curriculum), genres (fantasy, folklore, poetry, media, and theater), history, publishing, illustration, national and minority literatures, and other matters. The bibliography in volume 16 (1991–92) has nearly 2,000 items; the more selective one in volume 17 (1992–93) has somewhat less than 1,000.

(A1)   *MLA International Bibliography*

      Studies on specific authors and works are listed in their appropriate sections in volumes 1 and 2; general studies in children's literature are listed under "General Literature" in part 1, volume 4. See also the subject index under such subjects as children and adolescents. Before 1981 "Children's Literature" is a subsection within "Themes and Types" in the general literature division.

(B1)   *Annual Bibliography of English Language and Literature*

      "Literature for Children" is a subsection under "English Literature, General" starting with volume 50 for 1975 (1978) and is a subsection in the sections for literary periods starting with volume 60 for 1985 (1988).

D66   *Children's Literature Abstracts.* Birmingham: Intl. Federation of Library Assns., 1973– . 4/yr.

      An international, extensive, and classified bibliography of articles on children's literature, with brief descriptive summaries in English. Annual critic and subject index.

D67   *Children's Literature: Annual of the Modern Language Association Division on Children's Literature and the Children's Literature Association.* New Haven: Yale UP, 1972– . Annual. (Vols. 1–6, 1972–77, published by Temple UP, Philadelphia, and vol. 7, 1978, by Parousia, Windham Center.)

"Dissertations of Note" for 1974– , in volumes 5– (1976–), is drawn from listings in *Dissertation Abstracts International* (D154).

(D205) *ERIC*

Indexes an extensive range of topics dealing with children's and young adult literature.

(D280) *Library Literature: An Index to Library and Information Science*

Indexes an extensive range of topics dealing with children's and young adult literature.

D68   *Children's Literature Review: Excerpts from Reviews, Criticism, and Commentary on Books for Children and Young People.* Gale: Detroit, 1976– . Annual.

Excerpts current critical comment in books, reviews, and articles on writers and their works. British and American writers are emphasized, but other writers are selectively included. Cumulative indexes for authors, titles, and nationality of books discussed.

D69   *Phaedrus: An International Annual for the History of Children's and Youth Literature, Incorporating* Die Schieffertafel. Madison: Fairleigh Dickinson U, 1973–88. Annual. (Vols. 1–7, 2/yr.; vols. 8–12 published by the School of Library Service, Columbia U, New York; various subtitles.)

Each issue includes an international list of books, articles, dissertations, catalogs, and bibliographies.

D70   *Children's Book Review Index.* Detroit: Gale, 1975– . Annual.

Covers 1965– , with a five-volume cumulation for 1965–84, *Children's Book Review Index: Master Cumulation, 1965–1984* (Detroit: Gale, 1985). Entries are extracted from *Book Review Index* (D45) and arranged in an author list of books reviewed, with illustrator and title indexes.

D71   *Olderr's Young Adult Fiction Index.* Chicago: St. James, 1989– . Annual.

An author, title, and subject index to about 1,000 novels and story collections for young adults ages 10–18. Some young-adult books of 1987 were listed in the first edition of *Olderr's Fiction Index* (D131).

D72   *Children's Fiction Index.* Newcastle-under-Lyme: Assn. of Assistant Librarians, 1964– . Irregular. (Titled *Junior Fiction Index* for first five editions, 1964–85.)

An author, title, and subject index to recent, mainly British books for children.

D73   *Growing Point.* Northampton, Eng.: Fisher, 1962–92. 6/yr.

Each issue consists of reviews and review articles of some 50 mostly new, British books for children and young adults, providing a useful record of such publishing.

Classical Literature

See also in this chapter the sections on art, history, and philosophy and the entries in the medieval studies section covering Medieval Latin and Neo-Latin.

D75   *L'année philologique: Bibliographie critique et analytique de l'antiquité gréco-latine.* Paris: Belles Lettres, 1924– . Annual.

Electronic format: CD-ROM (Scholars, 1976–).

An annual, comprehensive, classified bibliography of international books and articles about all aspects of the classical world. Part 1 lists studies of individual authors and texts; part 2 lists, in classified form, studies on literature, language, archaeology, history, law, science, and classical studies. There are indexes for collective titles listed in part 1 (such as *Anthologia græca*), for classical names, for Renaissance and later humanists, and for critics.

The CD-ROM version, issued 1995– and titled *The Database of Classical Bibliography on CD-ROM*, starts with one disc containing the 12 volumes covering 1976–87, followed by annual updates that each add three to five volumes covering periods before and after those covered in the base set.

Coverage continues *Dix années de bibliographie classique: Bibliographie critique et analytique de l'antiquité gréco-latine pour la période 1914–1924*, 2 volumes (Paris: Belles Lettres, 1927, 1928), and *Bibliographie de l'antiquité classique 1896–1914. Part I* (Paris: Belles Lettres, 1951).

D76   *Gnomon: Kritische Zeitschrift für die gesamte klassische Altertumswissenschaft.* Munich: Beck'sche, 1925– . 8/yr.

"Bibliographische Beilage" in every other issue is a comprehensive, classified list of international books and articles on literature, philology, individual authors, history, and other aspects of classical culture.

D77   *Greece and Rome.* Oxford: Oxford UP, 1931– . 2/yr.

"Subject Reviews" in each issue, 1931– , consists of bibliographic reviews of international books in Greek and Roman literature, history, archaeology and art, philosophy, and general cultural studies.

D78   *Classical and Modern Literature.* Terre Haute: CML, 1980– . Annual. (Vols. 1–12, 1980–92, published 4/yr.)

"Bibliography of the Classical Tradition," annually for 1980– , in volumes 5– (1985–), is an extensive, classified bibliography of books and articles on classical figures and on classical tradition in modern literature and culture.

(A1)   *MLA International Bibliography*

The linguistics volume includes studies of Greek, Latin, and other ancient languages, but the bibliography does not cover the ancient literatures except as they influence modern literatures.

D79   *Vergilius.* Lynchburg: Vergilian Soc. of Amer. and Randolph-Macon Woman's Coll., 1956– . Annual.

"Vergilian Bibliography" for 1963– is an annotated, classified bibliography of international books and articles.

D80   *The Year's Work in Classical Studies.* Bristol, Eng.: Classical Assn.–Arrowsmith, 1906–47. Annual. (Publisher varied; 1938–45 and 1945–47 were covered in two volumes.)

Annual bibliographic essays on classical studies.

(D113) *Computing and the Classics*

Each issue includes a checklist of recent books and articles about computing and the classics.

(D355) *Oral Tradition*

Publishes at approximately two-year intervals an annotated author list of international books and articles on oral traditions in folklore, history, linguistics, literature, and religion and covering the classical, medieval, Renaissance, and modern worlds.

D81   *American Classical Review.* New York: City U of New York, 1971–73. 4/yr.

Each issue was intended to list all new international books relevant to classicists.

D82 *International Guide to Classical Studies: A Continuous Guide to Periodical Literature.* Darien: Amer. Bibliographic Service, 1961–78. 4/yr.

An international, extensive author list of articles for 1960–73, with annual cumulative author and subject index.

D83 *Quarterly Check-list of Classical Studies: An International Index of Current Books, Monographs, Brochures, and Separates.* Darien: Amer. Bibliographic Service, 1958–78. 4/yr.

An international, extensive author list for 1958–77 covering books on all aspects of the classical world. Annual author, editor, and translator index.

Communication

See the sections on journalism and mass communication and on speech communication.

Comparative Literature and Translation

Because comparative literature studies deal not only with relations between two or more literatures but also with relations between literature and other arts and subjects, see also the relevant bibliographies listed in other sections of this chapter (such as those on art, music, philosophy, psychology, religion, and science) as well as the bibliographies on the non-English literatures listed in chapter 4.

COMPARATIVE LITERATURE

D85 *Canadian Review of Comparative Literature / Revue canadienne de littérature comparée.* Edmonton: U of Alberta, 1974– . 4/yr.

Starting with volume 19, 1992, the journal carries "Review of Scholarship," an annual feature that provides bibliographic essays on relevant topics.

"Revue des revues," for 1973–88, in volumes 1–15

(1974–88), is an annual, classified, and annotated bibliography of international articles on comparative literature for 1973– , with sections for studies of literary history and relations, literary theory and critical methodology, and literature and the other arts.

"Preliminary Bibliography of Comparative Canadian Literature (English-Canadian and French-Canadian)," for 1976–86, in volumes 3–14 (1976–87), is an annual classified list of books, articles, and dissertations on relations between French Canadian and English Canadian literatures. The first bibliography is retrospective; subsequent ones cover each year's work in the field. Cumulated in Antoine Sirois et al., *Bibliography of Studies in Comparative Canadian Literature / Bibliographie d'études de littérature canadienne comparée, 1930–1987* (Sherbrooke, PQ: Université de Sherbrooke, 1989). One "Supplementary Bibliography of Comparative Canadian Literature" has appeared in the review since this cumulation.

D86   *Comparative Criticism: A Yearbook.* Cambridge: Cambridge UP, 1979– . Annual.

"Bibliography of Comparative Literature in Britain" is a classified list of books and articles published in Britain or by British scholars for 1975– . Arrangement follows that of the bibliography of comparative literature studies formerly carried in the *Yearbook of Comparative and General Literature* (D87).

D87   *Yearbook of Comparative and General Literature.* Bloomington: Indiana U, 1952– . Annual. (Vols. 1–9, 1952–60, were published at Chapel Hill as the University of North Carolina Studies in Comparative Literature.)

Carries the "Bibliography on the Relations of Literature and Other Arts," an extensive, classified, and annotated bibliography of international books and articles on the relations between literature and music, visual art, and dance and on the theory of comparative studies (the bibliographies for 1952–84 included film). Author and subject indexes (the latter for 1986–).

Originally compiled and issued annually by the MLA Division on Literature and the Other Arts (formerly General Topics 9) starting in 1953 (for 1952). This bibliography has been in the *Yearbook* since 1986 (for 1985–); earlier publication was as follows:

For 1977–84 the bibliography was published separately as *A Bibliography on the Relations of Literature and the Other Arts* (Hanover: Dartmouth Coll., 1978–85).

Coverage for 1973–75 is in volumes 6–8 of *Hartford Studies in Literature* (Hartford: U of Hartford, 1974–76). Coverage for 1952–67 is collected in *A Bibliography on the Relations of Literature and the Other Arts, 1952–67* (New York: AMS, 1968). This volume includes *Literature and the Other Arts: A Select Bibliography, 1952–1958* (New York: New York Public Library, 1959).

The *Yearbook* carried a bibliography of international and comparative literature studies for 1949–69 in volumes 1–20 (1952–70); the bibliography lists books, articles, and dissertations on themes and genres, on literary influences and relations, on individual authors and countries, and (in some years) on relations between literature and other arts and between literature and science. This bibliography updated Fernand Baldensperger and Werner F. Friederich, *Bibliography of Comparative Literature* (Chapel Hill: U of North Carolina, 1950).

(A1) *MLA International Bibliography*

Studies on comparative literature are listed under their own classifications in the section "Professional Topics" in part 1, volume 4; in the pre-1981 bibliographies they are listed under general 7 (1953–55), general 2 (1956), and general 3 (1957–80).

(B1) *Annual Bibliography of English Language and Literature*

Current coverage lists studies on comparative literature and translation within the linguistics section; coverage is more extensive in volumes 4–35 (1923–60).

D88 *Revue de littérature comparée*. Paris: Didier, 1921– . 4/yr.

Each quarterly issue, volumes 1–34 (1921–60), includes a bibliography of international comparative literature studies.

The bibliographies for 1949–58 were reprinted in *Bibliographie générale de littérature comparée* (Paris: Boivin, 1951–59).

(C90) *JEGP: Journal of English and Germanic Philology*
"Anglo-German Literary Bibliography," 1933–69, lists books and articles on Anglo-German literary relations.

TRANSLATION

(A1) *MLA International Bibliography*
Studies on the art and practice of literary translation are listed under "Literary Forms" in part 1, volume 4; studies on translation theory are found in the section "Translation" in part 1, volume 3. In the pre-1981 bibliographies the studies are listed under "Themes and Types."

D89 *Index translationum*. Paris: UNESCO, 1932– . Annual. (Published by the Intl. Inst. of Intellectual Cooperation, Paris, 1932–40; suspended 1941–47.)
An annual, classified bibliography of translations of books in all subjects and into all languages, arranged by country and then according to the universal decimal classification system. Author index.

D90 *Translation Review*. Dallas: U of Texas, 1976– . 3/yr.
"Annotated Books Received" in each issue lists new English translations, arranged by original language; includes some works of literary theory and criticism.

D91 *Babel: Revue internationale de traduction*. Gerlingen: Fédération Internationale des Traductions, 1955– . 4/yr.
Volumes through 1976 contain a biannual bibliography of international books and articles on translation, excluding works published in Fédération Internationale des Traductions journals.

(D87) *Yearbook of Comparative and General Literature*
Lists translations of literary works for 1960–79 in volumes 10–29 (1961–80).

D92 *Chartotheca translationum alphabetical / International Bibliography of Translations*. Bad Homburg: Bentz, 1962–72.
An author list of international translations for 1961–72.

(C137) *Bibliography of Modern Hebrew Literature in Translation*
The two issues each year list new translations from Hebrew into English and other languages for 1979– .

Composition, Rhetoric, and Technical Writing

There has been a comprehensive bibliography of composition
and rhetoric studies since the mid-1980s and good coverage is
also available into the 1970s for composition and into the 1950s
for rhetoric. See also the sections on education, linguistics, journalism and mass communication, social sciences, and speech in this
chapter and the relevant language bibliographies in chapter 4.

COMPOSITION, RHETORIC, READING

D95   *CCCC Bibliography of Composition and Rhetoric.* Carbondale:
        Southern Illinois UP, 1987– . Annual. (Vols. 1–2 titled
        Longman Bibliography of Composition and Rhetoric and pub-
        lished by Longman, New York.)
        Sponsored by the Conference on College Composition
        and Communication of the National Council of Teachers
        of English and providing coverage for 1984– , this clas-
        sified, annotated bibliography of international English-
        language books, articles, dissertations, and audiovisual
        materials covers written communication (nearly 2,000
        items each year), with author and subject indexes. The
        major sections on bibliography, theory and research, edu-
        cation of teachers, curriculum, and testing and measure-
        ment have appropriate subdivisions.
D96   *Research in the Teaching of English.* Urbana: Natl. Council
        of Teachers of English, 1967– . 4/yr.
        "Annotated Bibliography of Research in the Teaching
        of English" for 1966– is a biannual, classified bibliography
        of books, articles, dissertations, and papers.
(D205) *ERIC*
        Most of the relevant ERIC citations are included in the
        CCCC Bibliography, but for additional items and more pre-
        cise indexing also use ERIC itself.
D97   *Rhetorik: Ein internationales Jahrbuch.* Tübingen: Niemeyer,

1980– . Annual. (Vols. 1–4 published by Frommann-Holzboog, Stuttgart.)

Carries a bibliography of mainly German-language books, articles, and dissertations on rhetoric.

D98 *Rhetoric Society Quarterly.* St. Cloud: Rhetoric Soc. of America, 1968– . 4/yr. (Titled *Rhetoric Society Newsletter*, 1968–75.)

Most issues include a classified list of new books published in the United States.

(D470) *Style*

The annual bibliography of stylistics for 1966–90 includes items relevant to composition.

D99 *Composition Chronicle: Newsletter for Writing Teachers.* Livonia: Viceroy, 1988– . 9/yr.

"New Professional Books," in each issue, lists new books about composition, with brief descriptive annotations.

D100 *Writing Center Journal.* Bethlehem: Lehigh U, 1980– . 3/yr. (Sponsored by the Natl. Writing Centers Assn.; vols. 1–11 published by Utah State U, Logan.)

"Bibliography of Recent Writing Center Scholarship," an author list of recent articles with occasional books and other publications for 1983– , has been running annually since volume 5/6 (1985). This coverage is complemented by the annotated bibliography in *Focuses* (D101).

D101 *Focuses: A Journal Linking Composition Programs and Writing-Center Practice.* Boone: Appalachian State U, 1988– . 2/yr.

Starting in volume 2 (1989), the journal carries an annual "Annotated Bibliography of Scholarship on Writing Centers and Related Topics" for 1987– that lists United States books and articles about writing centers and related issues in composition.

D102 *Quarterly Review of Doublespeak.* Urbana: NCTE, 1974– . 4/yr. (Vols. 1–6 titled *Public Doublespeak Newsletter.*)

Each issue carries "Resources," a list of recent books and articles about the deliberate use of language to deceive or mislead an audience.

D103 *WPA: Writing Program Administrator.* Logan: Utah State U, 1987– . 3/yr. (Sponsored by the Council of College Writing Program Administrators; place and publisher have varied.)

"Bibliography of Writing Textbooks" is an annual list, with descriptive annotations, of new textbooks for courses in developmental, first-year-college, advanced, and professional writing.

(A1)   *MLA International Bibliography*

Studies on rhetoric are listed under "Literary Forms" in part 1, volume 4, and studies on reading under "Psycholinguistics" in volume 3.

(D467) *Bibliographic Annual in Speech Communication*

This annual and its predecessor list North American books and articles on rhetoric and public address for 1950–74.

D104 *College Composition and Communication: The Journal of the Conference on College Composition and Communication.* Urbana: NCTE, 1950– . 4/yr.

Volumes 26–30 (1975–79) include an annual, selective, annotated bibliography of books and articles on research in and teaching of composition for 1973–78.

TECHNICAL AND PROFESSIONAL WRITING

D105 *Technical Communication Quarterly.* Minneapolis: Assn. of Teachers of Technical Writing, U of Minnesota, 1992– . 4/yr. (Continues *Technical Writing Teacher*, Morehead, 1974–91.)

Carries "ATTW Bibliography," an annual, classified bibliography of international books and articles on various aspects of technical writing.

D106 *Technical Communication: Journal of the Society for Technical Communication.* Arlington: Soc. for Technical Communication, 1953– . 4/yr.

The section "Recent and Relevant," in each issue, 1976– , is a classified list of articles and abstracts from relevant journals in technical and professional communication.

(A18) *Biological and Agricultural Index*

See the subject headings for communication in science and for technical writing.

(A19) *Applied Science and Technology Index*

See the subject headings for communication in science and for technical writing.

(D438) *General Science Index*
See the subject headings for communication in science and for technical writing.

Computers

In addition to bibliographies of writing about computers and literature, this section includes several directories of electronic databases and texts.

BIBLIOGRAPHIES

D110 *Literary and Linguistic Computing*. Oxford: Oxford UP, 1986– . 4/yr.

"L'informatique et les humanities. Bibliographie [year], d'après quelques periodiques spécialisés" for 1979– is a biennial author list of international articles with indexes of subjects, methodologies, and languages studied (using French terms).

"Representatives' Reports," usually in two issues a year, consists of reports by members of the Association for Literary and Linguistic Computing on activities, conditions, and specific projects in different countries.

D111 *Computers and the Humanities*. Dordrecht, Neth.: Wolters, 1966– . 6/yr. (Various publishers.)

"Abstracts and Brief Reports," in volumes 1–18 (1966–84), lists international books and articles. Starting with volume 19 (1985) most issues carry reviews of new, relevant software, courseware, and hardware. Volumes 1–13 include an annual, classified bibliography of international books, articles, and dissertations for 1966–77; categories include archaeology, history, language and literature, and music. The "Directory of Scholars Active" is a triannual list of work in progress in the humanities involving computers. Each issue carries abstracts and brief notices of selected books and articles.

(A1) *MLA International Bibliography*
Studies on computer-assisted research in language and literature are listed under "Professional Topics" in part 1, volume 4, and under "Mathematical Linguistics" and

"Computational Linguistics" in volume 3; before 1981 they were listed under "Themes and Topics" in the general literature division.

(B1) *Annual Bibliography of English Language and Literature*
See "Language, Literature, and the Computer," volumes 46– (1971–).

D112 *Humanities Computing Yearbook.* Oxford: Clarendon, 1988– . Irregular. (Only two vols. published to date.)

Carries a classified bibliography of international books and articles dealing with computing and language, literature, and other areas of the humanities and fine arts; includes nonevaluative, annotated lists of new software, databases, and electronic tests.

D113 *Computing and the Classics.* Newark: Ohio State U, 1984– . 4/yr.

Each issue includes a checklist of recent books and articles about computing and the classics, language teaching, literary study, and the humanities.

(D323) *Medioevo latino: Bolletino bibliografico della cultura europea dal secolo VI al XIV*

"Elaborazione elettronica dei dati" lists items on computers and medieval studies.

(D116) *Directory of Electronic Journals, Newsletters, and Academic Discussion Lists*

Each annual volume includes "Bibliography of Current Articles Related to Electronic Journal Publications and Publishing."

DIRECTORIES

D114 *CD-ROMs in Print: An International Guide to CD-ROM, CD-I, CDTV, Multimedia, and Electronic Book Products.* Westport: Meckler, 1987– . Annual.

A title list of CD-ROMs with publisher and subject indexes. Updated in monthly issues of *CD-ROM World* (Meckler, Westport, 1986– ; vols. 1–7 titled *CD-ROM Librarian*).

D115 *Gale Directory of Databases.* Detroit: Gale, 1993– . Annual, with semiannual updates. (Combines and continues *Directory of Online Databases*, Cuadra, Santa Monica, 1979–92;

Directory of Portable Databases, Cuadra, Santa Monica, 1990–92; and *Computer-Readable Databases,* Gale, Detroit, 1985–92.)

A title list of international online databases (vol. 1) and CD-ROM, tape, handheld, and batch-access databases (vol. 2), with subject and producer indexes. Entries describe the database contents and format features.

D116   *Directory of Electronic Journals, Newsletters, and Academic Discussion Lists.* Washington: Assn. of Research Libraries, 1991– . Annual.

In addition to a classified directory of listservs and a list of electronic journals and newsletters, this directory also carries a checklist of current articles about electronic journals and publishing.

Creative Writing

The items listed here cover mainly North American writing and include both lists and surveys of new writing. See also the sections on African American literature, alternative press, children's literature, drama, ethnic and minority studies, little magazines, and women's studies in this chapter for additional specialized bibliographies of current creative writing, and see the general periodical indexes in chapter 2. Several bibliographies in chapter 4 also cover new writing.

INDEXES AND GENERAL SURVEYS

(D300)   *The American Humanities Index*

An author and subject index to over 500 mainly English-language, international little magazines, literary reviews, and scholarly literary journals, citing creative writing, scholarly articles, and reviews, with extensive listings under headings for plays, poems, and stories.

(B6)   *English Studies: A Journal of English Language and Literature*

Since 1925, the journal has published two bibliographic essays each year reviewing current English-language creative writing, one on drama and poetry, one on the novel and the short story.

D120   *Britannica Book of the Year.* Chicago: Encyclopedia Britannica, 1939– . Annual.

Covering 1938– , the section for literature (varying in arrangement) reviews the year's writing in Great Britain, the United States, Canada, France, Italy, Spain and Latin America, Portugal and Brazil, eastern Europe, Israel, Germany, Scandinavia, China, and Japan. Similar coverage was carried for 1898–1965 in *The New International Year Book* (New York: Dodd, then Funk, 1908–66) and *The International Year Book* (New York: Dodd, 1899–1903), for 1910–50 in *The American Year Book* (New York: Appleton, then Nelson, 1911–50), for 1861–1902 in *Appleton's Annual Cyclopaedia and Register of Important Events* (New York: Appleton, 1862–1902; titled *American Annual Cyclopaedia and Register of Important Events of the Year* for 1862–75), and for 1758– in the *Annual Register: A Record of World Events* (London: Longman, 1756– ; earlier publishers were Dodsely, then Rivington, then Longmans; slight variations in title and subtitle).

(B67)   *Contemporary Literary Criticism: Excepts from the Criticism of the Works of Today's Novelists, Poets, Playwrights, and Other Creative Writers*

One volume a year since 1985 includes survey articles covering the previous year's new American drama, fiction, and poetry and new international literature.

D121   *Dictionary of Literary Biography Yearbook.* Detroit: Gale, 1981– . Annual.

Each volume since 1984 includes survey articles on the previous year's new American drama, fiction, and poetry.

D122   *Magill's Literary Annual.* Englewood Cliffs: Salem, 1956– . Annual.

Each volume consists of four-page articles summarizing and commenting on some two hundred new books in the humanities and social sciences published in the United States, over half of which are fiction and poetry.

(D47)   *Book Review Digest*

Subject index includes headings of novels, poems, and plays.

POETRY

D123 *Index of American Periodical Verse.* Metuchen: Scarecrow, 1971– . Annual.

An author and title index to current poetry published in about 300 North American periodicals.

D124 *Directory of American Poetry Books.* Wakefield: Asphodel, 1993– . Annual.

Intended as an annual record of American poetry books, this directory lists entries by publisher with author and title indexes.

D125 *The Best American Poetry.* New York: Scribner's, 1988– . Annual.

In addition to a selection of the year's poetry, this volume also contains a list of another 100 poems of merit.

D126 *Poem Finder.* Great Neck: Roth, 1991– . Annual. CD-ROM format only.

An author, subject, title, and first- and last-line index to current poetry in periodicals, anthologies, and single-author collections, with further indexing for author nationality, religion, sex, and life dates. Continues *Roth's American Poetry Annual* (same publisher, 1988–90), which had been formed by the merger of *Annual Survey of American Poetry*, 1987–88 (an index to poetry in anthologies, 1985–86), the *Annual Index to Poetry in Periodicals*, 1985–88 (indexed from 6,200 to 14,000 poems a year for 1984–86), and *American Poetry Index*, 1983–87 (an index to single-author collections, 1981–86).

D127 *Anthology of Magazine Verse and Yearbook of American Poetry.* Beverly Hills: Monitor Book, 1980, 1984–85. Annual.

In addition to the anthology of poems, this title includes a yearbook section listing United States and Canadian books of poetry, biography, and criticism along with publishers and poetry magazines, societies, organizations, and prizes.

Earlier editions of this title provide comparable coverage for 1913–41: William Stanley Braithwaite, editor, *Anthology of Magazine Verse and Yearbook of American Poetry* (various publishers and places, 1913–29, 1959); *Anthology of Magazine Verse for 1931–1934* (New York: Praebar, 1932–35);

Alan F. Pater, editor, *Anthology of Magazine Verse and Yearbook of American Poetry* (New York: various publishers, 1936–42).

FICTION AND PROSE

D128   *The Best American Essays.* New York: Ticknor, 1986– . Annual.

In addition to a selection of the year's essays, this volume contains a list of another 150 essays appearing in American magazines. For an earlier version of this series, see *Essay Annual: A Yearly Collection of Significant Essays Personal, Critical, Controversial, and Humorous* (Chicago: Scott, 1933–41) and its annual "Bibliography of Outstanding Essays Which Have Appeared in American Periodicals."

D129   *Fiction Catalog.* New York: Wilson, 1901– . Five-year intervals, with annual supplements.

A selective, annotated author list (about 5,000 titles), with a title and subject index, of current and older English-language adult fiction, including translations. The annual supplements list mainly new fiction along with reissues and new translations of older fiction.

D130   *Fiction Index.* London: Assn. of Assistant Librarians, 1953– . Irregular, with five-year cumulations as *Cumulated Fiction Index.*

A subject list of current and older volumes of English-language fiction for 1945– .

D131   *Olderr's Fiction Index.* Chicago: St. James, 1988–90. Annual.

An author, title, and subject list of about 2,000 novels and short story collections a year published in the United States, with references to reviews in several book review periodicals.

D132   *Short Story Index.* New York: Wilson, 1953– . Annual, with five-year cumulations.

An author, title, and subject index to current and older short stories published in collections and in 45 periodicals indexed by the *Readers' Guide* (A20) and the *Humanities Index* (A8).

D133 *The Best American Short Stories.* Boston: Houghton, 1915– .
Annual. (Titled *Best Short Stories,* 1915–41.)

Most volumes through 1980 include "Yearbook of the
American Short Story," which lists about 100 additional
stories and a selection of fiction magazines and anthologies.

D134 *What Do I Read Next? A Reader's Guide to Current Genre Fiction.* Detroit: Gale, 1991– . Annual.

Lists the year's fantasy, horror, mystery, romance, science fiction, and western novels; entries contain descriptive
information and lists of books by other authors that a
reader who liked the original books might also like. Indexed by series, time period, geographic location and time
period, genre, character name, character description, author, and title.

D135 *Armchair Detective: A Quarterly Journal Devoted to the Appreciation of Mystery, Detective, and Suspense Fiction.* New York:
Armchair Detective, 1967– . 4/yr.

The "Checklist" section in each issue lists new books of
mystery, detective, and suspense fiction published in the
United States.

D136 *Best Detective Stories of the Year.* New York: Dutton, 1945– .
Annual.

Since 1963, includes "The Yearbook of the Detective
Story," a selective list of collections, anthologies, and books
of criticism and biography; necrology; and "honor roll" of
the previous year's stories.

(D450) *Science Fiction, Fantasy, and Horror: [year]: A Comprehensive
Bibliography of Books and Short Fiction Published in the English
Language*

Covering 1984– (the volume for 1985 was titled *Science
Fiction in Print*), this series attempts to record all new science
fiction, fantasy, and horror books and magazines published
or reissued during the year, with entries drawn from the
"Books Received" and "British Books" columns in *Locus*
(D137).

D137 *Locus: The Newspaper of the Science Fiction Field.* Oakland:
Locus, 1968– . 12/yr.

Each issue lists new English-language science fiction books in the "Books Received" and "British Books" columns. In addition, the issues contain extensive book reviews and news of publishing, authors, and prizes.

D138 *Science Fiction and Fantasy Book Review.* San Bernardino: Borgo, 1979– . 11/yr. (Incorporates *Fantasy Review*, 1978–83.)

Attempts to review most of the 1,000–1,500 English-language science fiction and fantasy books published each year.

D139 *Science Fiction and Fantasy Book Review Index.* Bryan: SFBRI, 1970– . Annual. (Titled *SFBRI: Science Fiction Book Review Index*, vols. 1–14; vols. 5– also available from Borgo, San Bernardino.)

An index to reviews of science fiction books in some 60 mainly United States periodicals. The reviews are listed by book author; a title index follows.

Cumulated in *Science Fiction Book Review Index, 1923–1973, Science Fiction Book Review Index, 1974–1979*, and *Science Fiction and Fantasy Book Review Index, 1980–1984*, all edited by Hal W. Hall (Detroit: Gale, 1974, 1981, and 1993).

D140 *Science Fiction Chronicle.* New York: Algol, 1979– . 12/yr.

Each issue includes a publisher list of new science fiction books.

D141 *The NESFA Index to Short Science Fiction.* Cambridge: New England Science Fiction Assn., 1966– . Annual. (Formerly titled *NESFA Index to the Science Fiction Magazines and Anthologies.*)

An author, title, and periodical and anthology index to creative writing, criticism, book reviews, and commentary on English-language science fiction and fantasy writing (including some translations).

Cumulated by *Index to the Science Fiction Magazines 1966–1970* (Cambridge: New England Science Fiction Assn., 1971). Continues coverage provided by Erwin S. Strauss, *The MIT Science Fiction Society's Index to the S-F Magazines, 1951–1965* (Cambridge: MIT Science Fiction Soc., 1965) and Donald B. Day, *Index to the Science Fiction Magazines, 1936–1950* (Portland: Perri, 1952).

(D453) *Science Fiction and Fantasy Book Review Annual*

Each volume carries bibliographic essays on new fantasy, horror, and science fiction writing; lists of recommended and prize-winning books, anthologies, and pieces in magazines; author profiles or interviews; and, especially, brief reviews of some 500–600 novels, story collections, and critical and scholarly works, all limited to English-language publications but including about 25 juvenile and 50–75 nonfiction books, and books from Australia, Canada, and Great Britain as well as the United States. Title index to books and stories mentioned.

D142   *Terry Carr's Best Science Fiction and Fantasy of the Year.* New York: Tor, 1972–87. Annual. (Originally titled *Best Science Fiction of the Year*; publishers and titles vary.)

"The SF [and Fantasy] Year in Review" in each volume reviews new books, publishing, motion pictures, and professional activities.

D143   *The Year's Best Science Fiction.* New York: St. Martin's, 1984– . Annual. (Published by Bluejay, New York, 1984–86.)

This anthology of stories also includes "Summation," a review essay on novels, stories, periodicals, anthologies, some criticism, and motion pictures; notes on professional activities; and "Honorable Mentions," a list of stories not anthologized in the volume. The anthology and "Summation" continue the coverage in *Best Science Fiction Stories of the Year* (New York: Dutton, 1972–81).

D144   *The Year's Best Fantasy and Horror.* New York: St. Martin's, 1988– . Annual. (Titled *The Year's Best Fantasy*, 1988–89.)

Each volume contains "Summation," a review of the year's publications in fantasy and horror, and "Honorable Mentions," a list of stories not anthologized in the volume.

D145   *Romantic Times.* Brooklyn: Romantic Times, 1981– . 12/yr.

Reviews popular romances, thus acting as a bibliography, but does not review books that rank below its three-hearts rating.

D146   *Heartland Critiques.* Independence: Heartland Critiques, 1980– . 12/yr.

Reviews some one hundred romances each month.

D147   *Romantic Spirit.* San Antonio: MJK, 1982– . Approximately
biennial.

Lists new books by author, omitting bibliographic infor-
mation but adding codes to indicate category of romance.
Appendixes list titles in about 20 numbered series. The
successive editions update the base volume, Mary June Kay,
*The Romantic Spirit: A Romance Bibliography of Authors and
Titles* (San Antonio: MJK, 1982).

DRAMA

In addition to the bibliographies of published plays listed here,
see also the subsection on reviews and calendars of performances under "Drama," below.

D148   *Play Index.* New York: Wilson, 1949– . Irregular.

An author, title, subject, and cast index to current and
older published plays.

(D193) *The Best Plays of [year]*

Covers 1894– . In addition to printing excerpts from
several Broadway plays, this yearbook variously lists drama
performances in New York and other United States cities;
provides information on runs, casts, awards, and recordings; and lists recently published plays.

(D194) *The Best American Short Plays*

Covering 1937– , this anthology of some 10 one-act or
short plays was accompanied during 1938–61 by a yearbook listing, variously, additional plays of the year, critical
and scholarly books, and publishers of short plays.

Dance

See the section on music and dance.

Dissertations and Theses

This list is selective; several bibliographies in chapters 3 and 4
also include citations for dissertations on specific literatures.

Theses, on the other hand, are seldom covered in bibliographies other than the specialized ones in this section. The listing for other countries is quite selective; for more complete information see the *Guide to Reference Books* (D402).

AMERICAN AND CANADIAN

D154 *Dissertation Abstracts International.* Ann Arbor: UMI, 1938– . 12/yr.

Electronic formats: CD-ROM (UMI, 1861–) and online (Dialog, OCLC, 1861–).

A monthly, classified compilation of abstracts of most North American doctoral dissertations; author and permuted title indexes in each issue are cumulated annually. The first issue included dissertations completed in 1935–38; coverage for the first years was very selective. Section A covers the social sciences and humanities. Section C covers foreign dissertations selectively. Within each subject division, dissertations are listed alphabetically by author. Citations provide information on author, title, length, director, school, and date as well as abstracts.

The online format includes master's theses from *Master's Abstracts International* (D158), chosen selectively before 1988; abstracts of United States and Canadian dissertations for 1980– are included, as are abstracts of international dissertations and master's theses for 1988– .

D155 *Comprehensive Dissertation Index.* Ann Arbor: UMI, 1973– . Annual.

Electronic formats: see previous entry.

An annual subject (permuted title) and author index to North American dissertations, 1861– , and to international dissertations listed in *Dissertation Abstracts International* (D154) part C. Keyed to abstracts in *Dissertation Abstracts International* and to listings in *American Doctoral Dissertations* (D156) and other dissertation bibliographies. Two multivolume sets cover 1861–1972 and 1973–1982 (1973 and 1983); each of the annual supplements for 1984– consists of five volumes, one an author index and the other four subject indexes. Literature, linguistics, and language dissertations are listed in volume 4.

D156 *American Doctoral Dissertations.* Ann Arbor: UMI, 1934– . Annual.

Lists most doctoral dissertations accepted by American and Canadian universities. Arranged by subject, then university, and then author; includes an author index.

D157 *Master's Theses Directories: The Arts and Social Sciences.* Cedar Falls: Master's Theses Directories, 1977– . Annual. (Vols. 1–13 titled *Master's Theses in the Arts and Social Sciences.*)

Provides a classified list of United States and Canadian theses for 1976– . Author and institution indexes.

D158 *Master's Abstracts International: A Catalog of Selected Master's Theses on Microfilm.* Ann Arbor: UMI, 1962– . 4/yr.

Electronic format: theses listed here for 1988– are included in the *Dissertation Abstracts International* CD-ROM and online database (D154).

A selective classified list of abstracts of master's theses from about 150 United States and Canadian universities as well as one university each in Australia, South Africa, and Venezuela. The author index in each issue is cumulated annually.

D159 *South Atlantic Review.* Tuscaloosa: Univ. of Alabama, 1935– . 4/yr. (Vols. 1–43, 1935–78, titled *South Atlantic Bulletin*; vols. 44–45, 1979–80, titled *SAB: South Atlantic Bulletin.*)

"Theses and Dissertations" is an annual list for 1936– (in issues 2.2– , 1936– , omitting 1970) of completed work at southern universities on English and American literature, comparative literature, modern languages, folklore, and linguistics.

D160 *Gypsy Scholar: A Graduate Forum for Literary Criticism.* East Lansing: Michigan State U, 1973–79. 3/yr.

"Bibliography of Doctoral Dissertations in British and American Literature" for 1974–78 is a classified list of about seventy percent of the year's American dissertations. Author index.

EUROPEAN AND OTHER

(D154) *Dissertation Abstracts International*
    Section C covers foreign dissertations selectively.
D161   *Répertoire des thèses de doctorat européenes.* Louvain: Dewallens, 1970– . Annual.
    An author index to western European doctoral dissertations (excluding Spain, Portugal, Italy, and, formerly, East Germany). Entries are arranged under three broad subject areas: humanities, medicine, and science.
D162   *Index to Theses with Abstracts Accepted for Higher Degrees by the Universities of Great Britain and Ireland and the Council for National Academic Awards.* London: ASLIB, 1950– . 4/yr. (Vols. 1–34 did not print abstracts or include the title phrase.)
    Electronic format: CD-ROM (Learned Information, 1970–).
    A classified list of theses accepted for advanced degrees (PhD, M. Litt., M. Phil., etc.). Information provided: author, title, degree, university, and date, with author and subject indexes.
D163   *Titles of Dissertations Approved for the Ph.D., M.Sc., and M.Litt. Degrees in the University of Cambridge.* Cambridge: Cambridge UP, 1958– . Annual.
    An author list of Cambridge dissertations, arranged under the departments for whom the students worked. Continues *Abstracts of Dissertations Approved for the Ph.D., M.Sc., and M.Litt. Degrees in the University of Cambridge* (Cambridge: Cambridge UP, 1927–59). Author index.
D164   *Successful Candidates for the Degree of D.Phil., B.Litt., and B.Sc., with Titles of Their Theses.* Oxford: Oxford UP, 1950– . Annual.
    A classified and author list of Oxford dissertations. Authors and titles are listed by subject areas. Author index.
    Continues *Abstracts of Dissertations for the Degree of Doctor of Philosophy*, 13 volumes (Oxford: Oxford UP, 1925–40).
D165   *Inventaire des thèses de doctorat soutenues devant les universités françaises.* Paris: Université de Paris I (Panthéon-Sorbonne), 1982– . Annual.

Continues the *Catalogue des thèses de doctorat soutenues devant les universités françaises* (Paris: Cercle de la Librairie, 1885–1984) and is a classified list of French university dissertations with author, subject, and university indexes. Entries list author, title, pagination, and university and frequently note whether there is a bibliography in the dissertation.

D166 *Deutsche Bibliographie: Hochschulschriften-Verzeichnis* and *Deutsche Bibliographie: Dissertationen und Habilitationsschriften.* Frankfurt: Buchhandler Vereinigung, 1950– . Annual.

List new German dissertations and other advanced academic writing, including *Habilitationsschriften* and *Hochschulschriften.*

D167 *Jahresverzeichnis der Hochschulschriften.* Leipzig: VEB, 1885–1987. Annual.

Lists German dissertations by university, with author and detailed subject indexes.

D168 *Gesamtverzeichnis österreichischer Dissertationen.* Vienna: Verband der Wissenschaftlichen Gesellschaften Österreichs, 1967– . Annual.

Dissertations are listed by university and then by school or faculty. Author and subject indexes.

D169 *Jahresverzeichnis der schweizerische Hochschulschriften.* Basel: Verlag der Universitätsbibliothek, 1898– . Annual.

Dissertations, as well as faculty books and articles, are listed by university and then by department; author and subject indexes are included (the latter until 1973).

D170 *Katalog doktorskikh i kandidatskikh dissertatsii, postupivskikh v Gosudarstvennuiu Biblioteku SSSR imeni V. I. Lenina i Tsentral'nuiu.* Moscow: Biblioteka, 1958– . 24/yr. (Titled *Katalog kandidatskikh i doktoratskikh,* etc., 1958–89.)

Classified catalog, with author and subject indexes, of dissertations in all subjects deposited in the Lenin Library and the Central State Library of Medicine. (Author has not examined the catalog.)

D171 *Nihon hakushiroku.* Tokyo, 1955– . Annual.

Annual compilation of titles and abstracts of Japanese dissertations. (Author has not examined the compilation.)

Don Juan Theme

D173 *West Virginia University Bulletin: Philological Papers.* Morgantown: West Virginia U, 1936– . Irregular.

Bibliographies in numbers 15 (1966), 17 (1970), 20 (1973), 23 (1975), and 26 (supp. 1980) continue Armand E. Singer, *The Don Juan Theme, Versions and Criticism: A Bibliography* (Morgantown: West Virginia UP, 1965).

Drama

The bibliographies listed here cover studies of drama as a genre and of specific plays, dramatists, and drama topics. See also most of the bibliographies in chapters 3 and 4 in which there are usually subsections for drama. For current bibliographies of published plays, see the subsection on drama under "Creative Writing," above, but for reviews and performance calendars or surveys of theater seasons, see "Reviews and Calendars of Productions" in this section.

CRITICISM AND SCHOLARSHIP

D174 *IBT: International Bibliography of Theatre.* Brooklyn: Theatre Research Data Center, Brooklyn Coll., 1984– . Annual.

This comprehensive, classified bibliography of international books and articles covers all aspects of the theater but emphasizes theater production more than drama-as-literature; it is the most important bibliography for the field. Author, subject, and geographical indexes.

(A1) *MLA International Bibliography*

Studies on drama as a genre and in general are listed in part 1 under individual national literatures and literary periods in volumes 1 and 2, and under "Dramatic Arts / Theater" in volume 4.

D175 *Theatre Journal.* Baltimore: Johns Hopkins UP, 1949– . 4/yr. (Titled *Educational Theatre Journal* and published by the Amer. Theatre Assn., 1949–78.)

"Books Received" in each issue is a classified list of new

English-language books on acting, stagecraft, criticism, as well as new plays and anthologies.

"Doctoral Projects in Progress in Theatre Arts" is an annual list of dissertation projects, beginning in volume 5 (1953) with coverage of 1952.

"Scholarly Works in Progress," 1974–80, is an annual list of studies and translations in press or in progress.

D176 *Bibliographic Guide to Theatre Arts.* Boston: Hall, 1976– . Annual.

An annual, international, comprehensive bibliography of all publications in theater cataloged by the New York Public Library, for 1975– , supplemented by entries from Library of Congress cataloging. Items listed by author, title, and subject.

D177 *Modern Drama.* Toronto: U of Toronto, 1958– . 4/yr.

"Modern Drama Studies: An Annual Bibliography" for 1972– , beginning in volume 17 (1974), is an annual classified list of international books and articles on areas, topics, and figures (playwrights and influential men and women other than performers) in modern drama since 1900. Covers drama of the United States, Great Britain, other English-language countries, Germany, France, Italy, Hispanic countries, Scandinavia, eastern Europe, Russia, and Asia (Near East, Israel, Far East, and south Asia). Cumulated in Charles A. Carpenter, *Modern Drama Scholarship and Criticism, 1966–1980: An International Bibliography* (Toronto: U of Toronto P, 1986).

"Modern Drama: A Selective Bibliography of Works Published in English" for 1959–67, in volumes 3–11 (1960–68), covers the same subject areas but a more limited range of publications.

D178 *Theatre History Studies.* Pella: Central Coll., 1981– . 2/yr. (Vols. 1–12 published by U of North Dakota, Grand Forks.)

"Books Received" in each issue is an extensive list of mainly English-language books on theater history, biography, and criticism.

D179 *Theater [year]: Jahrbuch der Zeitschrift* Theater heute. Berlin: Friedrich, 1961– . Annual. (Subtitle and place of publication vary before 1979.)

"Bibliographie die deutschsprachige Theaterliteratur" is a classified list of new German-language books and dissertations on all aspects of international theater, including history, stagecraft, playwrights and performers, dance, musical theater, and opera.

D180 *FIRT/IFTR-SIBMAS bulletin.* Leiden: Federation Internationale pour la Recherche Théâtral and Société Internationale des Bibliothèques et Musées des Arts du Spectacle, 1987– . 2/yr.

Each issue includes a section listing new international projects and publications.

D181 *Documenta: Mededelingen van het documentatiecentrum voor dramatische kunst.* Ghent: Het Centrum, 1983. 4/yr.

Includes a bibliography of international studies on the theater. (Author has not examined the bibliography.)

D182 *Revue d'histoire du théâtre.* Paris: Société d'Histoire du Théâtre, 1948– . 4/yr.

Through volume 34 (1982) the journal includes a comprehensive, classified bibliography of international books and articles on most aspects of the theater except stagecraft, citing articles on theory, history, literary aspects, and types of drama from about 1,800 periodicals. The bibliography appeared in each issue, 1948–65, and annually thereafter through volume 34, covering from the mid-1940s to 1980.

D183 *Dramatic Index.* Boston: Faxon, 1910–52. Annual.

An author and subject index to theater periodicals, along with a list of new books, covering scholarship, comment, reviews, and plays published in periodicals. The index reproduced in the quarterly issues of *Bulletin of Bibliography* for 1910–52 (cumulated annually), and then in the multiyear *Cumulated* Dramatic Index, *1909–1949: A Cumulation of the F. W. Faxon Company's* Dramatic Index, 2 volumes (Boston: Hall, 1965).

(B1) *Annual Bibliography of English Language and Literature*

Starting with volume 43 (1968) studies on English-language drama and theater history are listed in the chapter on literary history and criticism, and the chapters for literary periods each include a subsection for drama and theater.

(B23) *Medieval English Theater*

      Most issues include a list of books received and reports of recent productions of medieval plays.

(B36) *Research Opportunities in Renaissance Drama*

      Lists current research projects in medieval drama through volume 27 (1984) and frequently publishes bibliographies on figures and subjects of medieval drama.

      "Productions of Renaissance Drama," in volumes 15/16– (1974–), reviews recent international productions of English Renaissance plays, and "Productions of Medieval Drama," in volumes 10, 11, and 13– (1967–), does the same for English medieval plays.

(B37) Cahiers Elisabéthains: *Late Medieval and Renaissance English Studies*

      Each issue includes reviews of recent productions (mainly in Great Britain) of Renaissance Elizabethan and Stuart plays.

(B47) *Restoration and Eighteenth Century Theatre Research*

      Has carried a bibliography of studies of British theater of the period in volumes 1–16 and ns 4– , covering 1962–77 and 1986– .

(B59) *Nineteenth Century Theatre*

      Carries an annotated list of books received in each issue. Volumes 1–10 (1973–82), include an annual bibliography of international books, articles, and dissertations about nineteenth-century English-language theater, covering 1972–81.

D184 *New Theatre Quarterly*. Cambridge: Cambridge UP, 1974– . 4/yr. (Titled *Theatre Quarterly*, 1971–80; suspended 1981–84.)

      "Checklists," about one a year through 1990, are biobibliographic articles about current international playwrights.

D185 *South African Theatre Journal: SATJ*. Johannesburg, S. Afr.: U of the Witwatersrand, 1987– . 2/yr.

      "A Bibliography of South African Theatre" is a biennial list for 1987– . (Author has not examined the bibliography.)

(C66)   *Latin American Theatre Review*
"Recent Publications, Materials Received and Current Bibliography" for 1967– , in volume 1– (1967–), is a checklist of international books, articles, and unpublished papers on Latin American theater, largely from Latin America but including publications from other countries and including plays as well as criticism and scholarship.

(C91)   *Maske und Kothurn: International Beiträge zur Theaterwissenschaft*
Carries a bibliography of studies mainly on the German theater but including some items on international theater biography, history, bibliography, and stagecraft.

D186   *Annotated Bibliography of New Publications in the Performing Arts.* New York: Drama Book Specialists, 1971–80. 4/yr.
A classified bibliography of new books, mainly in English, on theater and other performing arts, including television, radio, film, musicals, and the circus. The bibliography supplements *Performing Arts Books in Print: An Annotated Bibliography* (New York: Drama Book Specialists, 1973).

(D467) *Bibliographic Annual in Speech Communication*
Continuing coverage that stated in 1934, this annual includes a comprehensive, classified bibliography for 1969–74 listing international books, articles, dissertations, and theses in various areas of speech communication studies and theatrical craft.

D187   *Theatre/Drama Abstracts.* Pleasant Hill: Theatre/Drama and Speech Information Center, 1974–80. (Titled *Theatre/Drama and Speech Index*, 1974; see D466.)
A comprehensive abstracting service for international articles, 1974–77. Author and subject index.

D188   *L'annuel du théâtre.* Meudon: L'Annuel du Théâtre, 1982–83. Annual.
"Revue des livres" is a classified bibliography of the year's French books about international theater along with new plays and translations. (Author has not examined the bibliography.)

D189   *Theatre [1–5]: The American Theatre [year].* New York: Scribner's, 1969–73. Annual. (Vols. of 1969–70 published by the Intl. Theatre Inst. of the US, who continued to sponsor the succeeding volumes.)

Covering 1967 through 1972, the compilers of the bibliography published in each volume attempted to list all new books published in America on the international theater, including stagecraft, acting and performance, history, reference, and criticism but not new plays.

Reviews and Calendars of Productions

D190   *National Theatre Critics' Reviews.* New York: Theatre Critics' Reviews, 1940– . 6/yr. (Titled *New York Theatre Critics' Reviews* through 1994.)

A compilation of reviews of New York theater productions (premieres, long-running productions, and revivals) from 9 newspapers, 6 weekly magazines, and 1 television station. Title index and an index of authors, producers, directors, composers and lyricists, set designers, choreographers, costume designers, and cast members.

D191   *Theatre Record.* Twickenham, Eng: Herbert, 1981– . 26/yr. (Vols. 1–10 titled *London Theatre Record.*)

A compilation of newspaper reviews of productions in London and regional England. Annual indexes of titles and production elements.

(D175)   *Theatre Journal*

"Theatre Review" in each issue reviews significant international academic and professional productions of new and classic plays.

D192   *Georgia Review.* Athens: U of Georgia, 1947– . 4/yr.

"American Theatre Watch" for 1977/78– , in volumes 32– (1978–), is an annual review of the year's new drama productions, predominantly in and near New York.

D193   *The Best Plays of [year].* New York: Limelight, 1899– . Annual. (Title varies but popularly known as *Best Plays*; published by Dodd, New York, 1899–1988, and then Applause, New York, 1990–93.)

Covers 1894– . In addition to printing excerpts from

several Broadway plays, this yearbook, variously, lists drama performances in New York and other United States cities, provides information on runs, casts, awards, and recordings, and lists recently published plays.

The listings are indexed cumulatively in Otis L. Guernsey, *Directory of the American Theater, 1894–1971: Indexed to the Complete Series of Best Plays Theater Yearbooks: Titles, Authors, and Composers of Broadway, Off-Broadway, and Off-Off Broadway Shows and Their Sources* (New York: Dodd, 1971).

D194   *The Best American Short Plays.* New York: Applause, 1991– . Annual. (Titled *Best One-Act Plays*, 1938–52, and *Best Short Plays*, 1952–89; published by Dodd, New York, 1938–55; Beacon, Boston, 1956–61; and Chilton, Philadelphia, 1968–85; suspended 1961–67.)

Covering 1937– , *Best American Short Plays* is an anthology of some 10 one-act or short plays accompanied during 1938–61 by a yearbook listing, variously, additional plays of the year, critical and scholarly books, and publishers of short plays.

D195   *John Willis' Theatre World.* New York: Applause, 1946– . Annual. (Published by Crown, New York, 1946–90; titled *Theatre World*, 1946–71.)

Prints calendars of Broadway, off-Broadway, and professional regional theaters and national touring companies for 1944/45– .

D196   *British Theatre Yearbook.* New York: St. Martin's, 1989– . Annual.

Provides calendars of the London and regional theaters and touring companies, with title index, for 1989– .

D197   *International Theatre Annual.* London: Calder, 1956–60. Annual.

In addition to articles surveying the year's theater in Great Britain, the United States, and other countries, variously, this annual included a list of world premieres and theatrical obituaries for 1955/56–60.

D198   *Australian and New Zealand Theatre Record.* Kensington, New South Wales: Australian Theatre Studies Centre, 1987– . 12/yr.

Reprints reviews of theater performances in Australia and New Zealand. (Author has not examined the periodical.)

D199 *Canada on Stage*. Toronto: PACT Communication Centre, 1974– . Annual. (Vol. 1 titled *Canadian Theatre Review Yearbook*; vols. for 1974–82 published by CTR, Downsview, ON.)

Surveys the year's theater work in Canada, with the record of professional and not-for-profit production arranged by province and then company or theater.

(D179) *Theater [year]: Jahrbuch der Zeitschrift* Theater heute

Most volumes since 1961 include a calendar of the year's German theater productions.

D200 *Année du théâtre [year]*. Paris: Hachette, 1992– . Annual.

A survey of the theatrical season in France, with a calendar of productions, cast and crew information, and brief articles about principal people, plays, and productions.

Economics and Business

The following bibliographies cover the field of economics, finance, and business and provide access to current information and to scholarly publication about economic history and theory, publishing, financial conditions affecting literature, and other literary matters. See also current newspaper and periodical indexes in chapter 2.

D201 *Business Periodicals Index*. New York: Wilson, 1958– . 11/yr., with annual cumulation. (Continues coverage in *Industrial Arts Index*, 1913–57.)

Electronic formats: CD-ROM (Wilson, 1984–) and online (OCLC and Wilson, 1984–).

A subject and author index to English-language articles from some 350 mainly North American periodicals on all aspects of business. Relevant subject headings include communication, copyright, fiction, and publishing.

D202 *ABI/Inform*. Louisville: UMI–Data Courier, 1971– .

Electronic formats only: CD-ROM (UMI–Data Courier, 1971–) and online (Dialog and OCLC, 1971–).

An index with abstracts to over 800 business and management periodicals.

(A30)   Lexis/Nexis
Provides the full text of hundreds of publications—periodicals, statutes, court rulings, government documents, reference books—in law, business, medicine, and current events.

(A40)   *Newspaper Abstracts*
An index, with abstracts, to 26 United States newspapers for 1985– .

D203   *Journal of Economic Literature.* Nashville: Amer. Economic Assn., 1963– . 4/yr. (Vols. 1–6 titled *Journal of Economic Abstracts*; place varies.)
Electronic formats: CD-ROM (SilverPlatter, 1969–) and online (Dialog and OCLC, 1969–).
Each issue includes an extensive list of new international books with abstracts, the contents of economics periodicals, a classified index to these contents, selected abstracts, and an author index. The journal provides good coverage of studies of economic history and theory, business, industrial, and labor economics, and consumer economics. Coverage cumulated and expanded in *Index of Economic Articles in Journals and Collective Volumes* (D204).

D204   *Index of Economic Articles in Journals and Collective Volumes.* Nashville: Amer. Economic Assn., 1961– . Annual. (Titled *Index of Economic Journals*, 1961–67; supplemented by *Index of Economic Articles in Collective Volumes*, 1969–72.)
A cumulation of the *Journal of Economic Literature* (D203), with coverage extended to edited books and with more detailed subject indexing.

(D458)   *International Bibliography of the Social Sciences*
Includes the *International Bibliography of Economics*, an annual, comprehensive, and classified bibliography of international books and articles on all aspects of economics.

(D440)   *Technology and Culture*
The annual bibliography of the history of technology includes a section on economic history and entries on technology and business and industry. See also the database *History of Science and Technology* (D436).

Editing

See the section on printing, publishing, book history and textual studies in this chapter.

Education

Education bibliographies cover educational theory and research as well as practical classroom issues and methods. See also the sections on composition, rhetoric, and technical writing and on linguistics, language, and language teaching in this chapter.

D205 *ERIC.* Washington: ERIC.

Electronic formats only: CD-ROM (SilverPlatter and Dialog, 1966–) and online (Dialog and OCLC, 1966–).

A comprehensive database with abstracts of international, predominantly English-language articles and of unpublished educational materials for 1966– collected in the Educational Resources Information Center clearinghouses. Books and book chapters excluded. Searchable by author, title, keyword, identifier, and descriptor. *ERIC* lists articles on such subjects as teaching methods and syllabi, literary criticism and bibliographies, literary genres and subjects, writing and journalism, specific writers, genres, themes, and so on, as well as on educational issues, developments, research, and methods. Originally made up of two print bibliographies, *Current Index to Journals in Education* (D206) and *Resources in Education* (D207).

D206 *Current Index to Journals in Education.* Phoenix: Oryx, 1969– . 12/yr., with biannual cumulations.

Electronic format: see *ERIC* (D205).

A classified index to articles in about 830 international English-language periodicals for 1966– . Organized into four parts: abstracts, subject index, author index, and tables of contents of indexed journals.

D207 *Resources in Education.* Washington: GPO, 1969– .

Electronic format: see *ERIC* (D205).

A classified list of abstracts of projects, reports, unpublished papers, and other materials with author and subject indexes for 1966– .

D208   *Education Index.* New York: Wilson, 1932– . 10/yr., with annual cumulation.

Electronic formats: CD-ROM (Wilson, 1984–) and online (OCLC and Wilson, 1984–).

An author and subject index to over 400 international English-language periodicals, related yearbooks, and some monographs, for 1929– . Coverage includes teaching methods, literary criticism, genres, bibliographies.

(D96)   *Research in the Teaching of English*

See the biannual bibliography on the teaching of English.

D209   *British Education Index.* London: British Library, 1961– . Annual. (Frequency varies for 1961–71; published by the Library Assn., London, 1961–81.)

Electronic format: online (Dialog, 1976–).

Indexes articles in about 175 periodicals published or distributed in Great Britain, for 1954– . Author index and two subject indexes.

(A2)   *FRANCIS bulletin signalétique 520. Sciences de l'education*

A classified bibliography of international books, articles, and other publications for 1947– , now accessible online and on CD-ROM.

(D289)   *Language Teaching*

Covers articles on language, language learning, and language teaching, 1965– .

(D292)   *Second Language Instruction/Acquisition*

An abstract journal recording international publications on language teaching and learning.

(D286)   *Linguistics and Language Behavior Abstracts*

Studies on nonnative-language learning and teaching and on bilingualism are listed in the section for applied linguistics.

(D293)   *ACTFL Annual Bibliography of Books and Articles on Pedagogy in Foreign Languages*

Covers books and articles on foreign language teaching.

D210   *Media Review Digest.* Ann Arbor: Pierian, 1971– . Annual with irregular supplements.

Indexes reviews of educational, instructional, and informational films, videos, filmstrips, educational and spoken audio recordings, slides, illustrations, kits, realia, and other media.

Ethnic and Minority Studies

See the sections in this chapter on African American studies, alternative press, folklore, history, Islamic studies, Jewish studies, regionalism, social sciences, and women's studies; also see under American literature (ch. 3) and under the general indexes and bibliographies (ch. 2).

D215   *Ethnic Newswatch: A Multicultural Database*. Stamford: Softline, 1992– . Annual. CD-ROM format only.

    A full-text compilation for 1991– of about 100 United States ethnic and minority newspapers and periodicals, some in Spanish, representing interests of African, Asian, European, eastern European, Jewish, Middle Eastern, and other ethnic Americans.

(A1)   *MLA International Bibliography*

    Before 1981 the MLA had several sections for ethnic and minority literatures in America: "Afro-American" (1970–80), "American Indian" (1974–80), and "Mexican American" (1973–80). "Americana Germanica" (title varied) was a subsection under "German Literature," 1926–80. Since 1981 these categories are included in the general American literature sections but are also indexed in part 2.

(A42)   *Black Newspapers Index*

    A subject index to some 20 current African American newspapers in the United States.

D216   *Minorities in America: The Annual Bibliography*. University Park: Pennsylvania State UP, 1985–86. Annual.

    The three volumes issued are a classified bibliography of the year's books, articles (from about 900 periodicals), dissertations, and government publications, arranged by ethnic group and then subject, with sections for literary history and criticism and subsections for genres and for individual authors; they include new writing. The volumes cover 1976–78 and continue Wayne Charles Miller, *Comprehensive Bibliography for the Study of American Minorities*, 2 volumes (University Park: Pennsylvania State UP, 1976).

D217   *Chicano Index*. Berkeley: U of California, Chicano Studies

Library, 1981– . 2/yr. (Titled *Chicano Periodical Index* for 1981–88; vols. 1–2 published by Hall, Boston, 1981 and 1983.)

Electronic format: CD-ROM (Chicano Studies Library, 1967–).

This publication, which started as *Chicano Periodical Index: A Cumulative Index to Selected Periodicals between 1967 and 1978*, is a subject index to over 30 Chicano periodicals, with selective indexing of another 250 periodicals. Author and title indexes. (Author has not examined the index.)

(C60) *HAPI: Hispanic American Periodicals Index*

Indexes criticism of Mexican American literature and new writing by Mexican Americans.

(D410) *Western American Literature*

The "Annual Bibliography of Studies in Western American Literature" lists books and articles about western writers, including Native Americans, for 1965– .

D218 *Index to Literature on the American Indian.* San Francisco: Indian Historian, 1970–73. Irregular.

An author and subject list of books and articles on or by Native Americans, which covers a wide range of subjects (such as games, agriculture, technology) in both scholarly and popular publications.

D219 *Yearbook of German-American Studies.* Lawrence: Soc. for German-Amer. Studies, 1981– . Annual. (Continues the *Journal of German-American Studies*, vols. 1–15, 1976–80.)

"Annual Bibliography of German-Americana: Articles, Books, and Dissertations" for 1979– is an extensive (about 500 items each year) author list, with subject index. Continues Arthur R. Schultz, *German-American Relations and German Culture in America: A Subject Bibliography, 1941–1980*, 2 volumes (Millwood: Kraus, 1984), and Henry A. Pochmann and Arthur R. Schultz, *Bibliography of German Culture in America to 1940*, revised edition (Millwood: Kraus, 1982). The latter in turn had developed from the continuing bibliography in *German Quarterly* and *American German Review* (see D220).

D220 *German Quarterly.* Cherry Hill: Amer. Assn. of Teachers of German, 1928– . 4/yr. (Place of publication has varied.)

"Bibliography Americana Germanica," 1967–69 (in vols. 41–43, 1968–70), an annual bibliography of books, articles, and dissertations on German American literary, historical, and cultural relations, continues coverage for 1941–66 in *American German Review* (Philadelphia: Natl. Carl Schurz Foundation).

(C90) *JEGP: Journal of English and Germanic Philology*
See the section "Anglo-German Literary Bibliography."

(C44) *Italica*
Lists Italian American and Italian Canadian studies for 1975– in volumes 52– , and volumes before 1985 list these categories in the general section of the bibliography.

Explication

See also the literary genre sections of this chapter, the general indexes and bibliographies in chapter 2, national and period bibliographies in chapters 3 and 4, and author bibliographies in chapter 6.

D223 *Explicator*. Washington: Heldref, 1942– . 4/yr.
A "Checklist of Explication" annually lists books and articles of explication covering mainly English-language writing. A separate annual index lists explication published in the journal.

Fiction

Although several journals—chiefly *Modern Fiction Studies* (D225), *Critique: Studies in Modern Fiction*, and *Studies in the Novel* (D227)—regularly publish bibliographical articles on specific aspects of fiction, there is no single, general bibliography of studies of long fiction. Short fiction scholarship, however, is recorded in *Studies in Short Fiction* (D228). See also the sections on comparative literature, creative writing, folklore, and science fiction in this chapter; national and period bibliographies in chapters 3 and 4; and relevant author bibliographies in chapter 6.

D225　*Modern Fiction Studies.* West Lafayette: Purdue U, 1955–. 4/yr. (Titled *Modern Fiction Newsletter* for vols. 1–14.)

"Recent Books on Modern Fiction," 1955– , is a biannual, classified list of recent, international books dealing with modern fiction in general and with individual authors, accompanied by book reviews and a bibliographic essay covering the books listed. Also regularly publishes checklists of criticism on the subjects of the journal's special-topic issues.

(A1)　*MLA International Bibliography*

Studies of prose fiction in general (fiction, novel, short story) are listed under "Genres" in part 1, volume 4, and under national literatures and literary periods in volumes 1 and 2. Coverage includes studies of fiction as a genre, science fiction, popular fiction types, and related critical issues. Before 1981 see "Prose Fiction" under "Themes and Types" in the general literature division.

(B1)　*Annual Bibliography of English Language and Literature*

Studies on fiction as a genre are listed under "Literary History and Criticism," in volumes 43– (1968–).

D226　*English Novel Explication.* Hamden: Shoe String, 1973– . Irregular. Five supplements to date, 1976–94.

An index to critical articles and chapters or passages in books about British novelists (i.e., novelists born in England, Scotland, Wales, Ireland, or the British Commonwealth who lived in Great Britain for a significant portion of their lives). Continues Inglis F. Bell and Donald Baird, *The English Novel, 1578–1956: A Checklist of Twentieth-Century Criticisms* (Denver: Swallow, 1958; rpt. Hamden: Shoe String, 1974).

D227　*Studies in the Novel.* Denton: North Texas State U, 1969– . 4/yr.

Regularly carries review articles on recent fiction criticism.

D228　*Studies in Short Fiction.* Newberry: Newberry Coll., 1963– . 4/yr.

Carries an annual bibliography of English-language books and articles on international short stories, with items arranged under the names of subject authors and including a list of books scanned.

These annual bibliographies have been cumulated and augmented in Warren S. Walker, comp., *Twentieth-Century Short Story Explication: Interpretations, 1900–1975, of Short Fiction since 1800*, 3rd ed. (Hamden: Shoe String, 1977, and 5 supps., 1980–91), and this cumulation is continued biennially by *Twentieth-Century Short Story Explication: New Series* (Hamden: Shoe String, 1993–).

D229 *Gothic: The Review of Supernatural Horror Fiction*. Baton Rouge: Gothic, 1979–87. Annual. (2/yr. for 1979–85).

Volumes 1 and 2 (1979–80) include an annual bibliography of criticism of Gothic fiction for 1978–80. A separate pamphlet, *The 1980 Bibliography of Gothic Studies* (Baton Rouge: Gothic, 1983) supplements this coverage. The bibliography was cumulated and extended by Frederick S. Frank, *Gothic Fiction: A Master List of Twentieth Century Criticism and Research* (Westport: Meckler, 1988).

Film

The general periodical and newspaper indexes in chapter 2 cover film studies and reviews, although indexing terms vary from *cinema* to *film* to *motion pictures* and *moving pictures*. The titles listed here, except for the last two, tend to stress film studies more than they stress film reviews.

D235 *Film Literature Index: A Quarterly Author-Subject Index to the International Periodical Literature of Film and Television*. Albany: Film and Television Documentation Center, 1973– . 4/yr.

An author and subject index to international periodicals; the subject headings include names, film titles, film genres, and topics in filmmaking, film criticism, and film study. Film reviews are also listed.

D236 *International Index to Film Periodicals: An Annotated Guide*. London: Intl. Federation of Film Archives, 1972– . Annual. (Publishers vary.)

A classified bibliography of articles in about 80 international periodicals on all aspects of film, including the film industry, distribution, society and cinema, aesthetics, history, individual films, biography, institutions, festivals, and conferences. Author, biography, subject, and director indexes.

D237 *Post Script: Essays in Film and the Humanities.* Jacksonville: Jacksonville U, 1981– . 3/yr.

"Annual Bibliography of Film Studies," 1981– , is a classified list of some 700 articles a year from 50 English-language periodicals.

(A1) *MLA International Bibliography*

Some 1,000 international books, articles, and dissertations on film are listed annually under "Dramatic Arts / Film" in part 1, volume 4; before 1981 see "Cinema" under "Themes and Topics" in the general literature division.

(D20) *Art Index*

An author and subject index to American and European periodicals dealing with art and aesthetics.

(B65) *Journal of Modern Literature*

The annual bibliography for 1970– includes a section of studies of film as literature.

(C28) *French XX Bibliography*

Beginning with volume 20 (1968) part 3 covers international books, articles, and dissertations on French film, with a subsection for general studies and for studies of specific directors and writers. In earlier volumes film studies are listed under "Theatre and Cinema." Film reviews are included.

(C15) *Bibliographie der französischen Literaturwissenschaft*

Studies on general issues (including film and literature) and specific individuals in French filmmaking are listed in section 1 "Généralités. Cinema," for 1956– .

D238 *Film Review Annual.* Englewood: Film Review, 1982– . Annual.

Reprints reviews from about 15 North American and British periodicals and newspapers of international feature-length films for 1981– , with additional reviews cited. Indexes for cast, directors, and production elements.

(D210) *Media Review Digest*

Indexes reviews of entertainment films as well as of educational, instructional, and informational media.

Folklore

Bibliographies listed here cover folklore in general or American, British, Irish, Scottish, or Welsh folklore specifically. See also the major national literature bibliographies in chapter 4 and the sections in this chapter on art, history, linguistics, music, names, regionalism, and social sciences. There has been good coverage of international folklore studies since 1917.

(A1)   *MLA International Bibliography*

International folklore studies are listed in part 1, volume 5, where there are sections for history and study, folk literature (subsections for speech, narrative, and poetry and further subdivisions for more specific forms and, within these, for geography), ethnomusicology, belief systems, rituals, and material culture. Before 1970 folklore studies were listed under "General Literature and Related Topics." Continues coverage in *Journal of American Folklore* (D243) and *Abstracts of Folklore Studies* (D244).

D240   *Internationale volkskundliche Bibliographie / International Folklore and Folklife Bibliography / Bibliographie internationale d'ethnographie.* Bonn: Habelt, 1949– . Annual.

A comprehensive, classified bibliography of international books and articles on folklore for 1939– . Coverage is comparable to that in the *MLA International Bibliography.* Continues coverage in *Volkskundliche Bibliographie* for 1917–36 (Berlin: Gruyter, 1917–41). Author and subject indexes.

D241   *Demos: Internationale ethnographische und folkloristische Informationen.* Berlin: Akademie, 1960–90. 4/yr.

A classified, annotated bibliography of mainly eastern European books and articles on international ethnology and folklore. Annual author, book review, and periodical index.

D242 *Folklore Bibliography for [1973–76]*. Bloomington: Research Center for Language and Semiotic Studies, Indiana U, 1975 and 1977; Philadelphia: Inst. for the Study of Human Issues, 1979 and 1981. Annual. (Indiana Folklore Inst. Monograph Series, vols. 28, 29, 31, and 33.)

An international bibliography of books and articles on all aspects of the folklore of the Western Hemisphere, including Latin America. Continues coverage for 1937–72 in *Southern Folklore Quarterly* (Gainesville: U of Florida, 1938–73).

(B1) *Annual Bibliography of English Language and Literature*

Beginning with volume 48 (1973), studies on English, American, and other English-speaking countries' folklore are listed in a separate section. Earlier, a few folklore studies are listed under "Auxiliary Studies" in volumes 15–47 (1934–72).

(B72) *American Literary Scholarship: An Annual*

The year's studies in American folklore were reviewed for 1965–74.

D243 *Journal of American Folklore*. Washington: Amer. Folklore Soc. 1888– . 4/yr.

"Work in Progress" is an annual list of scholarly projects, including dissertations, 1960– .

An annual, classified bibliography of international books and articles for 1954–62, in volumes 68–76 (1955–63), was published as a supplement; it was superseded by coverage in *Abstracts of Folklore Studies* (D244).

D244 *Abstracts of Folklore Studies*. Austin: Amer. Folklore Soc., 1963–75. 4/yr.

Lists abstracts of international articles on international folklore arranged under periodical titles; contains an annual subject index.

(C56) *Revista de dialectologia y tradiciones populares*

Carries an annual bibliography that includes studies of folklore in Spain and Spanish-speaking America.

Gay and Lesbian Studies

See also the sections for the alternative press, social sciences, and women's studies as well as the periodical indexes listed in chapter 2.

D245   *Gay/Lesbian Periodicals Index.* Charlotte: Integrity Indexing, 1993– . Annual. Microfiche format only.

Author and subject index to about 36 United States periodicals for 1990– with headings for literary forms (drama, poetry, short story) as well as literary criticism.

D246   *Forum Homosexualität und Literatur.* Sigen: Forschungsschwerpunkt Homosexualität und Literatur in Fachbereich Sprach- und Literaturwissenschaften an den Universität-Gesamthochschule Sigen, 1987– . 3/yr.

"Auswahl Bibliographie" in each issue is an international list of books and articles about homosexuality and literature for 1985– , mainly in English or German, including recent translations into German. (Author has not examined the bibliography.)

D247   *Lambda Book Report: A Review of Contemporary Gay and Lesbian Literature.* Washington: Lambda Rising, 1987– . 6/yr. (Titled *Lambda Rising Book Report,* 1981–91.)

A specialized book review journal. (Author has not examined the journal.)

Government Publications

The United States government publishes, or sponsors the publication of, an incredible range of materials, some of which is of interest to literary scholars. Covers such materials as bibliographies, exhibit catalogs, lectures, books and pamphlets, and information about national historical monuments and sites (which include homes of writers and artists), as well as the many official reports, announcements, and regulations of such federal agencies as the National Endowments for the Humanities and for the Arts.

D250   *Monthly Catalog of United States Government Publications.* Washington: GPO, 1895– . 12/yr.

Electronic format: CD-ROM (Auto-Graphics, SilverPlatter, 1976–).

Each issue lists documents published by all branches of the government; the catalog is arranged by department, bureau, or agency, with a subject index.

Cumulated by *Cumulative Subject Index to the* Monthly Catalog of United States Government Publications, *1900–71* (Washington: Carrollton, 1973), *Cumulative Subject Index to the* Monthly Catalog of United States Government Publications, *1895–1899*, 2 volumes (Washington: Carrollton, 1977), and *Cumulative Title Index to United States Public Documents, 1789–1976*, 16 volumes (Arlington: US Historical Documents Inst., 1979–82).

D251 *US Government Periodicals Index.* Bethesda: Congressional Information Service, 1994– . Annual.

Electronic format: CD-ROM (Congressional Information Service, 1994–).

An author and subject index to about 180 United States government periodicals for 1994– . Continues indexing in the *Index to US Government Periodicals* (Chicago: Infordata, 1975–89) for 1970–87. The years 1988–93 will eventually be included in the CD-ROM edition.

D252 *CIS / Index to Publications of the United States Congress.* Bethesda: Congressional Information Service, 1971– . 12/yr. (Subtitled *Index to Congressional Publications and Public Laws,* 1971–93.)

Electronic formats: CD-ROM (Congressional Information Service, 1978–) and online (Dialog, 1970– , and OCLC, 1976–).

An author and subject index, with abstracts, to congressional publications, such as House and Senate committee hearings, reports, and documents.

C253 *Monthly Checklist of State Publications.* Washington: Library of Cong., 1912– . 12/yr.

State government publications are listed by state and then agency, with a subject index in each issue.

History, Political Science, and Law

The items listed here emphasize English and American history, politics, and law; for the ancient and medieval worlds, see the sections on classical literature and medieval studies in this chapter. Also consult the major period bibliographies in chapter 3, appropriate sections of chapter 4, and other sections in this chapter, such as those on American studies, art, Caribbean studies, Celtic studies, ethnic studies, folklore, Jewish studies, manuscripts, printing, regionalism, Renaissance, science, and women's studies.

HISTORY

D255   *International Bibliography of Historical Sciences.* Munich: Saur, 1930– . Annual.

Produced under the auspices of the International Committee of Historical Sciences, this comprehensive, classified bibliography of international books and articles on world history, ancient and modern, for 1926– is arranged by time period and region, with indexes of authors, historical figures (e.g., Napoleon, Marx), and places. Editorial matter is in French.

D256   *Historical Abstracts: Bibliography of the World's Periodical Literature.* Santa Barbara: ABC-Clio, 1955– . 4/yr.

Electronic formats: CD-ROM (ABC-Clio, 1982–) and online (Dialog, 1973–).

An extensive, classified bibliography of international articles (with abstracts) on modern international history, in three parts: general (methodology, historiography, teaching, and study), topics (such as international relations, social and cultural history, and science and technology), and areas or countries. Studies on the United States and Canada are excluded starting with volume 16 (1970), and starting with volume 17 (1971) the bibliography is in two physical volumes, A for 1450–1914 and B for the twentieth century. Annual cumulated subject and author index.

D257   *America: History and Life.* Santa Barbara: ABC-Clio, 1964– . 7/yr.

Electronic formats: CD-ROM (ABC-Clio, 1982–) and online (Dialog, 1964–).

A classified bibliography of international books, articles,

dissertations, and reviews on the United States and Canada, arranged by format within the various subject sections. The book review listing also serves as a partial bibliography of books. Author and subject indexes in issues 1–3, cumulated in issue 5; five-year cumulations of the indexes.

D258   *Annual Bibliography of British and Irish History.* London: Harvester, 1976– . Annual.

A classified bibliography of international books and articles 1975– on the history of Britain, Ireland, medieval Wales, and Scotland before the union. Items arranged by period, with author and subject indexes.

(B1)   *Annual Bibliography of English Language and Literature*

"Related Historical Studies" are listed under the divisions for the sixteenth through the twentieth centuries, volume 46– (1971–).

D259   *History: Reviews of New Books.* Washington: Heldref, 1972– . 10/yr.

A book review journal with reviews arranged under the headings "Europe," "Asia," "General," and "America." Author index in each issue.

D260   *Reviews in American History.* Baltimore: Johns Hopkins UP, 1973– . 4/yr. (Through issue 3.2, published by Redgrave, Westport.)

A journal of lengthy reviews of new books in American history.

POLITICAL SCIENCE

D261   *ABC Pol Sci: Bibliography of Contents: Political Science and Government.* Santa Barbara: ABC-Clio, 1969– . 6/yr.

Electronic formats: CD-ROM (ABC-Clio, 1984–) and online (Dialog, 1971–).

Lists contents of articles of about 300 international periodicals, with author and subject indexes in each issue and cumulated annually.

D262   *International Political Science Abstracts / Documentation politique internationale.* Paris: Intl. Political Science Assn., 1951– . 6/yr.

A classified bibliography (with abstracts) of international articles on political science, arranged in sections covering methods and theory, thinkers and ideas, governmental and administrative institutions, political process, international relations, and national and area studies. Each issue has a subject index, and there is an annual author and subject index.

(D458) *International Bibliography of the Social Sciences*

Includes the *International Bibliography of Political Science*, an annual, comprehensive, and classified bibliography of international books and articles on all aspects of political science for 1952– .

D263 *Perspective: Monthly Reviews of New Books on Government, Politics, International Affairs.* Washington: Heldref, 1972– . 10/yr.

A book review journal with reviews listed under sections for the United States, Asia, Africa and the Middle East, the Western Hemisphere, comparative politics, international relations, and Europe. An author index is in each issue and is cumulated annually.

LAW

D264 *Index to Legal Periodicals.* New York: Wilson, 1909– . 11/yr. Electronic formats: CD-ROM and online (Wilson, 1981–).

An author and subject index to major articles in about 400 North American, United Kingdom, and Commonwealth journals. Book review index and table of cases included.

(A15) *Infotrac*

Includes *Legaltrac*, an author and subject index to some 800 legal periodicals and other materials.

(A30) Lexis/Nexis

The online service provides the full text of thousands of publications in over 120 files—periodicals, statutes, court rulings, government documents, reference books—in law, business, medicine, and current events. It is also a specialized professional resource for legal research, for which see also *Westlaw* (Saint Paul: West).

Humor

D265   *Studies in American Humor.* Elmira: Elmira Coll., 1982– .
Annual. (Series 3, no. 1, 1994– ; series 2, vols. 1–7,
1982–89; originally *American Humor: An Interdisciplinary
Newsletter,* Amer. Humor Studies Assn., Richmond,
1974–81.)

    "State of American Humor [year]," starting in the 1994
volume, is a compilation of articles about contemporary
American humor mainly from the popular press, listed in
categories for parody, race, women's humor, locale, political humor, and advertising. In *American Humor,* 1974–81,
"Criticism on American Humor: An Annotated Checklist"
lists articles and dissertations on American humor in literature, folklore, popular culture, mass media, education, and
other areas of American life.

(A1)   *MLA International Bibliography*

    Studies on humor in general are listed under "Literary
Forms" in part 1, volume 4.

Interviews

See the general periodical and newspaper indexes listed in
chapter 2 and, in this chapter, *The American Humanities Index*
(D300), in which interviews are listed under the names of the
people interviewed.

(D361) *Serials Review*

    "Little Magazine Interview Index" has appeared irregu-
larly, 1985– ; it indexes interviews with mainly literary figures in little magazines.

Islamic Studies

See the sections on history, medieval studies, philosophy, and
religion in this chapter and the Near and Middle Eastern literature section of chapter 4.

Jewish Studies

See also the sections on ethnic and minority studies, history, and religion in this chapter and the Near and Middle Eastern literature section in chapter 4.

D270   *Jewish Book Annual.* New York: Jewish Book Council, 1942– . Annual.

A review of Jewish books on such matters as juvenile literature, women, individual writers, and bibliographical subjects, along with selective, annotated bibliographies of current Jewish fiction, nonfiction, juvenile literature, and of award-winning Jewish books from the United States, Great Britain, and Israel written in English, Hebrew, and Yiddish.

D271   *Index to Jewish Periodicals.* Cleveland Heights: Index to Jewish Periodicals, 1963– . Annual.

An author and subject index to about 50 English-language periodicals of general and scholarly interest.

(A1)   *MLA International Bibliography*

In addition to work on Hebrew literature, lists studies on Yiddish literature, 1951– . For 1951–54, listed under "East European Literature"; for 1955, listed separately; for 1956–80, listed under "Germanic Literature," volume 2; for 1981– , listed as a subsection under "German Language (New High)." Articles on Jewish literature are included under the appropriate national literature. See also the subject index under "Jewish Writers" and related terms and under "Yiddish-Language Literature."

D272   *Judaica Book News.* New York: Book News, 1970– . 2/yr.

Each issue includes an annual classified bibliography of new or forthcoming books of Jewish interest, including a section of new literature and literary criticism.

D273   *Articles of Interest in Current Periodicals.* New York: Amer. Jewish Committee, c. 1940–93. 6/yr.

A classified list of recent articles generally dealing with social and religious but not literary issues.

Journalism and Mass Communication

The important and long-lasting bibliography in *Journalism and Mass Communication Quarterly* (D275) has recently ceased, regrettably. Comparable coverage appears in the *Humanities Index* (A8) and, to a lesser extent, in the *Social Sciences Index* (D455), *Infotrac* (A15), *Periodical Abstracts* (A16), *Readers' Guide* (A20), and other indexes in chapter 2. Most of the bibliographies listed in this section concern themselves more with the history of journalism than with current issues in journalism. See also the sections on the alternative press, censorship, little magazines, periodicals, printing and publishing, speech, and television in this chapter.

D275 *Journalism and Mass Communication Quarterly.* Columbia: Assn. for Educ. in Journalism, 1924– . 4/yr. (Vols. 1–4 titled *Journalism Bulletin*; vols. 5–71 titled *Journalism Quarterly: Devoted to Research in Mass Communication*; place varies.)

"Articles on Mass Communication in U.S. and Foreign Journals: A Selected Annotated Bibliography," 1930–92, volumes 7–69, is a classified, quarterly list of international articles. The subjects covered in the index include advertising, audience and communicator analysis, broadcasting, communication theory, community journalism, courts and law, criticism and defense of media, editorial policy and methods, education for journalism, government and media, history and biography, research methods, and technology.

D276 *Studies in Newspaper and Periodical History.* Westport: Greenwood, 1985– . Annual. (Vols. 1–8 titled *Journal of Newspaper and Periodical History* and published 2/yr.; vols. 1–5 published by the U of London.)

"Annual Review of Work in Newspaper History" lists international books, articles, and dissertations on international newspapers and periodicals for 1984, with an emphasis on the United States and Great Britain.

D277 *Journalism History.* Las Vegas: U of Nevada, 1974– . 4/yr. (Vols. 1–16 published by California State U, Northridge.)

"Recent Scholarship," in volumes 18– (1992–), preceded by "Communication History Abstracts," in volumes

4–13 (1977–86), lists current United States articles and dissertations about international communication history.

(D375) *ABHB: Annual Bibliography of the History of the Printed Book and Libraries*

The chapter on newspapers and journalism lists international books and articles for 1970– .

(B1) *Annual Bibliography of English Language and Literature*

Studies on journalism history and literary relations are listed under "Newspapers and Other Periodicals."

(B58) *Victorian Periodicals Review*

Carries an annual checklist of books and articles for 1971– about Victorian periodicals, newspapers, and journalism beginning in volume 6 (1973).

(D360) *American Periodicals: A Journal of History, Criticism, and Bibliography*

"American Periodicals: A Selected Checklist of Scholarship and Criticism" for 1985– lists books, articles, and dissertations from *Dissertation Abstracts International* about periodicals and newspapers.

D278 *Journalism Abstracts.* Columbia: U of South Carolina, 1963– . Annual. (Sponsored by Assn. for Educ. in Journalism; place of publication varies.)

An annual author list, with subject index, of abstracts of master's theses and doctoral dissertations written in United States universities.

D279 *Communication Abstracts: An International Information Service.* Newbury Park: Sage, 1978– . 4/yr.

A classified bibliography, with abstracts, of articles on communication research, journalism, broadcasting, mass communication, speech, and communication theory in about 115 English-language journals. Author and subject indexes.

(A2) *FRANCIS bulletin signalétique 521. Sociologie, ethnologie*

The section "Sociologie de la communication et des mass media" is an international, extensive bibliography of current articles.

(D467) *Bibliographic Annual in Speech Communication*

"Studies in Mass Communication: A Selected Bibliography" for 1972–74, in volumes 4–6 (1974–75), is a comprehensive, classified, and international list of books and articles on mass communication that are of interest to scholars in radio and television, journalism, speech, and mass communication.

Latin American Studies

See chapter 4.

Law

See the section on history, political science, and law.

Libraries

Bibliographies that list studies of, or information about, collections and recent library acquisitions are covered, as are bibliographies with studies in librarianship. Most major libraries publish newsletters or journals listing significant acquisitions and describing collections; *Library Literature* (D280) indexes these publications. See also the sections in this chapter on bibliography, censorship, children's literature, journalism and mass communication, manuscripts, printing and publishing, and reference books.

D280　*Library Literature: An Index to Library and Information Science.* New York: Wilson, 1934– . 6/yr.

Electronic formats: CD-ROM (Wilson, 1984–) and online (OCLC and Wilson, 1984–).

A comprehensive author and subject index to international books, articles, and pamphlets for 1921– dealing with libraries, library collections, librarianship, and information science, including issues involving archives, manuscripts, collections, bibliographic control, communications, censorship, and printing, publishing, and bookselling. Continues H. G. T. Cannons, *Bibliography of Library Economy* (Chicago: Amer. Library Assn., 1927), which covers 1876–1920.

(D205) *ERIC*

Provides good coverage of English-language library periodicals.

D281 *Library and Information Science Abstracts*. London: Library Assn., 1969– . 6/yr. (Supersedes *Library Science Abstracts*, 1950–68.)

Electronic formats: CD-ROM (SilverPlatter, 1969–) and online (Dialog and OCLC, 1969–).

A classified compilation of abstracts of international articles on bibliography, collections, manuscripts, archives, and printing, publishing, and bookselling. Annual author and subject index.

(D375) *ABHB: Annual Bibliography of the History of the Printed Book and Libraries*

An international, comprehensive, and classified bibliography of books and articles for 1970– , with one chapter listing studies of library history.

(D378) *Bibliographie der Buch- und Bibliotheksgeschichte: BBB*

A comprehensive bibliography of international books and articles on book and library studies for 1980– .

D282 *Libraries and Culture: A Journal of Library History*. Austin: U of Texas P, 1966– . 4/yr. (Vols. 1–22 titled *Journal of Library History, Philosophy, and Comparative Librarianship*; vols. 1–11 published by Florida State U, Tallahassee.)

Starting in volume 29, number 4 (1994), "The Literature of American Library History" is a biennial bibliographic essay citing books, articles, and dissertations; this coverage continues "The Year's Work in American Library History" for 1967–90 in volumes 3–27 (1968–92).

D283 *British Library History: Bibliography*. London: Library Assn.– Winchester Bibliographies, 1972– . Irregular.

Issued about every four years, this bibliography covers international books, articles, and dissertations on the subject, which includes private libraries and collections, for 1962– .

(A1) *MLA International Bibliography*

Studies of libraries in general are listed under "Bibliographical" in part 1, volume 4.

(B1)   *Annual Bibliography of English Language and Literature*
Studies on collecting and libraries are listed under "Bibliography."

Linguistics, Language, and Language Teaching

Many of the bibliographies listed in chapter 4 include language studies and language teaching items. See also the sections in this chapter on comparative literature, composition, computers, education, folklore, journalism and mass communication, and style. The *Arts and Humanities Citation Index* (A6) and *Humanities Index* (A8) cover journals that emphasize historical and analytical linguistics, language, and philology, while the *Social Sciences Index* (D455) and the *Social Sciences Citation Index* (D456) cover journals dealing with psycho- and sociolinguistics.

LINGUISTICS AND LANGUAGE

D285   *Linguistics Bibliography for the Year [date] / Bibliographie linguistique de l'année [date].* Dordrecht: Kluwer, 1947– . Annual. (Publisher varies.)
An annual, comprehensive classified bibliography of international books, reviews, and articles, 1939– . Subjects include bibliography, general linguistics and related fields of study (such as stylistics, translation, psycholinguistics, and onomastics), and the major language groups. Lists some 21,000 entries a year.

(A1)   *MLA International Bibliography*
Covers all aspects of linguistics, including theoretical, descriptive, and comparative linguistics, and the language families, listing some 11,000 entries a year. The separate section for linguistics began with the 1968 bibliography and is now volume 3 in part 1; before 1968 linguistics coverage was included under the separate sections for individual literatures.

(A2)   *FRANCIS bulletin signalétique 522. Sciences du langage*
A comprehensive, classified bibliography of international books, articles, and other publications, 1947– , now online and on CD-ROM. See sections on psycholinguistics,

sociolinguistics, linguistic theories, communication, literary semiotics, applied linguistics, and history of linguistics and comparative grammar.

D286 *Linguistics and Language Behavior Abstracts.* San Diego: Sociological Abstracts, 1967– . 4/yr.

Electronic formats: CD-ROM (SilverPlatter, 1974–) and online (Dialog, 1973–).

A comprehensive, classified bibliography with abstracts of international books, articles, and dissertations on language and language behavior, especially applied linguistics; socio-, psycho-, and anthropological linguistics; and communication. Among the categories included are verbal learning, poetics and literary theory, philosophy of language, speech and hearing, and special education. Annual cumulated subject and author indexes and annual book review index.

D287 *Bibliographie linguistischer Literatur (BLL): Bibliographie zur allgemeinen Linguistik und zur anglistischen, germanistischen und romanistischen Linguistik.* Frankfurt: Klostermann, 1976– . 4/yr., with annual cumulation. (Titled *Bibliographie unselbständiger Literatur-Linguistik*, vols. 1–3.)

Electronic format: online (STN, 1971–).

A comprehensive, classified, international bibliography for 1971– covering books, articles, and published proceedings on German, English, and the Romance languages and on linguistics. Author and subject indexes.

D288 *Linguistics Abstracts.* Oxford: Blackwell, 1985– . 4/yr.

Each issue consists of abstracts of current books and articles on international linguistics. (Author has not reviewed the periodical.)

(C1) *The Year's Work in Modern Language Studies*

Volumes 35–49 (1974–87) include a chapter on general linguistics, and the sections on individual literatures often include chapters on linguistics studies in those languages.

D289 *English World-wide: A Journal of Varieties of English.* Heidelberg: Goosm, 1980– . 2/yr.

The second issue in each year includes summaries of international dissertations on worldwide varieties of English for 1978– .

(B1)   *Annual Bibliography of English Language and Literature*
Covers books, reviews, and articles on the English language, with sections for history, phonetics, grammar, vocabulary, lexicography, names, meaning, medium and register, dialects, and translation.

(C10)   *Revue de linguistique romane*
"Chronique bibliographique," 1950–83, is a classified list of reviews of recent international books on Romance linguistics.

(D470) *Style*
The annual bibliography for 1966–90 includes coverage of language aspects of literature.

D290   *Quarterly Check-list of Linguistics: An International Index of Current Books, Monographs, Brochures, and Separates.* Darien: Amer. Bibliographic Service, 1958–72. 4/yr.
A comprehensive author list of international books and other publications, with an annual author, editor, and translator index.

LANGUAGE TEACHING

D291   *Language Teaching.* London: Cambridge UP, 1968– . 4/yr. (Titled *Language-Teaching Abstracts*, vols. 1–7, 1968–74, and *Language Teaching and Linguistics: Abstracts*, vols. 8–14, 1975–81.)
A classified bibliography with abstracts of international articles on language, linguistics, and language learning and teaching drawn from some 400 periodicals. There are author and subject indexes in each issue; those in the fourth issue are cumulative for the volume.
Lists of current research projects in Britain and in Europe appear in alternate issues.

D292   *Second Language Instruction/Acquisition.* San Diego: Sociological Abstracts, 1991– . 2/yr.
An abstract journal recording international publications on language teaching and learning.

(D205) *ERIC*
Covers international periodicals and educational documents.

(D286) *Linguistics and Language Behavior Abstracts*
   Studies on nonnative-language learning and teaching and on bilingualism are listed in the section for applied linguistics.

(A1) *MLA International Bibliography*
   Studies on the teaching of language are listed under "Professional Topics" in part 1, volume 3, and studies on second-language learning are listed under "Psycholinguistics" in the same volume.

D293 *ACTFL Annual Bibliography of Books and Articles on Pedagogy in Foreign Languages.* New York: ACTFL, 1978–82. Annual.

   A classified bibliography of international books and articles, with coverage extending back to 1875. Its publishing history is somewhat complex. The bibliographies for 1975–79 were published as above; 1974 was published in the ERIC system (D205, document no. 125268); 1973 was published separately by ACTFL but is also available in the ERIC system (no. 134002); 1967–72 were published in *Foreign Language Annals* (New York: ACTFL), and 1969–72 were also published as volume 4 of the *MLA International Bibliography* (A1). Direct predecessors of these versions were Emma Marie Birkmaier and Dale L. Lange, "A Selective Bibliography on the Teaching of Foreign Languages, 1920–1966," in *Foreign Language Annals* 1 (1967): 318–53; "Annotated Bibliography of Modern Language Methodology," covering 1915–59, annually in *Modern Language Journal,* volumes 1–45 (1916–61); James B. Tharp, *Annotated Bibliographies of Modern Language Methodologies for the Years 1946, 1947, 1948* (Columbus: Ohio State UP, 1952); and Charles H. Handschin, "Work on the Teaching of Modern Languages" for 1875–1912, in *The Teaching of Modern Languages in the United States* (Washington: GPO, 1913), 107–49.

Literary Theory and Criticism

Although there is no single, extensive bibliography devoted exclusively to literary theory and literary criticism, *Style* (D470) carries a useful annotated list, and the major literary bibliographies include sections specifically listing studies on the theory of literature and literary criticism. See also bibliographies on art, comparative literature, philosophy, and social sciences, as well as the current indexes listed in chapter 2.

(D470) *Style*

"Recent Work in Critical Theory" is an annual, annotated bibliography of mainly English books covering 1992– in volumes 27– (1993–), with entries arranged under headings for general literary theory; semiotics, narratology, rhetoric, and language systems; postmodernism and deconstruction; reader-response and phenomenological theory; feminism; psychoanalytic theory; and historical criticism. A bibliographic essay of the same title appeared in volumes 24–26 (1990–92), covering 1989–92 and citing articles as well as books.

(A1) *MLA International Bibliography*

Studies on literary and critical theory in general are listed under "Literary Theory and Criticism" and under "Literary Movements" in part 1, volume 4, and under the sections for literary periods in volumes 1 and 2. For 1961–80 see under "Literary Theory" in the general literature division, where there are subheadings for aesthetics, literary criticism, and literary theory. Before 1961 see the sections on aesthetics and literary criticism.

(B1) *Annual Bibliography of English Language and Literature*

Studies on literary theory are listed under "English Literature, General" and within the sections for literary periods. Before volume 48 (1973), this section was titled "Literature, General"; it had subsections for literary history and literary criticism.

(B4) *Abstracts of English Studies*

Studies on theory are listed under the sections for general studies, aesthetics, literary theory, and theory of criticism.

(B72) *American Literary Scholarship: An Annual*

The chapter "Themes, Topics, and Criticism" covers literary theory for 1966– .

(B2)   *The Year's Work in English Studies*
Includes a chapter for literary theory starting with volume 62 (1984), covering 1981– ; in earlier volumes see "Literary History and Criticism: General Works."

(B6)   *English Studies: A Journal of English Language and Literature*
See the annual review article on literary theory, criticism, history, and biography, 1925– .

D295   *Unisa English Studies.* Pretoria: U of South Africa, 1968– . 2/yr.
Starting in volume 17 (1979), the journal carries an annual annotated list of international English-language articles on literary theory, critical methodology, and literary aesthetics for 1977– .

(C15) *Bibliographie der französischen Literaturwissenschaft*
Various relevant sections include "Critiques et methodes," "Poétique," "Stylistique," "Theorie du texte," "Textologie," "Structuralism," and "Sémiotique (et sémiologie)."

(C81) *Bibliographie der deutschen Sprach- und Literaturwissenschaft*
Studies on theory have been listed under "Literaturwissenschaft" since 1980.

(C51) *Nueva revista de filología hispánica*
Has included studies on theory since the 1985 volume.

(A2)   *FRANCIS bulletin signalétique 523. Histoire et sciences de la littérature*
In addition to the subject index see section B, on theory of literature and poetics, and section C, on theoretical studies of literature, within the division on sciences of literature, both in the classified part.

(D286) *Linguistics and Language Behavior Abstracts*
See the sections for poetics and literary theory, semiotics, and the philosophy of language. The poetics and theory section was titled "Poetics and Stylistics" for 1977–89, and before 1977 simply "Stylistics."

D296   *Œuvres et critiques: Revue internationale d'étude de la réception critique des œuvres littéraires de langue française.* Tübingen: Narr, 1976– . 2/yr.
Most issues include a bibliography of North American, English, French, and German books, articles, and dissertations on reception studies; occasionally the lists are limited

to studies dealing with a specific century's writing or with specific topics.

(D365) *Philosopher's Index: An International Index to Periodicals and Books*

Starting with 1970 there is a heading for literary criticism and starting in 1978 one for literary theory; see the section on literary theory in the retrospective volume for United States publications and the section on literary theory and literary criticism in the retrospective volume for non–United States publications.

(D87) *Yearbook of Comparative and General Literature*

The "Bibliography on the Relations of Literature and the Other Arts" includes sections for theory and general studies.

(D85) *Canadian Review of Comparative Literature / Revue canadienne de littérature comparée*

"Revue des revues," 1974–88, includes annotated entries on theory.

D297 *Structuralist Review: A Journal of Theory, Criticism, and Pedagogy*. New York: Queens Coll. P, 1978–84. 3/yr.

Includes an annual bibliography of structuralist criticism and theory.

Little Magazines and Small Presses

Coverage by the *American Humanities Index* (D300), which now indexes over 500 international English-language periodicals, is extended by that of the current indexes described in chapter 2. See also the specialized indexes for African American studies, the alternative press, creative writing, ethnic and minority studies, and women's studies in this chapter, along with bibliographies listed in chapters 3 and 4. Small-press books present a problem because they have not been consistently reviewed or listed in trade bibliographies.

LITTLE MAGAZINES

D300 *The American Humanities Index*. Troy: Whitston, 1975– . Annual.

Originally a complement to the *Humanities Index* (A8), this publication is now an author and subject index to over 500 mainly English-language, international little magazines, literary reviews, and scholarly literary journals, citing creative writing, scholarly articles, and reviews, with extensive listings under headings for plays, poems, and stories.

Coverage is extended by the *Index to Little Magazines* for 1948–67 (Denver: Swallow, 1949–70), 1943–1947 (Denver: Swallow, 1965), and 1940–1942 (New York: Johnson, 1967); by the *Index to American Little Magazines, 1920–1939* (Troy: Whitston, 1969); and by the *Index to American Little Magazines, 1900–1919* (3 vols., Troy: Whitston, 1974). In addition, the *Comprehensive Index to English-Language Little Magazines, 1890–1970,* 8 volumes (Millwood: Kraus, 1976), covers 100 American, British, and other English-language titles.

(B92) *Canadian Literary Periodicals Index*

An author and subject index for 1992– to 95 Canadian literary periodicals and the literary articles in the Toronto *Globe and Mail*. Continues coverage of the *Canadian Literature Index*, 1984–87 (B93).

D301 *Index to Commonwealth Little Magazines*. Troy: Whitston, 1964– . Biennial.

An author and subject index to creative writing, criticism, bibliographical articles, and book reviews in about 15 little magazines from Britain, Australia, Ireland, Africa, and Wales.

D302 *Access to Little Magazines*. Evanston: Burke, 1976–78. Annual.

An author, title, and subject index to about 70 American little magazines for 1974–78. Subject index includes book reviews and interviews.

SMALL PRESSES

D303 *Small Press Record of Books*. Paradise: Dustbooks, 1969– . Annual.

An author list of mainly American small-press books in print, with subject, title, and publisher indexes.

(D124) *Directory of American Poetry Books*
A list by publisher (including many small presses) of new books published in the United States.

D304 *Private Press Books: A Checklist of Books Issued by Private Presses in the Past Year.* Pinner, Eng.: Private Libraries Assn., 1960– . Annual.
Annual publisher list of mainly British private-press books. Author index.

D305 *Small Press Review.* Paradise: Dustbooks, 1967– . 12/yr.
Reviews new small-press books and new little magazines and lists new books and magazines received.

D306 *American Book Review.* New York: Amer. Book Review, 1978– . 6/yr.
Each issue reviews about 15 books of literature and current thought, mainly published by small, university, regional, and specialist presses.

D307 *Small Press Book Review.* Southport: Greenfield, 1985– . 4/yr. (Vols. 1–8, 6/yr.)
A classified compilation of reviews of new United States small-press books. See regular sections for drama, fiction, literature, and poetry in most issues and occasional feature sections.

Manuscripts and Archives

Although scholars need information about the locations of manuscripts and archives, as well as studies of them, there is no complete, up-to-date, and continuous inventory. The *National Union Catalog of Manuscript Collections* (D311) and the annual index in *College and Research Libraries* (D312) are the most helpful regular bibliographies of additions to or announcements about North American library holdings. Also see relevant articles in *American Literary Scholarship* (B72), the two *Year's Work* volumes (B2 and C1), and the quarterly *Resources for American Literary Study* (University Park: Pennsylvania State P, 1971–), as well as the journals and annual reports of major libraries. For studies of individual manuscripts, see the period and author

bibliographies. See also the sections on libraries and on microforms and reprints in this chapter.

D310 *English Manuscript Studies, 1100–1700.* Oxford: Blackwell,
1989– . Annual.

Each volume contains a list of manuscripts offered at
auction in the previous year and an index to manuscripts
cited in articles in the volume.

D311 *The National Union Catalog of Manuscript Collections.* Washington: Library of Cong., 1959–93. Annual.

The print version lists manuscript collections in United
States libraries and museums that are open to scholarly
researchers. The print format has ceased, but the bibliographic information continues to be entered into national
databases. Access to the print volumes is through the annual (formerly biennial) subject and author indexes and
two cumulated author and subject indexes, the *Index to
Personal Names in the National Union Catalog of Manuscript
Collections, 1959–1984,* 2 volumes (Alexandria: Chadwyck-
Healey, 1988), and the *Index to Subjects and Corporate Names
in the National Union Catalog of Manuscript Collections,
1959–1984,* 3 volumes (Alexandria: Chadwyck-Healey,
1994).

D312 *College and Research Libraries.* Chicago: Amer. Library
Assn., 1939– . 6/yr., with monthly newsletter.

"News from the Field" notes the acquisition of books,
manuscripts, and collections by United States and Canadian libraries; it appears in most issues and then in each
monthly *College and Research Libraries News* (started as a
newsletter supplement to vol. 27, 1966, and now separate).
This feature has been indexed annually under the heading
"Acquisitions"; items are listed by author, subject, and institution, starting with the *Index to Volumes 26 to 40
(1965–1979) of* College and Research Libraries *and* College
and Research Libraries News, compiled by Eldon W.
Tamblyn (Chicago: Amer. Library Assn., 1980), and annually thereafter.

(D280) *Library Literature*

See headings for manuscripts, special collections, acquisitions, and archives.

D313 *American Archivist.* Chicago: Soc. of Amer. Archivists, 1938– . 4/yr.

"Writings on Archives" for 1988– in volumes 53– (1990–) is a resumption of the annual bibliography "Writings on Archives, Historical Manuscripts, and Current Records" for 1942–78 (in 1943–82). Bibliographic coverage for the 1980s is irregular: it appears in *Writings on Archives, Historical Manuscripts, and Current Records: 1979–82* (Washington: Natl. Archives and Records Administration, 1985) and in annual bibliographies for 1983 and 1984 in volume 49, numbers 3 and 4 (1986). "Writings" is a bibliography of international books, pamphlets, and articles on the management and use of archives, on editing, and on general issues relating to archives; it also lists reports of acquisitions and descriptions of archive collections. The bibliography emphasizes historical rather than strictly literary materials.

D314 *Scriptorium: Revue internationale des études relatives aux manuscrits.* Brussels: Centre d'Etudes des Manuscrits, 1946– . 2/yr. (Publishers vary.)

"Bulletin codicologique" is an international, annotated bibliography of books and articles about manuscript studies and facsimile editions. Annotations, usually in the language of the book or article, note which manuscripts are cited (if any). Generally covers European medieval manuscripts.

(A1) *MLA International Bibliography*

Studies on manuscripts in general are listed under "Bibliographical" in part 1, volume 4; before 1981 the "Bibliographical" section appears in the general literature division. See also the subject index under "Manuscript Study" or under the name of the library where a manuscript is preserved.

(B1) *Annual Bibliography of English Language and Literature*

Studies on manuscripts in general are listed under the bibliography section.

D315 *National Inventory of Documentary Sources in the United States.* Teaneck: Chadwyck-Healey, 1983– . 2/yr.

The *Inventory* consists of a basic set of of catalogs and finding aids on microfiche for a range of federal, state, academic, and other institutions; this set is supplemented by twice yearly updates and accompanied by indexes in microfiche and on CD-ROM. (Author has not examined the set.)

Medicine

See the section on science, technology, and medicine.

Medieval Studies

The comprehensive bibliographies and the specialized bibliographies covering cross-national topics are listed here, including bibliographies of Medieval Latin and Neo-Latin. See chapters 3 and 4 for additional bibliographies devoted to national aspects of medieval studies. See also the sections in this chapter on art; Arthurian, classical, Islamic, and Jewish studies; manuscripts; philosophy; and religion. See the sections on Chaucer and Dante in chapter 6.

GENERAL BIBLIOGRAPHIES

D320   *International Medieval Bibliography*. Leeds: Intl. Medieval Bibliography, 1968– . 2/yr. (Originally published by the U of Leeds)

    A comprehensive, classified bibliography for 1965– covering international books and articles on all aspects of medieval Europe and of the Middle East and Christian North Africa, 450–1500. Categories include art, folk studies, language, and literature (subdivided by genre and then by country or region). Critic and subject indexes in each issue.

D321   *Deutsches Archiv für Erforschung des Mittelalters*. Cologne: Böhlau, 1937– . 2/yr. (Titled *Deutsches Archiv für Geschichte des Mittelalters*, 1937–44.)

    Each issue carries a comprehensive, classified, and annotated bibliography of international books and articles from the early 1930s covering all aspects of medieval life.

D322 *Cahiers de civilisation médiévale X^e–XIIe siècles: Bibliographie.*
Poitiers: Centre d'Etudes Supérieures de Civilisation Médiévale, 1958– . 5/yr.
Carries a bibliography of international books and articles
for 1969– . Volumes 1–11 include the bibliography in each
issue; in volumes 12– it appears annually in a fifth issue.
Name, subject, and critic index.

D323 *Medioevo latino: Bolletino bibliografico della cultura europea dal
secolo VI al XIV.* Spoleto: Centro Italiano di Studi sull'Alto
Medioevo, 1980– . Annual.
A comprehensive, classified bibliography, annotated in
Italian, of international books, articles, and reviews on all
aspects of the medieval world.
"Elaborazione elettronica dei dati" lists items on compu-
ters and medieval studies.

(A1) *MLA International Bibliography*
See the sections for 400–1099 and 1100–1499, for Old
English, and for Middle English in part 1, volume 1, and
see the appropriate sections in volume 2 for the non-
English literatures. Before 1981 see the sections for Old
English and Middle English, the division for Medieval
Latin and Neo-Latin literature, and the medieval subsec-
tion under "Literature, General and Comparative" within
the general literature division.

D324 *Envoi: A Review Journal of Medieval Literature.* New York:
AMS, 1988– . 2/yr.
Each issue consists of a review article on a medieval topic,
length book reviews, brief notices of new books, and a list
of mainly English-language books received on medieval
studies.

(B24) *Speculum: A Journal of Medieval Studies*
A classified list of American periodical literature on medieval studies appears in most issues from 1934 to 1972.
"Bibliography of Editions and Translations in Progress
of Medieval Texts," volumes 48– (1973–), is an annual
subject list of mainly North American and British projects.

D325 *International Guide to Medieval Studies: A Continuous Index to*

Periodical Literature. Darien: Amer. Bibliographic Service, 1962–77. 4/yr.

Provided extensive coverage of international periodicals, Festschriften, and published proceedings on all aspects of the medieval world. Items arranged by author, with annual author index. A detailed subject index in each issue was cumulated annually.

D326 *Quarterly Check-list of Medievalia.* Darien: Amer. Bibliographic Service, 1958–78. 4/yr.

An extensive list for 1957–77 of international books (studies, reprints, translations) on all aspects of the medieval world. Entries are arranged alphabetically by author. Annual author, editor, and translator index.

SPECIALIZED TOPICS

(B1) *Annual Bibliography of English Language and Literature*
See the sections on Old English and Middle English for general subjects and individual writers.

(B2) *The Year's Work in English Studies*
See chapters on Old English and Middle English.

(B20) *Neuphilologische Mitteilungen: Bulletin de la Société Néophilologique / Bulletin of the Modern Language Society*
Includes an annual list of international work in progress in Old English (for 1964–85/86), Middle English (for 1963–84/85), and Chaucer (for 1968–). The Chaucer list is also carried in *Chaucer Review* (E25).

(B21) *Old English Newsletter*
Publishes two annual bibliographies: "Old English Bibliography," 1969– , a classified bibliography of international books, articles, and dissertations, and "The Year's Work in Old English Studies," 1969– , an evaluative bibliographic essay.

(B22) *Anglo-Saxon England*
Carries an annual, extensive, and classified bibliography of international books, articles, and significant reviews on all aspects of Anglo-Saxon culture, placing greater emphasis on history, archaeology, and Anglo-Saxon culture than does *OEN* (B21).

D327 *Bulletin bibliographique de la Société Rencesvals.* Paris: Nizet, 1958– . Annual.

A classified bibliography of international books, reviews, and articles on the medieval romance. Offers occasional annotations in French. Items are arranged by subject country. Critic and subject indexes.

D328 *Olifant: A Publication of the Société Rencesvals, American-Canadian Branch.* Winnipeg: Société Rencesvals, American-Canadian Branch, 1973– . 4/yr.

Carries a quarterly checklist of books, articles, reviews, and North American dissertations on the medieval romance for 1966– . Published in mimeograph format by the Société Rencesvals, 1966–72.

(B23) *Medieval English Theatre*

Most issues since 1979 include a list of books received and reports of recent productions of medieval plays.

(B36) *Research Opportunities in Renaissance Drama*

Lists current research projects in medieval drama for 1956–84 and continues to publish bibliographies on figures and subjects of medieval drama.

D329 *Encomia: Bibliographical Bulletin of the International Courtly Love Society.* Philadelphia: Int. Courtly Love Soc., 1975– . Annual.

Includes a classified, annotated bibliography of international books, articles, and dissertations, of book reviews, and of new editions and translations. Author and subject indexes.

(D30) *Bibliographical Bulletin of the International Arthurian Society / Bulletin bibliographique de la Société Internationale Arthurienne.*

A comprehensive, classified, annotated bibliography of international books and articles on Arthurian matters.

(E100) *The Yearbook of Langland Studies*

The section "Annual Bibliography" lists new international books, articles, dissertations, and book reviews covering medieval alliterative poetry as well as Langland studies.

(D355) *Oral Tradition*

Publishes in approximately two-year intervals an annotated author list of international books and articles on oral traditions in folklore, history, linguistics, literature, and religion that covers the classical, medieval, Renaissance, and modern worlds.

(D429) *Mystics Quarterly*

The section "Publications and Reviews," in each issue through 17.2 (1992), is an annotated list of North American books, articles, and dissertations on mysticism, especially mysticism in literature.

D330 *Medieval Feminist Newsletter.* New York: Fordham U, 1986– . 2/yr.

Each issue carries a bibliography of relevant international books and articles.

(D314) *Scriptorium: Revue international des études relatives aux manuscrits*

Annotations in the "Bulletin codicologique" note which manuscripts are cited (if any).

(C1) *The Year's Work in Modern Language Studies*

Medieval Latin studies are covered beginning with volume 1 (1931), and Neo-Latin studies are covered beginning with volume 32 (1970).

(B33) *Seventeenth-Century News*

"Neo-Latin News," in each issue, 1952– , lists summaries of recent books, articles, and dissertations.

(B31) *Studies in Philology*

The Renaissance bibliography for 1917–68 includes studies of Neo-Latin.

D332 *Bibliographie annuelle du moyen age tardif. Auteurs et textes latins.* Paris: Brepols, 1991– . Annual.

An annual bibliography emphasizing studies of Medieval Latin literature. (Author has not examined the bibliography.)

D333 *Bulletin de philosophie médiévale.* Louvain: Intl. Soc. for the Study of Medieval Philosophy, 1959– . Annual.

Carries a list of new international translations and European editions of medieval texts.

(B25) *The Year's Work in Medievalism*

Projected annual.

Microforms and Reprints

D335 *Guide to Microforms in Print.* Munich: Saur, 1961– . Annual. (Published by Microcard, Englewood, 1961–77; Microform Review, Westport, 1978–81; Meckler, Westport, 1982–90.)

An international author, title, and subject list of microforms in print on all topics (the subject list appears in a separate volume).

D336 *Microform Review.* Munich: Saur, 1972– . 4/yr. (Vols. 1–11 published by Microform Review, Westport; vols. 12–19 by Meckler, Westport.)

Each issue carries reviews of microform publications and books about micropublishing, and "Recent Articles on Micro Publishing," through volume 11 (1982), lists international articles.

D337 *Guide to Reprints.* Kent: Guide to Reprints, 1967– . Annual.

An international author and title list of current reprints in print on all subjects.

D338 *Reprint Bulletin: Book Reviews.* Dobbs Ferry: Glanville, 1955–80. 4/yr.

Includes reviews of current, reprinted books in all subjects from mainly North American publishers; the reviews are arranged by Dewey classification categories. Author index in each issue is cumulative for the volume.

D339 *Bulletin of Reprints.* Munich: Dokumentation, 1964– . 4/yr. (Titled *Bibliographia anastatica*, vols. 1–10, 1964–73.)

An author, title, and subject list of reprints of international books and serials. Updates Christa Gnirss, editor, *Internationale Bibliographie der Reprints / International Bibliography of Reprints* (Munich: Dokumentation, 1976).

Minorities

See the section on ethnic and minority studies.

Music and Dance

The bibliographies here cite current musicological studies and reviews as well as information about librettists, literary-musical collaborations, and specific poets and other writers whose work has been set to music.

D340   *Music Index: A Subject-Author Guide to Current Music Periodical Literature.* Detroit: Information Coordinators, 1949– . 12/yr.

Electronic   format: CD-ROM   (Chadwyck-Healey, 1981–).

This author and subject index covers articles in over 300 international periodicals on classical, popular, jazz, folk, and ethnic music, on musicology, and on performance and pedagogy; it lists reviews of books, performances, and recordings. For literary subjects, see under subject headings for specific authors, literature, genres, themes, and subjects (such as the Faust legend).

D341   *RILM Abstracts: Répertoire Internationale de Littérature Musicale / International Repertory of Music Literature.* New York: Intl. RILM Center, 1967– . 4/yr.

Electronic format: CD-ROM (see *Muse*, D342).

A comprehensive, classified bibliography with abstracts for 1966– covering international books, articles, reviews, dissertations, catalogs, and other publications on all aspects of music. See "Poetry and Other Literature" in the section on music and other arts and the entire section on ethnomusicology. Author index in each issue and annual subject index.

D342   *Muse: Music Search.* Baltimore: Natl. Information Services, 1989– . Annual. CD-ROM format only.

Combines into one computer file the bibliographic information about books cataloged by the Library of Congress for 1960– and the periodical literature cited by *RILM Abstracts* (D341) for 1970– .

(D87)   *Yearbook of Comparative and General Literature*

Issues since 1986 include the "Bibliography on the Relations of Literature and Other Arts," an extensive, classified, and annotated bibliography of international books and articles on the relations between literature and music, visual art, dance, and film; see the main entry for earlier versions, 1952– .

D343   *Guide to the Performing Arts.* Metuchen: Scarecrow, 1960–72.

(Continues the *Guide to the Musical Arts: An Analytical Index of Articles and Illustrations, 1953–1956,* Scarecrow, Metuchen, 1957; also continues the *Guide to Dance Periodicals,* D348.)

Indexes some 40 international but mainly North American periodicals for 1957–68 covering music, dance, theater, and television.

DANCE

D344   *Index to Dance Periodicals.* Boston: Hall, 1990– .

(Author has not examined the index.)

D345   *Bibliographic Guide to Dance.* Boston: Hall, 1976– . Annual.

A classified bibliography of international publications for 1975– covering dance, with materials ranging widely from books to films, photos, and drawings to manuscripts and scores to tapes and playbills and more, arranged by author or performer, title, and subject. Continues *Dictionary Catalog of the Dance Collection: A List of Authors, Titles, and Subjects of Multi-media Materials in the Dance Collection of the Performing Arts Research Center of the New York Public Library,* 10 volumes (Boston: Hall, 1974).

D346   *Dance Abstracts and Index.* Los Angeles: Dance Database Project, 1989– .

(Author has not examined the publication.)

D347   *Dance Research Journal.* New York: Committee on Research in Dance, 1976– . 2/yr.

Most issues include reports of conferences, meetings, resources (e.g., recent acquisitions of the New York Public Library's dance collection), and other relevant items, along with lists of books and journals received.

D348   *Guide to Dance Periodicals: An Analytical Index of Articles.* Metuchen: Scarecrow, 1948–63. (Vols. 3–4 for 1941–50 issued in 1948 and 1951 by Stephens, Asheville; vols. 1–2 for 1931–40 and vols. 5–7 for 1951–56 by U of Florida P, Gainesville, 1955–59.)

An index to from 10 to 20 English-language periodicals covering ballet and folk, square, and ballroom dance for 1931–62. Continued by *Guide to the Performing Arts* (D343).

Names

In addition to these bibliographies see the major bibliographies listed under linguistics in this chapter, most of which have a section on onomastics.

D350   *Names: Journal of the American Name Society.* Vermillion: Amer. Name Soc. 1953– . 4/yr. (Place varies.)

"Bibliography of Personal Names" was an annual, extensive, international list of books and articles about worldwide personal names in volumes 1–24 (1952–75). This bibliography updated Elsdon C. Smith, *Personal Names: A Bibliography* (New York: New York Public Library, 1952).

"Place-Name Literature," 1952 and then biennially 1965–79, listed books and articles about place-names. These have been cumulated, most recently, in Richard B. Sealock, Margaret M. Sealock, and Margaret Sealock Powell, *Bibliography of Place-Name Literature, United States and Canada*, 3rd edition (Chicago: Amer. Library Assn., 1982), and have been updated in Margaret S. Powell and Stephen D. Powell, "Bibliography of Placename Literature, United States and Canada, 1980–1988," *Names* 38 (1990): 49–141.

D351   *Onoma: Bibliographical and Information Bulletin / Bulletin d'information et de bibliographie.* Louvain: Intl. Centre of Onomastics, 1950– . 3/yr.

"Bibliographia Onomastica" is an annual, classified bibliography of international books and articles on place-names and personal names, with items arranged by subject country.

(A1)   *MLA International Bibliography*

Studies on names are listed under "Onomastics" in part 1, volume 3.

(B1)   *Annual Bibliography of English Language and Literature*
       Studies on names are listed within the linguistics section.

Naturalism

(E293)   *Les cahiers naturalistes. Bulletin*
         Each annual issue carries a bibliography of international
         books and articles about Zola and naturalism.

Near and Middle Eastern Studies

See the section on Asian literatures in chapter 4.

News and Current Events

See chapter 2.

Oral Literature

D355   *Oral Tradition.* Columbus: Slavica, 1986– . 3/yr.
       Publishes at approximately two-year intervals an anno-
       tated author list of international books and articles on oral
       traditions in folklore, history, linguistics, literature, and
       religion of the classical, medieval, Renaissance, and mod-
       ern worlds.

Periodicals

This section lists bibliographies of studies and reviews of periodicals, but not periodical directories. See also the sections on
journalism, little magazines and small presses, printing, and
television and radio, as well as many of the bibliographies in
chapters 3 and 4.

(A1)   *MLA International Bibliography*
       Studies on periodicals in general are listed under
       "Genres" in part 1, volume 4, and under relevant literary

periods in all the sections for English, American, and other literatures; before 1981 they are listed under "Themes and Types" in the general literature division.

(B1)   *Annual Bibliography of English Language and Literature*
Includes "The Newspaper and Periodical" for 1973– , in volumes 48– (1976–), as a subsection under "Bibliography."

(D276) *Journal of Newspaper and Periodical History*
"Annual Review of Work in Newspaper History" for 1984– lists international books, articles, and dissertations on international newspapers and periodicals, with an emphasis on the United States and Great Britain.

(B58)   *Victorian Periodicals Review*
Carries an annual checklist of books and articles about Victorian periodicals for 1971– in volumes 6– (1973–).

(B2)   *The Year's Work in English Studies*
Starting with 1978 *The Year's Work* includes periodicals in its survey of studies of Victorian prose.

D360   *American Periodicals: A Journal of History, Criticism, and Bibliography.* Denton: Research Soc. for Amer. Periodicals, U of North Texas P, 1991– . Annual.
"American Periodicals: A Selected Checklist of Scholarship and Criticism" for 1985– lists books, articles, and dissertations from *Dissertation Abstracts International.*

D361   *Serials Review.* Ann Arbor: Pierian, 1975– . 4/yr.
"Serials Review Index" for 1974– , in every other issue, 1975– , indexes reviews in some 150 periodicals.

D362   *Literary Magazine Review.* Manhattan: Kansas State U Writers Soc., 1982– . 4/yr.
In addition to review discussions of individual magazines and to articles on broad topics, one article each year lists newly started American little magazines.

(D121) *Dictionary of Literary Biography Yearbook*
"New Literary Periodicals: A Report" for 1987– in each annual, 1988– , describes about 25 new titles a year, covering new scholarly journals, little magazines, and literary reviews.

Philosophy

See also *L'année philologique* (D75) for works on Greek and Roman philosophers, and see the sections in this chapter on art, aesthetics, and architecture; comparative literature and translation; linguistics, language, and language teaching; literary theory and criticism; religion and theology; and social sciences, sociology, and anthropology.

D365   *Philosopher's Index: An International Index to Periodicals and Books.* Bowling Green: Philosophy Documentation Center, 1967– . 4/yr.

Electronic formats: CD-ROM and online (Dialog, 1940–).

A comprehensive index to international books, articles, and reviews, selectively abstracted. In the print edition the subject index refers the user to an author list with abstracts; there is a separate book review section. Coverage has been extended back to 1940.

(A2)   *FRANCIS bulletin signalétique 519. Philosophie*

A comprehensive, classified bibliography of international books, articles, and other publications, 1947– , now accessible online and on CD-ROM.

D366   *Bibliographie de la philosophie / Bibliography of Philosophy.* Paris: Vrin, 1937– . 4/yr.

A comprehensive, classified bibliography of international books, with annotations, usually in the language of the book. Categories include logic, semantics, philosophy of science, philosophical psychology, aesthetics, ethics, social philosophy, philosophy of history, philosophy of religion, history of philosophy, annuals, and reference books. Author, subject, and publisher indexes in every fourth issue.

D367   *International Philosophical Bibliography / Répertoire bibliographique de la philosophie / Bibliografisch repertorium van de wijsbegeerte.* Louvain: Editions de l'Institut Supérieur de Philosophie, 1949– . 4/yr. (Continues the *Répertoire bibliographique de la philosophie,* 1949–90, which had been formed from *Répertoire bibliographique*, a supplement to *Revue néo-scolastique de philosophie* and then to *Revue philosophique de Louvain*, 1934–45 and 1946–48, and from the *Bibliografisch repertorium van de wijsbegeerte*, appearing in *Tijdschrift voor filosofie*, 1939–90.)

An international, comprehensive, classified bibliography of books, articles, and reviews. Each issue is in two parts, one covering the history of philosophy and the other covering a variety of philosophical topics. Every fourth issue contains a book review index and a name index.

Poetry

There is no single bibliography of poetry criticism; therefore, in addition to the following items, see also the relevant national, period, and author bibliographies. For bibliographies of new poetry, see the section on creative writing in this chapter.

(A1)   *MLA International Bibliography*

Studies on poetry in general are listed under "Genres" and under "Figures of Speech" in part 1, volume 4, under the various literary periods in volumes 1 and 2, and under "Prosody" and the prosody subsections within individual languages in volume 3. Before 1981 the studies are listed under "Themes and Types" within the general literature division.

(B1)   *Annual Bibliography of English Language and Literature*

Studies on poetry as a genre are included under "English Literature, General" and under the various literary periods; studies of poetics are listed under "Medium and Register" within the linguistics section.

D369   *Eidos: The International Prosody Bulletin.* Suffern: Gall, 1984–90. 4/yr. Includes "Studies in Verseform" for 1979–90. (Author has not examined the bulletin.)

(D286) *Linguistics and Language Behavior Abstracts*

See the sections for poetics and literary theory, semiotics, and the philosophy of language.

(B57)   *Victorian Poetry: A Critical Journal of Victorian Literature*

"Guide to the Year's Work in Victorian Poetry" is a bibliographic essay on the year's international books and articles on Victorian poetry for 1962– .

(D126) *Poem Finder*

Roth American Poetry Annual includes a selective list of new books of poetry criticism for 1988–90.

(D127) *Anthology of Magazine Verse and Yearbook of American Poetry*

Includes a selective list of new books of poetry criticism for 1979, 1983, and 1984.

Political Science

See the section on history, political science, and law.

Popular Culture

See also the sections on art, creative writing, fiction, film, folklore, history, humor, music, periodicals, printing, science fiction, and social sciences in this chapter, as well as relevant sections in the *Bibliographie der deutschen Sprach- und Literaturwissenschaft* (C81) and the *Bibliographie der französischen Literaturwissenschaft* (C15). *Contemporary Literary Criticism* (B67) covers contemporary popular literature starting with volume 13.

D370 *Abstracts of Popular Culture: A Quarterly Publication of International Popular Phenomena*. Bowling Green: Popular Culture, 1976–77. 4/yr.

Lists books and articles on various aspects of popular culture.

Printing, Publishing, History of the Book, and Textual Studies

Bibliographies listed here cover analytical bibliography, printing, publishing, and the book trade, along with textual studies and editing, and tend to cover the historical aspects of publishing;

for more current topics see *Library Literature* (D280), *Library and Information Science Abstracts* (D281), *Business Periodicals Index* (D201), and *ABI/Inform* (D202). See also the major bibliographies for national literatures and literary periods and the sections on bibliography, journalism and mass communication, libraries, little magazines and small presses, periodicals, and reference books and research tools.

D375   *ABHB: Annual Bibliography of the History of the Printed Book and Libraries.* Dordrecht: Wolters, 1973—. Annual. (Vols. 1–15 published by Nijhoff, The Hague, 1975–83; Dordrecht, 1984–86.)

A classified bibliography of international books, articles, and reviews for 1970– . Chapters list items about the history of books and libraries, printing materials, calligraphy and type, printing, book illustration, bookbinding, publishing and the book trade, collecting, institutions and libraries, the legal, economic, and social aspects of books and libraries, newspapers and journalism, and related subjects. A name index provides access to studies on specific writers.

D376   *SHARP News.* Madison: Soc. for the History of Authorship, Reading, and Publishing, 1992– . 4/yr.

"Recent Publications" in each issue is a checklist of international books and articles on authorship, reading, and publishing for 1991– starting in volume 1, number 2 (1992).

D377   *In octavo: Bulletin international d'information sur l'histoire du livre et de l'édition.* Paris: IMEC, 1992– . 2/yr.

"Publications" in each issue is a classified list of new international books and articles on printing, publishing, and the history of the book.

D378   *Bibliographie der Buch- und Bibliotheksgeschichte: BBB.* Bad Iburg: Meyer, 1981. Annual.

An extensive international bibliography of books and articles on book and library studies for 1980– .

(A1)   *MLA International Bibliography*

Studies on printing, publishing, the book trade, analytical bibliography, and textual studies are listed under

"Bibliographical" in part 1, volume 4. See also under the bibliography subsections of the national literatures and literary periods in volumes 1 and 2. Before 1981 "Bibliographical" appeared in the general literature division.

(B1)   *Annual Bibliography of English Language and Literature*
Studies on printing, publishing, the book trade, analytical bibliography and textual studies are listed under "Bibliography"; coverage is extensive starting with volume 48 (1973).

(B2)   *The Year's Work in English Studies*
Starting with 1978 *The Year's Work* includes publishing history in its survey of studies of Victorian prose.

D379   *Library: The Transactions of the Bibliographical Society.* London: Bibliographical Soc., 1899– . 4/yr.
Each issue since volume 20 (1965), has two sections of note: "Recent Books" lists recent studies in analytical and descriptive bibliography, with brief summaries, and "Recent Periodicals" selectively lists the contents of North American and European literary, historical, and bibliographical journals.

(D37) *Index to Reviews of Bibliographical Publications: An International Annual*
An annual classified bibliography for 1976–85 covering international reviews of international bibliographical publications, including editions of literary texts and materials (such as letters and manuscripts), concordances, indexes, bibliographies, and books on textual and editorial theory.

D380   *Direction Line: A Newsletter for Bibliographers and Textual Critics.* Austin: U of Texas, 1975–77. 2/yr.
Each issue lists dissertations in progress and new or forthcoming literary bibliographies, critical editions, and bibliographic or textual studies, and the journal includes a bibliographic essay surveying mainly British and North American work in 1975–77 on bibliography and on textual studies.

(B35) Manuscripta: *A Journal for Manuscript Research*
Volumes 7–28 (1963–84) include an annual review of English Renaissance textual studies for 1962–83.

(E109) *Luther Jahrbuch*

The annual "Lutherbibliographie" for 1927– , in volumes 1929– , includes useful listings on printing and related aspects of the Reformation.

(B42) *The Eighteenth Century: A Current Bibliography*

This annual bibliography of international scholarly work on eighteenth-century life worldwide includes "Printing and Bibliographic Studies," a major section that covers printing, publishing, libraries, textual and bibliographic scholarship, and new enumerative bibliographies.

(B54) *Victorian Studies*

The annual bibliography includes "Bibliographical Material," a section that lists textual studies; enumerative bibliographies; and books and articles on Victorian printing, publishing, book trade, libraries, periodicals, and journalism.

(D38) *Literary Research*

"Record of Current Publication" in each issue lists new critical editions as well as international literary reference books, specialized dictionaries and encyclopedias, and, especially, secondary and primary author bibliographies for 1985–90.

D381 *Studies in Bibliography*. Charlottesville: Bibliographical Soc. of Virginia, 1948– . Annual.

"A Selective Checklist of Bibliographical Scholarship" for 1949–71, in volumes 3–26 (1950–73), lists international books and articles dealing with incunabula, early printing, bibliographies, checklists and enumeration, printing and publishing, and bibliography and textual scholarship.

The checklists for 1949–54 were reprinted in *Studies in Bibliography* volume 10 (1957) along with the checklist for 1955 and an author and subject index; those for 1956–62, with an added author and subject index, were reprinted separately in Howell J. Haney and Rudolf Hirsch, editors, *Selective Check Lists of Bibliographical Scholarship, Series B, 1956–1962* (Charlottesville: UP of Virginia, 1966).

D382 *Proof: The Yearbook of American Bibliographical and Textual Studies*. Columbia: Faust, 1971–77. Annual.

"The Register of Current Publications" in volumes 1–4 (1971–75) lists books, monographs, and pamphlets of interest to textual critics. The section covers editions, subject and author checklists, national bibliographies, and studies, and lists scholarly tools on literature, writing, printing, publishing, bookselling, libraries and collecting, and bibliographic theory and practice.

Prose

(A1) *MLA International Bibliography*
Studies on prose in general, including travel literature, autobiography, and biography, are listed under "Genres" in part 1, volume 4, and under literary periods in volumes 1 and 2; before 1981 they are listed under "Themes and Types" within the general literature division.

(B1) *Annual Bibliography of English Language and Literature*
Studies on prose in general are listed under "English Literature, General" and in the sections for literary periods.

(B2) *The Year's Work in English Studies*
Starting with 1978 *The Year's Work* includes a section surveying studies of Victorian prose.

D385 *Prose Studies: History, Theory, Criticism.* London: Frank Cass, 1977– . 3/yr. (Vols. 1–2 published at U of Leicester, Leicester, Eng.)
"Nineteenth-Century Non-fictional Prose: A Bibliography of Work" for 1977–78 lists books and articles on English and American writers and on literary aspects of nonfiction prose.

Psychology

See also *Linguistics and Language Behavior Abstracts* (D286) and items under social sciences in this chapter.

D390 *IPSA Abstracts and Bibliography in Literature and Psychology.* Gainesville: Inst. for Psychological Study of the Arts, U of Florida, 1986– .

See the sections "Bibliography—Articles" and "Bibliography—Books." (Author has not examined the bibliography.)

D391   *Literature and Psychology.* Providence: Rhode Island Coll., 1951– . 4/yr. (Vols. 1–17, U of Hartford; vols. 17–31, Fairleigh Dickinson U, Teaneck; vols. 32–33, Illinois State U, Normal.)

Includes an annual bibliography of articles on literature and psychology through 1970 in volumes 1–23 (1951–73).

D392   *Psychological Abstracts.* Washington: Amer. Psychological Assn., 1927– . 12/yr.

Electronic formats: CD-ROM (SilverPlatter and Dialog, 1974– for articles and 1987– for books) and online (Dialog, 1974– and 1987– , OCLC Epic, 1967– , and OCLC First-Search, latest three years).

A comprehensive, classified bibliography with abstracts of international books, articles, dissertations, and some unpublished papers (books not covered during 1982–91; see *Psycbooks*, D393). Author and subject indexes appear in each issue and are cumulated semiannually. Relevant index headings include "Literature," "Poetry," "Prose," "Autobiography," and "Biography."

D393   *Psycbooks.* Arlington: Amer. Psychological Assn., 1989–91. Annual, each in 5 volumes.

A classified bibliography with abstracts of chapters in collections and monographs for 1987–90.

D394   *Contemporary Psychology.* Washington: Amer. Psychological Assn., 1956– . 12/yr.

Each issue is a classified arrangement of reviews of recent, international, English-language books in psychology; items are classified in such categories as sexuality, social and personality psychology, and history of philosophy and psychology.

Reference Books and Research Tools

Reference books having to do with individual authors and certain broader subjects are frequently reviewed in *The Year's Work in English Studies* (B2), *The Year's Work in Modern Language Studies* (C1), and *American Literary Scholarship* (B72).

D400 *Reference Services Review: A Quarterly Guide to the World of Reference.* Ann Arbor: Pierian, 1973– . 4/yr.

"Reference Sources" in each issue is a selectively annotated list of new reference books in all subjects. Reviews of new reference books are indexed. The index supplements Shirley Smith, editor, *Reference Book Review Index, 1970–1972* (Ann Arbor: Pierian, 1975) and M. and S. Balachandran, eds., *Reference Book Review Index, 1973–1975* (Ann Arbor: Pierian, 1979).

D401 *American Reference Book Annual.* Englewood: Libraries Unlimited, 1970– . Annual.

A classified bibliography of some 1,800 new reference books published in the United States and Canada. The section for literature lists titles by form (such as bibliography, handbook, and biography), by genre, and then by national literature. Author, subject, and title index.

(D45) *Book Review Index*

Provides extensive coverage of reference book reviews, although without a subject index. Cumulated in *Reference Book Review Index: A Cumulated Index to More Than 87,000 Reviews of Approximately 40,000 Reference Titles That Have Been Cited in* Book Review Index (Detroit: Gale, 1986).

D402 *Guide to Reference Books.* Chicago: Amer. Library Assn., 1902– . Irregular, with supplements.

Now in its tenth edition, first supplement, this volume is a comprehensive, classified, annotated bibliography of international reference books in all subjects, with author, title, and subject index. In addition to supplements, *Guide to Reference Books* is updated once or twice yearly in *College and Research Libraries* (D312).

(D37) *Index to Reviews of Bibliographical Publications: An International Annual*

Includes reviews of new literary reference books for 1976–85.

D403 *Reference Book Review.* Dallas: Reference Book Review, 1976– . 4/yr.

Lists 100–150 recent reference books in most fields, except medicine, technology, and agriculture, with descriptive and evaluative annotations.

D404 *Zeitschrift für Bibliothekswesen und Bibliographie.* Frankfurt: Klostermann, 1954– . 4/yr.

"Ausgewählte Bibliographien und andere Nachschlagewerke" in each issue lists new international reference books and bibliographies in the humanities, with extensive annotations in German.

(A1) *MLA International Bibliography*

Books and articles about research tools are listed under "Professional Topics" in part 1, volume 4.

(D38) *Literary Research*

"Record of Current Publication" lists new literary bibliographies, specialized dictionaries and encyclopedias, and other literary reference books for 1986–90.

D405 *American Notes and Queries.* Owingsville: Erasmus, 1962–86. 10/yr. (Vols. 1–12 published in New York; continued by *ANQ: A Journal of Short Articles, Notes, and Reviews,* U of Kentucky, Lexington, 1988– .)

The reviews and lists of books received in each issue from 1962 to 1986 emphasize reference books in literature and related subjects.

D406 *Informationsmittel für Bibliotheken.* Berlin: Deutsches Bibliotheksinstitut, 1993– . 4/yr.

A review journal covering about 600 recently published international reference books a year in all fields, about half in English and the remainder in German and other European languages. (Author has not seen this periodical.)

Supplemented by *IFB Astracts,* an electronic journal on the Internet (http://library.upenn.edu/ifba) that provides English-language abstracts of reviews for 1994– of the non-English-language reference books.

(D382) *Proof: The Yearbook of American Bibliographical and Textual Studies*

"The Register of Current Publications," 1971–77, lists editions, subject and author checklists, national bibliographies, and studies; it also lists scholarly tools on literature, writing, printing, publishing, bookselling, libraries and collecting, and bibliographic theory and practice.

Regionalism (US)

Except for the section in *Abstracts of English Studies* (B4) that covers regionalism in Great Britain and the United States, only bibliographies for American regional studies are listed here. See also the sections on African American studies, ethnic and minority studies, folklore, and history in this chapter.

(B4)   *Abstracts of English Studies*

     See the sections for regionalist studies of both English and American literature.

D410 *Western American Literature.* Logan: Western Amer. Lit. Assn., Utah State U, 1966– . 4/yr.

     The "Annual Bibliography of Studies in Western American Literature" for 1965– lists books and articles about western writers, including Native Americans, and about western literature in general.

D411 *Mississippi Quarterly: The Journal of Southern Culture.* Mississippi State: Mississippi State U, 1947– . 4/yr.

     "A Checklist of Scholarship on Southern Literature," 1968– , is an annual list of books and articles on southern writers, arranged in five parts: colonial, antebellum, postbellum, contemporary (1920–), and general.

     The bibliographies for 1968–75 have been collected, cumulated, and supplemented in Jerry T. Williams, editor, *Southern Literature, 1968–1975: A Checklist of Scholarship* (Boston: Hall, 1978).

D412 *Midamerica.* East Lansing: Center for the Study of Midwestern Lit., Michigan State U, 1973– . Annual.

     "Annual Bibliography of Studies in Midwestern Literature" lists American books and articles on general literary topics and on individual writers for 1973– .

D413 *North Carolina Historical Review.* Raleigh: North Carolina Div. of Archives and History, 1924– . 4/yr.

     "North Carolina Bibliography," 1933– , is an annual,

classified bibliography of books and articles by North Carolinians or about North Carolina; among the categories are philosophy and literary studies and poetry, fiction, and other creative writing.

D414 *New England Quarterly: A Historical Review of New England Life and Letters.* Boston: New England Quarterly, 1928– . 4/yr.

"A Bibliography of New England" for 1927–65, in volumes 1–39 (1928–66), lists recent work on New England history, literature, and culture.

D415 *Great Lakes Review: A Journal of Midwest Culture.* Mount Pleasant: Central Michigan U, 1974– . 2/yr. (Published at Northeastern Illinois U, Chicago, 1974–78; continued as *Michigan Historical Review*, Mount Pleasant, 1986– .)

Volumes 1–4 (1974–77) include an annual bibliography of creative writing and studies of literary and related topics centered on the Great Lakes region and its people.

Religion and Theology

See also bibliographies listed in the sections in this chapter on comparative literature, history, Islamic studies, Jewish studies, and medieval studies, philosophy, and social sciences, as well as those listed under the national literatures in chapters 3 and 4.

D420 *Religion Index One: Periodicals.* Evanston: Amer. Theological Library Assn. (ATLA), 1949– . 4/yr., with annual cumulation. (Titled *Index to Religious Periodicals*, 1949–77.)

Electronic formats: *ATLA Religion Database* on CD-ROM and online (Wilson, 1949– , including the ATLA indexes to periodicals for 1949– , books for 1960– , book reviews for 1949– , and publications on the ministry for 1981–) and a reduced version of the database on CD-ROM as *Religion Indexes: RIO/RIT/IBRR, 1975– , on CD-ROM* (ATLA, 1975–) and online as *Religion Index* (Dialog, 1975–).

An author and subject index to over 500 international periodicals, including indexes of books reviews through 1985. Broad coverage of literary and humanities subjects, as well as of religious and theological issues. Supplemented by *Religion Index Two* (D421) and *Index to Book Reviews in Religion* (D422); new editions of early volumes feature expanded coverage and improved accuracy.

D421　*Religion Index Two: Multi-author Works.* Evanston: Amer. Theological Library Assn., 1978– . Annual.

An author and subject index to international collective volumes on religion, 1960– ; subject terms are identical with *Religion Index One.*

D422　*Index to Book Reviews in Religion.* Evanston: Amer. Theological Library Assn., 1986– . 6/yr.

Continues the book review indexing previously carried in *Religion Index One* for 1977–86. A three-volume cumulation, incorporating corrections, additions, and greater detail in its subject indexing, covers 1949–75: *Index to Book Reviews in Religion*, 3 volumes (Evanston: Amer. Theological Library Assn., 1991–93).

D423　*Science of Religion: Abstracts and Index of Recent Articles.* Amsterdam: Inst. for the Study of Religion, Free Univ., 1976– . 4/yr. (Supersedes *International Bibliography of the History of Religions / Bibliographie internationale de l'histoire des religions*, covering 1952–73 and published by Brill, Leiden.)

A classified bibliography of international articles on religion, with abstracts in English, author and title indexes, and annual subject and author indexes, covering religion in general and specific prehistoric, ancient, and modern religions.

D424　*Religious and Theological Abstracts.* Myerstown: Religious and Theological Abstracts, 1958– . 4/yr.

Electronic format: CD-ROM (Innotech, 1957–).

A classified bibliography of international periodical articles for 1957– with abstracts and annual, cumulated author, subject, and scripture indexes. The abstracts are arranged in five main parts, on biblical, theological, historical, practical (such as ministry, pastoral care, church administration), and sociological subjects; each part is divided into subsections.

D425　*Elenchus of Biblica.* Rome: Pontifical Biblical Inst., 1920– .

Annual. (Titled *Elenchus Bibliographicus Biblicus*, with editorial matter in Latin, vols. 1–59.)

An international, comprehensive, and classified bibliography of books, reviews, articles, and dissertations on biblical (but not necessarily Christian) matters. Author and subject indexes.

(A2) *FRANCIS bulletin signalétique 527. Histoire et sciences des religions*

A comprehensive, classified bibliography of international books, articles, and other publications on religion in general, the ancient religions, Judaism, Christianity, and the Bible for 1947– , now accessible online and on CD-ROM.

D426 *Christianity and Literature*. Carrollton: West Georgia Coll., 1952– . 4/yr. (Formerly *Conference on Christianity in Literature Newsletter*, published at Adrian Coll., Adrian.)

Through volume 37, number 4 (1988), the journal includes an annual, annotated author list of articles on literature and Christianity.

D427 *Catholic Periodical and Literature Index*. Haverford: Catholic Library Assn., 1930– . 6/yr.

This author, title, and subject index to periodical articles and books by, or of interest to, Catholics covers about 120 periodicals and 50 books in each issue. Book review index.

D428 *Christian Periodical Index*. Cedarville: Assn. of Christian Librarians, 1956– . 3/yr.

A general author and subject index to some 90 conservative Christian periodicals, with headings for poems and short stories as well as for literary topics.

D429 *Mystics Quarterly*. Cincinnati: U of Cincinnati, 1975– . 4/yr. (Titled *Fourteenth-Century Mystics Newsletter*, vols. 1–9; through issue 17.2, published by U of Iowa, Iowa City.)

The section "Publications and Reviews," in each issue until volume 17, number 2, is an annotated list of North American books, articles, and dissertations on mysticism, especially mysticism in literature.

(C132) *Quarterly Index Islamicus: Current Books, Articles, and Papers on Islamic Studies*

A comprehensive, classified bibliography of international studies, continuing and cumulated by the *Index Islamicus*.

(D271) *Index to Jewish Periodicals*

An author and subject index to about 50 English-language periodicals of general and scholarly interest.

(C149) *Quarterly Check-list of Oriental Studies*

Continues the *Quarterly Check-list of Biblical Studies* (Darien: Amer. Bibliographical Service, 1958–73). Coverage provided for 1958–78.

Renaissance

In addition to the bibliographies listed here, see those for the Continental literatures in chapter 4 and for art, history, philosophy, religion, and science and technology in this chapter.

D432 *Bibliographie internationale de l'humanisme et de la Renaissance.* Geneva: Droz, 1960– . Annual.

A comprehensive, classified bibliography for 1965– covering international books and articles on all aspects of the Renaissance—history (political, geographic, social, and economic), religion and philosophy, the arts, literature and language, and science and technology. The bibliography is arranged in a section for studies of authors and works and a section for studies of subjects, the latter subdivided for the subjects and then for individual countries. Critic index. A less comprehensive version of this bibliography for 1956–65 appears in *Bibliothèque d'humanisme et Renaissance* (Paris: Droz, 1934–).

(A1) *MLA International Bibliography*

See the sections for English literature for 1500–1599 and 1600–1699 in volume 1 and see the comparable sections in volume 2 for French, Italian (1400–1499), German, Scandinavian, and Spanish literature. In addition there is a section for the Renaissance under "Literary Movements" in volume 4. See also the subject index under "Renaissance." Comprehensive coverage of the period dates from the 1969 bibliography; before 1969 the major Renaissance literary bibliography appeared in *Studies in Philology* (B31).

(B31) *Studies in Philology*

Volumes 14–66 (1917–69) include an annual, international, comprehensive, and classified bibliography of books and articles on Renaissance literature for 1917–68. Coverage of literature of Germany, France, Italy, Spain, and Portugal and related subjects began with year 1938 (vol. 36, 1939).

D433 *Renaissance Quarterly*. New York: Renaissance Soc. of America, 1948– . 4/yr. (Titled *Renaissance News*, vols. 1–19, 1946–66; vols. 1–6 published by Dartmouth Coll. Library, Hanover.)

"Books Received" in each issue records 200–300 international books each year dealing with the Renaissance; for 1952–80 this list, titled "Renaissance Books," is an extensive, classified list of new international books drawn from entries in national bibliographies.

"Recent Bibliographical Tools," an annotated list of relevant international publications, appears in one issue a year starting in the early volumes, but sometimes appears more often and sometimes includes new critical editions and other scholarly tools.

"Reports on Scholarship," which appear irregularly throughout volumes 16–21 (1963–68), are review articles on current work in a wide range of Renaissance topics.

D434 *Quarterly Check-list of Renaissance Studies: An International Index of Current Books, Monographs, Brochures, and Separates*. Darien: Amer. Bibliographic Service, 1959–76. 4/yr.

An international author list of books on Renaissance subjects, with an annual author, editor, and translator index.

Reprints

See the section on microforms and reprints.

Rhetoric

See the section on composition, rhetoric, and technical writing.

Science, Technology, and Medicine

SCIENCE

D435 *Configurations: A Journal of Literature, Science, and Technology.* Baltimore: Johns Hopkins UP, 1993– . 3/yr.
"Relations of Literature and Science: A Bibliography of Scholarship," 1992– , is an annual, international classified bibliography of books and articles, now arranged under headings for topics (e.g., theory, rhetoric) and types of science, with a name index for authors, scientists, and others who are the subjects under discussion. Formerly arranged by time period. The bibliography has been published serially, with cumulations, since 1939, as follows:

> *PSLS: Publication of the Society for Literature and Science.* Troy: Rensselaer Polytechnic Inst., 1985– . 4/yr. Includes the bibliography "Relations of Literature and Science" for 1983–91.

> *Relations of Literature and Science: A Bibliography of Scholarship.* Worcester: Clark U, 1981–83. Annual. Covers 1979–80 (1981), 1980–81 (1982), and 1981–82 (1983).

> Walter Schatzberg, Ronald A. White, and Jonathan K. Johnson. *The Relations of Literature and Science: An Annotated Bibliography of Scholarship, 1880–1980.* New York: MLA, 1987. Cumulates earlier bibliographies and extends coverage back to 1880.

> *Clio: An Interdisciplinary Journal of Literature, History, and the Philosophy of History.* Fort Wayne: Indiana U–Purdue U, 1971– . 3/yr. Includes the bibliography for 1972–79 in volumes 4–10 (1974–80).

> Fred A. Dudley, *The Relations of Literature and Science: A Selected Bibliography, 1930–1967.* Ann Arbor: UMI, 1968. A cumulation of coverage for 1951–67 in *Symposium: A Quarterly Journal of Modern Foreign Literatures* (Syracuse: Syracuse UP) and for 1939–50 in *Relations of Literature and Science: A Bibliography of Scholarship,* an annual bibliography mimeographed by the MLA.

(D87)   *Yearbook of Comparative and General Literature*
        See the annual bibliographies for 1949–69 for occasional
        coverage of the relations between literature and science.

D436   *History of Science and Technology.* Mountain View: RLIN,
       1976– . Continual updating. Computer file only.

       This online computer file contains references from the
       "Bibliography of the History of Science and Its Cultural
       Influences" carried in *Isis* (D437), 1976– , and the current
       bibliography on the history of technology in *Technology and
       Culture* (D440), 1987– . Records describe journal articles,
       conference proceedings, books, book reviews, and dis-
       sertations.

D437   *Isis: An International Review Devoted to the History of Science
       and Its Cultural Influences.* Washington: History of Science
       Soc., 1913– . 5/yr.

       Electronic format: see *History of Science and Technology,*
       D436.

       "Bibliography of the History of Science and Its Cultural
       Influences," 1913– (published as a supplement, vols. 58– ,
       1969–), is an annual, classified, and comprehensive bibli-
       ography of international books and articles, with a sep-
       arate book review index and name index for authors and
       subjects.

       Cumulated in Magda Whitrow, Isis *Cumulative Bibliogra-
       phy: A Bibliography of the History of Science Formed from* Isis
       Critical Bibliographies 1–90, 1913–1965, 6 volumes (Lon-
       don: Mansell, 1971–84); John Neu, Isis *Cumulative Bibliog-
       raphy, 1966–1975: A Bibliography of the History of Science
       Formed from* Isis *Critical Bibliographies 91–102,* 2 volumes
       (London: Mansell, 1980, 1985); and John Neu, Isis *Cumula-
       tive Bibliography, 1976–1985: A Bibliography Formed from* Isis
       Critical Bibliographies, 2 volumes (Boston: Hall, 1989).

(A2)   *FRANCIS bulletin signalétique 524. Histoire des sciences et des
       techniques*

       A comprehensive, classified bibliography of interna-
       tional books, articles, and other publications on the history
       of science and technology for 1947– , now accessible online
       and on CD-ROM.

(B44) *Johnsonian News Letter*

The bibliography in each issue has a section for studies of science and medicine in the Restoration and in the eighteenth century.

D438 *General Science Index.* New York: Wilson, 1978– . 10/yr.

Electronic formats: CD-ROM (Wilson, 1984–) and online (OCLC and Wilson, both 1984–).

An author and subject index to articles and reviews in about 90 English-language science magazines. See, for example, the headings for history and philosophy of science and for science and literature.

(A18) *Biological and Agricultural Index*

A subject index to 225 English-language periodicals covering agricultural and biology but not medicine; includes a separate section of book reviews.

(A19) *Applied Science and Technology Index*

A subject index to 400 English-language periodicals in all areas of mathematics, physical sciences, and engineering; includes a separate section of book reviews.

D439 *Science Books and Films.* Arlington: Amer. Assn. for the Advancement of Science, 1965– . 9/yr.

Each issue consists of reviews of books and films on all aspects of science, medicine, and certain social sciences (psychology, sociology, anthropology, economics, and folklore) for adults, teenagers, and children. Annual author and film indexes.

TECHNOLOGY

D440 *Technology and Culture: The International Quarterly of the Society for the History of Technology.* Chicago: U of Chicago P, 1961– . 4/yr.

Electronic format: see *History of Science and Technology,* D436.

Volumes 4– (1964–) include an annual, classified bibliography of international books and articles for 1961– with items arranged by subject under broad chronological periods. Frequent, brief annotations; author index and biennial subject index.

D441 *Journal of American Culture*. Bowling Green: Bowling Green State U, 1978– . 4/yr.

"Technology in American Culture: Recent Publications" for 1979–80 in volumes 3–4 (1980–81) is an annotated list of mainly American books and articles.

D442 *Environment Abstracts*. Bethesda: Congressional Information Service, 1971– . 12/yr. (1971–87, published by Environment Information Access, New York, as *Environment Index* and *Environment Information Access*, then *Environment Abstracts*; 1988–93, published by Bowker A and I, New Providence.)

Electronic formats: CD-ROM (Congressional Information Service, 1971–) and online (Dialog, 1971–).

A comprehensive, classified list of abstracts from international periodicals, proceedings, and reports, with author, subject, and source indexes.

D443 *Agricultural History: The Quarterly Journal of the Agricultural History Society*. Berkeley: U of California P, 1927– . 4/yr.

Starting with volume 27 (1953) the journal includes an annual list of new international books on worldwide agricultural history; a list of publications on the history of American agriculture appears in the most issues of volumes 1–15 (1927–41).

D444 *Agricultural History Review*. Oxford: British Agricultural History Soc., 1953– . 2/yr.

Starting with the first volume and covering 1952– each issue includes either a bibliographic essay and list of recent articles or a list of recent books and pamphlets on English agricultural history.

MEDICINE

D445 *Cumulated Index Medicus*. Bethesda: Natl. Library of Medicine, 1961– . Annual.

Electronic formats: Several electronic versions available, notably *Medline* in CD-ROM (SilverPlatter, 1966–) and online (Dialog, 1960– , and OCLC, 1985–).

A cumulation of the monthly *Index Medicus* (Bethesda: Natl. Library of Medicine, 1960–) with comprehensive, classified coverage of international books and articles.

D446 *Bibliography of the History of Medicine.* Bethesda: Natl. Library of Medicine, 1965– . Annual, with five-year cumulations.

Comprehensive, classified bibliography of international books and articles for 1964– . Section 1 covers studies on individuals, arranged alphabetically by the subject's name (e.g., Goethe, Rousseau, Shakespeare). Section 2 covers subjects (e.g., "Literature and Medicine"). Author index.

D447 *Bulletin of the History of Medicine.* Baltimore: Johns Hopkins UP, 1933– . 4/yr.

"Bibliography of the History of Medicine in the United States and Canada" for 1939–65 in volumes 8–40 (1940–66) lists books and articles. Cumulated in Genevieve Miller, *Bibliography of the History of Medicine of the United States and Canada, 1939–1960* (Baltimore: Johns Hopkins UP, 1964).

Science Fiction

International science fiction criticism has been covered serially since 1970, with cumulations back to 1878, and the field has attracted several bibliographers who have produced a rich but confusing array of serial bibliographies and indexes. There are now a detailed subject index to international publication, a more selective list of English-language studies, and an annual bibliographic essay. In addition, the standard bibliographies, especially the *MLA International Bibliography* (A1), provide extensive coverage.

For indexes to current science fiction writing, see under the fiction subsection of the creative writing section in this chapter.

D450 *Science Fiction, Fantasy, and Horror: [year]: A Comprehensive Bibliography of Books and Short Fiction Published in the English Language.* Oakland: Locus, 1988– . Annual.

"Research Index" continues for 1988– the annual *Science Fiction and Fantasy Research Index* (D451) and is an extensive subject index to international books, articles, and dissertations; it uses some 300 subject terms, as well as author and title headings, and has a critic index.

This index and its predecessor are cumulated in Hal W. Hall, editor, *Science Fiction and Fantasy Reference Index, 1985–1991: An International Author and Subject Index to History and Criticism* (Englewood: Libraries Unlimited, 1993), and Hal W. Hall, editor, *Science Fiction and Fantasy Reference Index, 1878–1985: An International Author and Subject Index to History and Criticism*, 2 volumes (Detroit: Gale, 1987).

The indexers also attempt to record all new science fiction, fantasy, and horror books and magazines published or reissued during the year; these listings are drawn from the "Books Received" and "British Books" columns in *Locus* (D137).

D451 *Science Fiction and Fantasy Research Index*. San Bernardino: Borgo, 1980– . Annual. (Vols. 1–6, Bryan: SFBRI; vol. 1 titled *Science Fiction Research Index*.)

An extensive subject index to international books, articles, and dissertations for 1980– .

D452 *JFA: Journal of the Fantastic in the Arts*. Liverpool: Orion, 1988– . 4/yr.

"The Year's Scholarship in Fantastic Literature and the Arts" for 1988– , which started in volume 2 (1990) but continues coverage extending to 1972, is an annual, classified, partially annotated bibliography of American books, articles, dissertations, and reference books. Carried for 1972–79 in *Extrapolation* 17–22 (1975–81), published separately for 1980–82 (three annual editions) as Marshall B. Tymn, editor, *The Year's Scholarship in Science Fiction, Fantasy, and Horror Literature* (Kent: Kent State UP, 1983–85), and then for 1983–87 returned again to *Extrapolation* 26–29 (1985–88).

The bibliography is cumulated by Marshall B. Tymn and Roger C. Schlobin, *The Year's Scholarship in Science Fiction and Fantasy, 1972–1975* and *1976–1979* (Kent: Kent State UP, 1979 and 1982), and continues Thomas Clareson, *Science Fiction Criticism: An Annotated Checklist* (Kent: Kent State UP, 1982).

D453 *Science Fiction and Fantasy Book Review Annual*. Westport: Greenwood, 1988– . Annual. (Vols. 1 and 2 published by Meckler, Westport.)

"A Critical Survey of Fantastic Literature and Film Scholarship" for 1987– is a bibliographic essay covering the year's English-language books about science fiction and fantasy and books on film, television, illustration, and magazines. Includes a bibliography of works cited.

In addition, each volume carries bibliographic essays on new fantasy, horror, and science fiction writing; lists of recommended and prizewinning books, anthologies, and pieces in magazines; author profiles or interviews; and, especially, brief reviews of novels, story collections, and critical and scholarly works, all limited to English-language publications. Title index to books and stories mentioned.

(D137) *Locus: The Newspaper of the Science Fiction Field*

Each issue lists new English-language science fiction books in the "Books Received" and "British Books" sections. In addition, *Locus* publishes extensive book reviews and news of publishing, authors, and prizes.

(D141) *The NESFA Index to Short Science Fiction*

In addition to new writing, this publication indexes criticism, book reviews, and commentary.

(A1) *MLA International Bibliography*

Studies of science fiction are listed in part 1, volume 4, "General Literature and Related Topics," under the heading "Prose Fiction" within "Themes" and under the twentieth-century sections of the English and American literature sections.

(C15) *Bibliographie der französischen Literaturwissenschaft*

The bibliography contains a subsection on science fiction under "Généralités," volumes 12– (1974–). Only French-language books and articles are listed.

(D139) *Science Fiction and Fantasy Book Review Index*

In addition to reviews of new writing, this publication indexes reviews of reference books and criticism.

Social Sciences, Sociology, and Anthropology

See also the sections in this chapter on the alternative press, economics and business, education, ethnic and minority studies, history, psychology, religion, and women's studies.

D455   *Social Sciences Index.* New York: Wilson, 1974– . 4/yr. (Formerly *Social Sciences and Humanities Index,* 1965–74, and *International Index,* 1916–65.)

Electronic formats: CD-ROM (Wilson, 1983–) and online (OCLC and Wilson, 1983–).

An author and subject index to over 400 predominantly North American periodicals in the social and behavioral sciences, excluding history, which is covered in *Humanities Index* (A8). See such headings as autobiography, literature and society, politics and literature, and psychological aspects of literature. Book reviews listed separately.

D456   *Social Sciences Citation Index.* Philadelphia: Inst. for Scientific Information, 1973– . 3/yr., including annual cumulation.

Electronic formats: CD-ROM (ISI, 1986–) and online (Dialog, 1973– ; OCLC, 1980–).

An author, citation, permuted title, and institution index to articles, correspondence, and notes in about 4,600 international periodicals (1,400 covered fully, 3,200 partially), monographic series, and collections in the social sciences, excluding history, which is covered in the *Arts and Humanities Citation Index* (A6).

Complemented by the weekly *Current Contents: Social and Behavioral Sciences* (Philadelphia: ISI, 1969–) in which tables of contents of journals received are listed and indexed.

(A2)   *FRANCIS bulletin signalétique 521. Sociologie, ethnologie*

A comprehensive, classified bibliography of international books, articles, and other publications for 1947– . See particularly the sections "Sociologie de l'art de la littérature" and "Sociologie de la communication et des mass media." The bibliography is accessible online and on CD-ROM.

D457   *Sociological Abstracts.* San Diego: Sociological Abstracts, 1952– . 6/yr.

Electronic formats: CD-ROM (SilverPlatter, 1974–) and online (Dialog and OCLC, 1974–).

A classified, comprehensive bibliography with abstracts of international articles in sociology. Categories include history, theory, and methodology of sociology; areas of sociological study, such as organizations, the family, political institutions, and the arts; and more specialized subjects such as violence, feminism, Marxism, and the sociology of knowledge. Author and subject indexes.

D458   *International Bibliography of the Social Sciences.* London: Routledge, 1952– . Annual in four subseries. (1952–61 published by UNESCO, Paris; 1962–63 by Stevens, London; 1963–87 by Tavistock, London.)

The bibliography is in four subseries, each a classified, comprehensive, international list of books and articles with subject and author indexes. It was sponsored by the Fondation Nationale de Sciences Politiques, Paris, from 1952 to 1989, and then by the British Library of Political and Economic Science, London, 1990– , at which time it incorporated the *London Bibliography of the Social Sciences* (London: Mansell, 1931–90), a comprehensive bibliography of new books.

International Bibliography of Sociology, 1951– .

International Bibliography of Economics, 1952– .

International Bibliography of Political Science, 1952– .

International Bibliography of Social and Cultural Anthropology, 1955– .

D459   *Contemporary Sociology: A Journal of Reviews.* Washington: Amer. Sociological Assn., 1972– . 6/yr.

A classified arrangement (including such categories as theory and methods, sociology of culture, and political processes and institutions) of reviews of new international books and a classified list of publications received, with an annual index.

D460   *Abstracts in Anthropology.* Amityville: Baywood, 1970– . 4/yr.

International, classified bibliographical abstracts of articles. Categories of special relevance to literary studies are arts (folklore, graphic arts, literature, music) and symbol systems (religion, ritual, and worldview). Author and subject indexes.

(D436) *History of Science and Technology*

This electronic database includes studies on technology and culture for 1976– and continues coverage in *Isis* (D437) and *Technology and Culture* (D440).

(D441) *Journal of American Culture*

"Technology in American Culture: Recent Publications" for 1979–80 in volumes 3–4 (1980–81) is an annotated list of mainly American books and articles.

Speech Communication

See also the sections in this chapter on censorship; composition, rhetoric, and technical writing; drama; journalism and mass communication; linguistics, language, and language teaching; psychology; and social sciences, sociology, and anthropology, as well as the general periodical indexes listed in chapter 2.

D465 *Southern Communication Journal.* Knoxville: Southern States Communication Assn., 1935– . 4/yr. (Titled *Southern Speech Bulletin,* 1935–42, *Southern Speech Journal,* 1942–71, *Southern Speech Communication Journal,* 1971–88.)

"A Bibliography of Speech, Theatre, and Mass Communication in the South" for 1954–77 and 1980–82, through volume 49 (1983/84), is an annual, classified bibliography of books, reviews, articles, and dissertations on public address, theater, speech education, and mass communication published in southern journals or about people and conditions in the South.

D466 *Speech Communication Abstracts.* Pleasant Hill: Theatre/Drama and Speech Information Center, 1975–80. (Titled *Theatre/Drama and Speech Index,* 1974; see D187.)

An international, comprehensive abstracting service for articles, 1974–77. Author and subject index.

D467 *Bibliographic Annual in Speech Communication.* Falls Church: Speech Communication Assn., 1970–75. Annual.

Continuing coverage that started in 1934, this annual includes a comprehensive, classified bibliography for 1969–74 listing international books, articles, dissertations, and theses in various areas of speech communication studies, mass communication, rhetoric, public address and oral interpretation, and theatrical craftsmanship.

The bibliography was previously carried in *Speech Monographs* (Falls Church: Speech Communication Assn.,

1934–75). Theses are listed for 1902–68 in volumes 1–36 (1934–69); theses are abstracted for 1945–68 in volumes 13–36 (1946–69); and books, articles, and dissertations are listed for 1950–68 in volumes 18–36 (1951–69).

Style

See also the sections in this chapter on art and aesthetics, composition and rhetoric, linguistics and language, and the literary genres.

D470   *Style*. De Kalb: Northern Illinois U, 1967– . 4/yr. (Vols. 1–16 published by U of Arkansas, Fayetteville.)

Volumes 1–25 (1967–91) include an annual, classified, and annotated bibliography of international books, articles, and dissertations on style in English, American, and European literatures for 1966–90. Subject categories vary but generally deal with theoretical issues, individual works and authors, and social contexts. Volume 26 (1992) initiates an annual series of bibliographic reviews. Author, title, and subject indexes in volumes 16–24.

Technical Writing

See the section on composition, rhetoric, and technical writing.

Technology

See the section on science, technology, and medicine.

Television and Radio

See also the sections in this chapter on American studies and on journalism and mass communication, as well as the news and current events indexes in chapter 2.

D475   *International Index to Television Periodicals*. London: Intl. Federation of Film Archives, 1983– .

An author and subject index to international periodicals for 1979– . (Author has not examined the index.)

(D235) *Film Literature Index: A Quarterly Author-Subject Index to the International Periodical Literature of Film and Television*

Starting with volume 14 (1986) the index includes a separate section for television and video that lists international articles on topics and individual shows and titles.

(A1) *MLA International Bibliography*

Studies on television as a genre and on television in general are listed under "Dramatic Arts / Television" in part 1, volume 4.

(D343) *Guide to the Performing Arts*

An index to some 40 international but mainly North American periodicals for 1957–68, covering music, dance, theater, and television.

Textual Studies and Scholarly Editing

See the section on printing, publishing, history of the book, and textual studies.

Theater

See the section on drama.

Women's Studies

See also the bibliographies listed in this chapter in the sections on the alternative press, ethnic and minority studies, history, literary theory and criticism, psychology, and the social sciences.

D480 *Women Studies Abstracts*. Rush: Rush, 1972– . 4/yr.

A classified list of articles, chiefly from United States journals, with abstracts provided for about one-quarter of the citations. A subject index in each issue contains headings for art, literature, and feminist criticism.

D481 *Women's Studies Index*. Boston: Hall, 1991– . Annual.

An author and subject index to about 80 popular and scholarly periodicals (mostly American), starting with the 1989 issue of the publications indexed. Headings include poems, plays, short stories, individual writers, and literary subjects.

D482   *Studies on Women Abstracts*. Abingdon, Eng.: Carfax, 1983– . 6/yr.

An author and subject index to abstracts of books and articles in over 500 international periodicals covering a wide range of women's issues, from health, social sciences, politics, and social policy to history and literary criticism.

D483   *Signs: A Journal for Women in Culture and Society*. Chicago: U of Chicago P, 1965– . 4/yr.

The section "New Scholarship" regularly publishes bibliographic essays on a variety of subjects including literary criticism.

D484   *New Books on Women and Feminism*. Madison: U of Wisconsin, 1979– . 2/yr.

Classified bibliography of new English-language books by and about women, with subject and author indexes. Includes drama, literary history and criticism, and poetry but not novels and short story collections, except for reissued classics, new translations, international anthologies, and works by rediscovered women writers.

D485   *Feminist Periodicals: A Current Listing of Contents*. Madison: Phyllis Homan Weisbard, 1981– . 4/yr.

Provides tables of contents of about 115 English-language feminist scholarly journals and small-press periodicals in all fields, of which some 20 publish literature and literary criticism.

D486   *Women's Review of Books*. Wellesley: Wellesley Coll. Center for Research on Women, 1983– . 11/yr.

"The Month's Bookshelf" in each issue is an author list of books received in editorial offices.

(B75)   *Legacy: A Journal of American Women Writers*

The "Legacy Bookshelf" in each issue is a classified list of current books, articles, and dissertations on nineteenth-century American women writers.

D487   *Women and Literature: A Journal of Women Writers and Literary Treatment of Women.* New York: Holmes, 1972– . Annual. (Titled *Mary Wollstonecraft Newsletter*, 1972–74; published 4/yr., 1972–79.)

"Bibliography of Literature in English by and about Women" for 1972–78 in volumes 3–7 (1975–79) is an annual, classified, international bibliography of books, reviews, and articles on women writers and on the treatment of women in literature. Occasional brief annotations.

(D330)   *Medieval Feminist Newsletter*

Each issue carries a bibliography of relevant international books and articles.

(B44)   *Johnsonian News Letter*

The Restoration and eighteenth-century bibliography in each issue has a section for women's studies.

Chapter Six

Authors

This chapter describes author newsletters, journals, and yearbooks that regularly carry checklists of criticism, reviews of current scholarship, or enough book reviews and news to be reliable sources of up-to-date information about scholarly activities on individual authors. Many other author journals, valuable as they are, have been excluded because they do not provide regular bibliographies of consistent quality. James K. Bracken's *English and American Writers*, volume 2 of *Reference Works in British and American Literature* (Englewood: Libraries Unlimited, 1991), offers an extensive list of current author journals in English and American literature, while the most complete list, which covers all literatures, is Margaret C. Patterson's *Author Newsletters and Journals* (Detroit: Gale, 1979), with supplements in *Serials Review* 8.4 (1982): 61–72; 10.1 (1984): 51–59; and 11.3 (1985): 31–44.

An author bibliography, especially one published in an author journal that also carries book reviews and news, has virtues not found in a more general and comprehensive bibliography. It can be at once broad and specialized; it can be very current (even to the point of listing forthcoming publications and suggestions for further research); and it can provide information about archives, collections, meetings, and other matters of interest to scholars and enthusiasts. Its breadth comes from its ability to cite not only scholarly books, articles, and dissertations but also newspaper articles, media presentations and materials, unpublished papers, forthcoming books and articles, mentions of the author in works on other subjects, and other out-of-the-way items. Its specialization comes from its having bibliographers familiar enough with the subject to be able to provide critical or evaluative annotations and bibliographic essays and even, as in the *Keats-Shelley Journal* (B52) and the *Stendhal Club* (E170), thorough subject indexing of the bibliography. Of course, author bibliographies can be impressionistic, provincial, unsympathetic to new approaches and interpretations, and overloaded with trivia, but these faults can coexist with the virtues of breadth, specialization, and timeliness.

Despite the happy proliferation of author journals and secondary bibliographies, however, students looking for current serial author bibliographies must still consult the standard literary bibliographies and the relevant period, subject, and genre bibliographies. Exemplifying this need most vividly perhaps are the many seventeenth-and eighteenth-century British writers (including Austen, Behn, Defoe, Donne, Dryden, Fielding, Milton, Pope, Richardson, Smollett, Sterne, and Swift) covered in the *Johnsonian News Letter* (B44), *Restoration* (B46), the *Scriblerian and the Kit-Cats* (B45), and *Seventeenth-Century News* (B33) as well as in *The Eighteenth-Century: A Current Bibliography* (B42). See, therefore, chapters 2–5.

Bibliographies are listed alphabetically by subject authors.

Andersen

E1   *Anderseniana*. Odense, Den.: Hans Christian Andersen Museum, 1933– . Annual, but volumes frequently combined.
      Has carried a review of research for 1960– in volumes 1961– .

Anderson

E2   *Winesburg Eagle*. Blacksburg: Virginia Polytechnic Inst. and State U, 1975– . 2/yr.
      "A Sherwood Anderson Checklist," usually in the first issue of a volume, includes books, articles, dissertations,

new editions, reprints, and translations appearing since 1972.

Apollinaire

(C29) *La revue des lettres modernes: Histoire des idées et des littératures Guillaume Apollinaire* is a subseries, 1962– .

Arnold

E3 *Arnoldian.* Annapolis: US Naval Acad., 1974–89. 3/yr. (Continues as *Nineteenth-Century Prose*, Niwot: UP of Colorado.)

An annual bibliographic essay is in the third issue of each volume; coverage extends through spring 1988.

Atwood

E4 *Newsletter of the Margaret Atwood Society.* Oxford: Miami U, 1984– . 2/yr.

"Current Atwood Checklist [year]" is an extensive, annual list of new publications by Atwood, interviews, international reviews of her books, and new international books, articles, and dissertations about Atwood. The checklist first appeared in 1986 and covers 1986– .

Balzac

E5 *L'année balzacienne.* Paris: Garnier, 1960– . Annual. (Supersedes *Etudes balzaciennes*, 1951–60, and *Le courrier balzacien*, 1948–50.)

Carries an annual bibliography, 1960– , of international books (including new editions), articles, and dissertations.

Barbey d'Aurevilly

(C29) *La revue des lettres modernes: Histoire des idées et des littératures Barbey d'Aurevilly* is a subseries, 1966– .

Baudelaire

E6   *Bulletin baudelairien.* Nashville: Vanderbilt U, 1965– . 2/yr.
An annual bibliography in the first issue of each volume lists international books, articles, dissertations, and theses.

Beckett

French XX (C28) provides extensive coverage of Beckett studies, with perhaps twice as many entries as in the *MLA International Bibliography* (A1) or the *Bibliographie der französischen Literaturwissenschaft* (C15).

E7   *Beckett Circle: Newsletter of the Samuel Beckett Society.* Tallahassee: Florida State U, 1978– . 2/yr. (Place of publication and publisher vary.)

"New and Forthcoming" in each issue lists international books and articles on Beckett, including new editions and translations of his work, and lists new international productions of his plays.

Bellow

E8   *Saul Bellow Journal.* West Bloomfield: Saul Bellow Journal, 1981– . 2/yr.

"Selected Annotated Critical Bibliography" for 1980– , in volumes 4– (1985–), lists international books, articles, interviews, and reviews. Recent theses and dissertations were also listed in most of the issues in volumes 1–3.

Bergman

E9   *Hjalmar Bergman samfundet-årsbok.* Stockholm: Hjalmar Bergman Samfundet, 1959–85. Annual.

"Hjalmar Bergman bibliografi," a list of international works by and about Bergman, appeared biennially, 1959–69, and triennially, 1970–85.

Bernanos

(C29)   *La revue des lettres modernes: Histoire des idées et des littératures*
Etudes Bernanos is a subseries, 1960– .

Beyle

See Stendhal.

Blake

See also these two important annotated bibliographies: *The Eighteenth Century: A Current Bibliography* (B42) and *The Romantic Movement: A Critical and Selective Bibliography* (B51). Blake entries are listed in the eighteenth-century sections of both the *MLA International Bibliography* (A1) and the *Annual Bibliography of English Language and Literature* (B1).

E10   *Blake: An Illustrated Quarterly.* Rochester: U of Rochester, 1967– . 4/yr. (Formerly *Blake Newsletter: An Illustrated Quarterly*, vols. 1–10; vols. 1–20 published at the U of New Mexico, Albuquerque.)

Since volume 1 the quarterly has carried an annual, extensive, and extensively annotated bibliography of international books, articles, dissertations, reviews, exhibit catalogs, and new editions for 1966– . The bibliography has been titled "Blake and His Circle: An Annotated Checklist of Recent Publications" since volume 13 (1979). Blake's circle includes artists and authors Henry Fuseli, William Godwin, Angelica Kaufmann, Thomas Paine, Benjamin West, and Mary Wollstonecraft.

Bloy

(C29)   *La revue des lettres modernes: Histoire des idées et des littératures*
Bloy has been included since 1989.

Boccaccio

E11   *Studi sul Boccaccio.* Florence: Sansoni, 1963– . Annual.
An extensive list of international books, articles, and translations. The first three volumes gather studies done since 1938. Editorial matter in Italian.

Boswell

(B44)   *Johnsonian News Letter*
The "Précis of Articles on Johnson and Boswell" contains listings, many of them annotated, for international articles.

Brontës

E12   *Brontë Society Transactions.* Haworth, Eng.: Brontë Soc., 1895– . 2/yr. (Frequency has varied.)
"A Brontë Reading List" for 1969– has been a regular annual feature since 1970, listing international English-language books and articles, often with brief annotations.
See also *Dickens Studies Annual* (E42) for coverage of 1975–87 in volumes 10 (1982) and 18 (1989).

Brownings

Elizabeth Barrett Browning and Robert Browning are given separate sections in the annual bibliographies of *Victorian Studies* (B54) and *Victorian Poetry* (B57).

E13   *Studies in Browning and His Circle: A Journal of Criticism, History, and Bibliography.* Waco: Armstrong Browning Library, 1973– . 2/yr. (Continues *Browning Newsletter,* 1968–72.)
"Checklist of Publications," in each issue since 1968, is an extensive list of international books, reviews, articles, bibliographies, and dissertations. Each issue also lists research in progress (including dissertations), performances, symposia, exhibits, and desiderata.

E14   *Victorian Literature and Culture.* New York: AMS, 1973– .

Annual. (Titled *Browning Institute Studies* and published by the Browning Inst., New York, vol. 1–18.)

"Robert and Elizabeth Barrett Browning: An Annotated Bibliography," an annual, extensive bibliography for 1971– , lists international books, articles, reviews, exhibit catalogs and reference books. The bibliography supplements William S. Peterson, *Robert and Elizabeth Barrett Browning: An Annotated Bibliography, 1951–1970* (New York: Browning Inst., 1974). Index of critics, book reviewers, and titles of the Brownings' works.

Büchner

E15   *Georg Büchner Jahrbuch*. Tübingen: Niemeyer, 1981– . Annual. (Vols. 1–7 published by Europäische and then Hain, Frankfurt.)

Regularly carries a classified bibliography for 1977– of international books, articles, broadcasts, films, and new editions and translations.

Bunyan

E16   *Bunyan Studies: John Bunyan and His Times*. London: Counter Productions, 1988– . 2/yr.

Each issue carries a checklist of recent articles on Bunyan.

Byron

(B52)   *Keats-Shelley Journal: Keats, Shelley, Byron, Hunt, and Their Circles*

Carries an annual, extensive bibliography of international books and articles on Byron, his circle, Romanticism, and the other younger Romantics. Subject index.

Camus

(C29)   *La revue des lettres modernes: Histoire des idées et des littératures Albert Camus* is a subseries, 1961– .

Carlyle

E19   *The Carlyle Annual.* Flushing: Queens Coll. P, 1989– . Annual. (Titled *Carlyle Newsletter,* 1979–80.)
Carries a bibliography of books and articles.

Cather

E20   *Willa Cather Pioneer Memorial Newsletter.* Red Cloud: Willa
Cather Soc., 1957– . 4/yr.
The annual bibliographical issue carries a review article
surveying the year's international books and articles, starting with 1989 in volume 34.

Céline

E21   *L'année Céline.* Tusson, Fr.: Editions du Lérot, 1991– . Annual.
"Bibliographie critique" in each volume includes annotated listings of new international books, articles, and dissertations; "Adaptions" lists theater, television, and other
productions of Céline's works; and "Echos et mentions"
lists books and articles in which Céline is mentioned.

(C29)   *La revue des lettres modernes: Histoire des idées et des littératures
L.-F. Céline* is a subseries, 1974– .

Cendrars (Sauser)

(C29)   *La revue des lettres modernes: Histoire des idées et des littératures
Blaise Cendrars* is a subseries, 1985– .

Cervantes

E22   *Anales cervantinos.* Madrid: Consejo Superior de Investigaciones Científicas, Instituto de Filología, 1951– . Annual.
"Bibliografía cervantina" is a classified bibliography of
international books, reviews, and articles, with annotations

in Spanish. Items are arranged under sections for bibliographies, general studies, biography, *Don Quixote*, and the other works.

Chateaubriand

E23   *Société Chateaubriand: Bulletin.* Paris: Société Chateaubriand, 1930– . Annual.
       Carries an international list of books and articles for 1958– .

Chaucer

Both the *Annual Bibliography of English Language and Literature* (B1) and the *Year's Work in English Studies* (B2) devote a section to Chaucer studies.

E24   *Studies in the Age of Chaucer.* Columbus: New Chaucer Soc. and Ohio State U, 1979– . Annual. (Vols. 1–4 published by New Chaucer Soc. and the U of Oklahoma, Norman, and vols. 5–13 by New Chaucer Soc. and the U of Tennessee, Knoxville.)
       "An Annotated Chaucer Bibliography" is a classified, annotated bibliography of international books, reviews, articles, and dissertations for 1975– .

E25   *Chaucer Review: A Journal of Medieval Studies and Literary Criticism.* University Park: Pennsylvania State UP, 1966– . 4/yr.
       "Chaucer Research Report" is an annual list of books (including editions), articles, and dissertations, chiefly by North Americans. The list was published in mimeograph form by the MLA's Chaucer Group from 1941 to 1965. A list of works in progress, projects completed but unpublished, and desiderata is carried here and in *Neuphilologische Mitteilungen* (B20).

Claudel

E26   *Cahiers Paul Claudel.* Paris: Gallimard, 1959–68. Annual.

Each volume includes a brief list of recent international books and articles within the section "Claudeliana" for 1957–68.

(C29)   *La revue des lettres modernes: Histoire des idées et des littératures Paul Claudel* is a subseries, 1964– .

Clemens (Twain)

Clemens receives a separate chapter in *American Literary Scholarship* (B72). See also the bibliographies listed under "Regionalism (US)" in chapter 5.

(D411) *Mississippi Quarterly: The Journal of Southern Culture*
The annual "Checklist of Scholarship on Southern Literature" for 1968– includes a significant compilation of Clemens scholarship.

E27   *Mark Twain Circular: Newsletter of the Mark Twain Circle of America*. Charleston: The Citadel, 1987– . Monthly but irregular.
"Current Books and Articles" in each issue is an annotated author list of international books, chapters, and articles; it continues the similar bibliography published in *American Literary Realism* (E28) from 1977 to 1983.

E28   *American Literary Realism*. Arlington: U of Texas, 1967– . 4/yr.
Volumes for 1977–83 include annual list of international books, articles, and dissertations, that updates Thomas Asa Tenney, *Mark Twain: A Reference Guide* (Boston: Hall, 1977).

Cocteau

E29   *Cahiers Jean Cocteau*. Paris: Gallimard, 1969– . 4/yr.
"Bibliographie" is an annual, selective list of editions (including translations) and of French-language books and articles.

(C29)   *La revue des lettres modernes: Histoire des idées et des littératures Jean Cocteau* is a subseries, 1970– .

Coleridge

(E208) *Wordsworth Circle*
"Coleridge Scholarship: An Annual Register" for 1971–79 in volumes 3–11 (1972–80) lists books, reviews, articles, and dissertations.

Colette

E30   *Cahiers Colette*. Paris: Société des Amis de Colette, 1977– . Annual.
"Bibliographie" appears in each issue.

Conrad

E31   *Conradiana: A Journal of Joseph Conrad Studies*. Lubbock: Texas Tech U, 1968– . 2/yr.
"Conrad Bibliography: A Continuing Checklist" is an annual list of international books (including editions), reviews, articles, and dissertations for 1967– .

E32   *Conradian*. Hull, Eng.: Joseph Conrad Soc., 1975– . 2/yr.
"Conrad in Some Recent General Studies and Collections," 1974–87, describes monographs and collections while "The Year's Work in Conrad Studies: A Survey of Periodical Literature," also 1974–87, covers articles.

Constant

E33   *Annales Benjamin Constant*. Lausanne, Switz.: Institut Benjamin Constant, 1980– . Annual.
Includes bibliographies for 1980–86 in numbers 3–6 (1983–86) and for 1986–90 in number 12 (1991) that are annotated, extensive lists of international books and articles, including new editions of Constant's works. These bibliographies update *Bibliographie analytique des écrits sur Benjamin Constant* (Oxford: Voltaire Foundation, 1980).

Crane

E34   *Stephen Crane Newsletter.* Columbia: U of South Carolina, 1966–70. 4/yr.

"Quarterly Checklist" of criticism appears in each issue, along with reviews of books, films, and plays.

E35   *Thoth.* Syracuse: Syracuse U, 1959–77. 3/yr.

"Stephen Crane Bibliography," 1963–75, is an annual list of critical and biographical studies (books and articles) and of editions and manuscripts. The lists for 1963–69, with additional items, are cumulated and included in "A Bibliography of Stephen Crane Scholarship: 1893–1969," published as a special supplement in *Thoth*, volume 10 (1970) but bound in volume 11 (1971). This bibliography continued Robert N. Hudspeth, "A Bibliography of Stephen Crane Scholarship: 1893–1962," *Thoth* 4 (1963): 31–58.

Dante

Dante studies have been surveyed in a separate chapter in the *Year's Work in Modern Language Studies* (C1) starting in volume 27 for 1965 (1966), and most earlier volumes have a major section on him.

E36   *Dante Studies.* Albany: Dante Soc. of America, 1882– . Annual.

"American Dante Bibliography," 1953– , is an annotated list of books, reviews, articles, and dissertations published in North America.

E37   *Studi danteschi.* Florence: Sansoni, 1920– . Annual. (Supersedes *Bullettino della Società Dantesca Italiana*, Società Dantesca Italiana, Florence, 1890–1921.)

"Notizie," in each volume, 1920–34, is a brief list of current international publications; starting with volume 13 (1928) the section includes an annual, comprehensive bibliography of international books and articles, annotated in Italian. Issues of the *Bullettino* from 1890 to 1918 include an annual bibliography of Dante criticism.

E38   *Lectura Dantis: A Forum for Dante Research and Interpretation.*
       Charlottesville: U of Virginia, 1987– . 2/yr.
       "Dante in North America [year]" is a biennial review
       essay covering North American books for 1990– , starting
       in number 11 (1992).

E39   *L'Alighieri: Rassegna bibliografica dantesca.* Rome: Rassegna
       bibliografica dantesca, 1960– . 2/yr.
       Carries an annual bibliography of Italian Dante studies.
       (Author has not examined the bibliography.)

Dickens

E40   *Dickens Quarterly.* Louisville: Dickens Soc., 1984– . 4/yr.
       (Continues *Dickens Studies Newsletter*, Dickens Soc., Louis-
       ville, 1970–83.)
       "The Dickens Checklist," in each issue, is an extensive
       list of international editions, studies (books, reviews, arti-
       cles, and dissertations), and miscellaneous items such as
       audiovisual programs, screenplays, and teaching aids.

E41   *Dickens Studies Annual: Essays on Victorian Fiction.* New York:
       AMS, 1970– . Annual. (Vols. 1–7 published by Southern
       Illinois UP, Carbondale.)
       "Recent Dickens Studies," starting in volume 8 (1980),
       is a review article covering English-language books and
       articles for 1977– .

E42   *Dickensian.* London: Dickens Fellowship, 1905– . 3/yr.
       An annual bibliographic essay, "Year's Work in Dickens
       Studies," 1968–75, lists books and surveys the year's peri-
       odical literature.

Dickey

E43   *James Dickey Newsletter.* Dunwoody: De Kalb Coll., 1984– .
       2/yr.
       "Continuing Bibliography," in the first issue of each vol-
       ume, lists current books, articles, dissertations, and reviews
       as well as new work by Dickey.

Dickinson

A separate chapter is devoted to Dickinson and Whitman in *American Literary Scholarship* (B72).

E44   *Dickinson Studies*. Brentwood: Higginson, 1968–93. 2/yr. (Titled *Emily Dickinson Bulletin*, 1968–78.)

An annual bibliography starting in 1968 lists books, articles, dissertations, and reviews.

Diderot

E45   *Diderot Studies*. Geneva: Droz, 1949– . Annual.

Starting with volume 21 (1983), carries a list of international books, articles, and dissertations that supplements Robert A. Spears, *Bibliographie de Diderot* (3 vols., Geneva: Droz, 1980–89).

E46   *Recherches sur Diderot et sur l'*Encyclopédie. Paris: Klincksiek, 1986– . 2/yr. (Published for 1986–89 by Aux Amateurs de Livres, Paris.)

"Carnet bibliographie" in each issue lists new European books, articles, and dissertations dealing with Diderot, the *Encyclopédie*, and the Encyclopédistes.

Doolittle (H. D.)

E47   *H. D. Newsletter*. Dallas: Dallas Inst. of the Humanities, 1987– . 2/yr.

Each issue lists recent books, articles, and dissertations.

Dostoevsky

E48   *Dostoevsky Studies: Journal of the International Dostoevsky Society*. Klagenfurt, Aus.: International Dostoevsky Soc. and U of Klagenfurt, 1980– . Annual. (Supersedes the *International Dostoevsky Society Bulletin*, Washington, 1971–79.)

The "Current Bibliography" for 1970– in each volume since 1971 is an extensive author list of international books, articles, and dissertations, with good coverage of east European and Russian publications.

Doyle

E49   *Baker Street Journal: An Irregular Quarterly.* New York: Baker Street Irregulars, 1946– . 4/yr. (Vols. 25–42, 1975–92, published by Fordham UP, New York.)
       "Baker Street Inventory" in each issue lists new books and articles about, and new periodicals devoted to, Doyle, although its selection is more for devotees than for scholars.

Dreiser

E50   *Dreiser Studies.* Terre Haute: Indiana State U, 1970– . 2/yr. (Titled *Dreiser Newsletter* through no. 17.2, 1970–86.)
       Each fall issue carries an annotated list of international books, articles, and dissertations as well as of new Dreiser editions.

Durrell

E51   Deus Loci: *The Lawrence Durrell Quarterly.* Kelowna, BC: Okanagan Coll., 1977–84; ns, 1992– . Annual.
       An annual bibliography of primary and secondary materials, starting in volume 7, number 3, may continue in the new series (not seen).

Eichendorff

E55   *Aurora: Jahrbuch der Eichendorff-Gesellschaft.* Würzburg: Eichendorff-Gesellschaft, 1929– . Annual. (Subtitle varies.)
       "Eichendorff-Bibliographie" lists books, articles, editions, and musical settings of Eichendorff's works.

Eliot

T. S. Eliot is listed in the English literature sections of the *MLA International Bibliography* (A1) and *The Year's Work in English*

Studies (B2) and is the subject, along with Pound, of a chapter in *American Literary Scholarship* (B72) since the volume for 1974.

E56   *Yeats Eliot Review: A Quarterly Journal of Scholarship, Criticism, and Opinion*. Little Rock: U of Arkansas, 1974– . 4/yr., irregular. (Titled *T. S. Eliot Review*, 1974–78, and published at U of Alberta, Edmonton, 1974–82.)

"Bibliographical Update" in each issue, volume 1–7 (1974–82) is an extensive list of international books, articles, and dissertations.

Emerson

Emerson has received a chapter in *American Literary Scholarship* (B72) since the first volume.

E57   *American Transcendental Quarterly*. Kingston: U of Rhode Island, 1969– . 4/yr. (Nos. 1–32 published by Transcendental, Hartford.)

"Current Bibliography" for 1972–77 in numbers 17 (1973), 23 (1974), 32 (1976), and 36 (1977) lists books, articles, and dissertations (including some in progress) and continues "Current Bibliography" for 1955–72 in *ESQ: Journal of the American Renaissance* (Pullman: Washington State U).

Erasmus

E58   *Erasmus in English*. Toronto: U of Toronto P, 1970–88. Irregular.

"Recent Publications" in each issue lists international books and articles.

Faulkner

Faulkner has received a chapter in *American Literary Scholarship* (B72) since the first volume.

E59   *Faulkner Newsletter and Yoknapatawpha Review*. Oxford: Yoknapatawpha, 1981– . 4/yr.

Most issues include "Checklist," which describes recent books and articles.

(D411) *Mississippi Quarterly: The Journal of Southern Culture*
The annual bibliography of studies of southern literature includes an extensive list of Faulkner studies. In addition, "Faulkner [year]: A Survey of Research and Criticism," an annual review article in volumes 31–40 (1978–88), covers books and articles for 1977–86.

Fitzgerald

Fitzgerald and Hemingway have received a chapter in *American Literary Scholarship* (B72) since the first volume.
E61 *Fitzgerald/Hemingway Annual*. Detroit: Gale, 1969– . Annual. (Vols. are dated 1969–79; continues *Fitzgerald Newsletter*, 1958–68; vols. for 1969–75 published by Microcard Editions, Washington and then Englewood; vols. for 1976–79 published by Information Handling Services, Englewood.)
Includes an extensive list of international books, articles, and newspaper stories for 1957–79 starting in the first issue of the *Fitzgerald Newsletter*. Each volume of the *Annual* for 1973–79 also notes addenda to Matthew J. Bruccoli, *F. Scott Fitzgerald: A Descriptive Bibliography* (Pittsburgh: U of Pittsburgh P, 1972).

Flaubert

E62 *Les Amis de Flaubert*. Rouen: Amis de Flaubert, 1951– . 2/yr.
"Bibliographie" is an annual list of international books and articles for 1951– .
(C29) *La revue des lettres modernes: Histoire desidées et des littératures Gustave Flaubert* is a subseries, 1984– .

Frost

E63 *Robert Frost Review*. Rock Hill: Winthrop Coll., 1991– . 2/yr.
"Current Frost Scholarship" lists books, articles, and dissertations on Frost and continues similar lists for 1986–90 in *South Carolina Review* 22.2 (1989) and 23.1 (1990).

Gide

E64   *Bulletin des Amis d'André Gide.* Lyon: Centre d'études gidiennes de l'université Lumière, 1968– . 4/yr.
       Each issue includes a checklist of recent international books and articles.

(C29)   *La revue des lettres modernes: Histoires des idées et des littératures André Gide* is a subseries, 1970– .

Giono

(C29)   *La revue des lettres modernes: Histoire des idées et des littératures Jean Giono* is a subseries, 1973– .

Giraudoux

E65   *Cahiers Jean Giraudoux.* Paris: Grasset, 1972– . Annual.
       Most volumes carry a bibliography of current international books and articles about Giraudoux.

Gissing

E66   *Gissing Newsletter.* Dorking, Eng.: Gissing Newsletter, 1965–90. 4/yr.
       "Recent Publications," in each issue, lists books, articles, and newspaper stories as well as new Gissing editions.

Glasgow

E67   *Ellen Glasgow Newsletter.* Knoxville: U of Tennessee, 1974– . 2/yr.
       "Recent Scholarship on Ellen Glasgow," in most issues, lists new books, articles, dissertations, and papers.

Goethe

Both the *Bibliographie der deutschen Sprach- und Literaturwissenschaft* (C81) and *Germanistik* (C82) devote separate sections to Goethe and the *Goethezeit*.

E68   *Goethe-Jahrbuch.* Weimar: Böhlaus, 1936– . Annual.
"Goethe-Bibliographie" is an extensive list of international books and articles, including new editions of primary materials, for 1951– . Critic index.

Gracq (Poirier)

(C29)   *La revue des lettres modernes: Histoire des idées et des littératures Julien Gracq* is a subseries, 1991– .

Grillparzer

E69   *Grillparzer-Forum Forchtenstein.* Vienna: Grillparzer-Forum, 1965– . Annual.
"Grillparzer Bibliographie" is an annual list of international books, articles, and dissertations.

Hardy

E75   *Thomas Hardy Annual.* London: Macmillan, 1982–87. Annual.
"A Hardy Bibliography" in each volume lists English-language books and articles, including new editions and textual studies, for 1978–85.

E76   *Thomas Hardy Yearbook.* Guernsey: Toucan, 1970– . Annual.
"Thomas Hardy: A Bibliography" in each annual issue through volume 7 (1977), lists international books, articles, and dissertations.

Hawthorne

Hawthorne has received a chapter in *American Literary Scholarship* (B72) since the first volume.

E77   *Nathaniel Hawthorne Review.* Brunswick: Bowdoin Coll., 1986– . 2/yr. (Formerly *Hawthorne Society Newsletter*, 1975–85.)

The "Current Hawthorne Bibliography," a regular feature since 1985, lists English-language books, articles, and dissertations. "Hawthorne at Scholarly Meetings" lists papers read at conferences for 1987– , and the *Review* frequently includes abstracts of papers read at conferences.

E78   *Nathaniel Hawthorne Journal.* Detroit: Gale, 1971–84 (in 8 vols. dated 1971–78). Annual. (Vols. 1–6 published by Microcard Editions, Washington and then Englewood, and Information Handling Services, Englewood.)

"Recent Hawthorne Scholarship: A Checklist," in volumes 1–7 for 1967–76, provides comprehensive coverage of international editions, translations, and critical books, articles, and dissertations.

Hazlitt

(B52)   *Keats-Shelley Journal: Keats, Shelley, Byron, Hunt, and Their Circles*

Carries an annual, extensive bibliography of international books and articles. Hazlitt items were listed in the Keats section of the bibliography until volume 24 (1977; for 1975), in which they were put into a separate section on Hazlitt and Hunt. Subject index.

H. D.

See Doolittle.

Hebbel

E79   *Hebbel-Jahrbuch.* Heide in Holstein: Westholsteinische Verlagsanstalt Boyens, 1939– . Annual.

"Literaturbericht," in most volumes, 1953– , is a bibliographic essay in German discussing mainly German books, articles, and dissertations. There are also irregular bibliographic checklists and, notably, decade-long bibliographies, comprehensive and international, for 1970–80 (1983) and 1980–90 (1992) that update U. Henry Gerlach, *Hebbel-Bibliographie 1910–1970* (Heidelberg: Winter, 1973).

Heine

E80　*Heine-Jahrbuch.* Hamburg: Hoffmann, 1962– . Annual.
　　　"Heine Literatur [year] mit Nachträgen" is a list of international books, reviews, articles, and mentions of Heine in works on other subjects.

Hemingway

Hemingway and Fitzgerald have received a chapter in *American Literary Scholarship* (B72) since the first volume.

E81　*Hemingway Review.* Pensacola: U of West Florida, 1981– .
　　　2/yr. (Continues *Hemingway Notes*, vol. 1–6, 1971–78, published at Northern Ohio U, Ada, 1971–81.)
　　　"Bibliography," in each issue 1971– , is an extensive list of international books, journal articles, and newspaper and magazine stories on Hemingway for 1970– .

(E61)　*Fitzgerald/Hemingway Annual*
　　　"Hemingway Checklist," in volumes dated 1972–79, covers international books, articles, reviews, newspaper stories, and primary materials for 1969–79.

Hesse

E82　*Hermann-Hesse-Literatur.* Mittelbrüchen: Hermann-Hesse-Literatur, 1964– . Annual.
　　　A list of international books, articles, and dissertations, which is cumulated in Martin Pfeifer, *Hermann-Hesse-Bibliographie: Primär und Sekundarschriftum in Auswahl* (Berlin: Schmidt, 1973).

Hofmannsthal

E83　*Hofmannsthal Blätter.* Frankfurt: Hugo von Hofmannsthal-Gesellschaft, 1968– . 2/yr.
　　　Each volume carries a list of Hofmannsthal texts and letters and of international books, articles, and dissertations about him.

Hölderlin

E84 *Hölderlin-Jahrbuch.* Tübingen: Friedrich-Hölderlin Gesellschaft, 1947– . Annual. (Titled *Iduna: Jahrbuch der Hölderlin-Gesellschaft*, (1944–46.)

"Hölderlin Bibliographie" is an irregular, classified bibliography of international editions, translations, and critical books, articles, and dissertations. The years 1966–70 are covered in the 1973–74 volumes; the years 1971–73 are covered in volumes for 1975–77. Future installments are planned. Additional coverage through 1988 is provided in Maria Kohler, Werner Paul Sohnle, and Marianne Schütz, *Internationale Hölderlin-Bibliographie* (2 vols., Stuttgart: Fromann-Holzboog, 1985 and 1991) with entries based on holdings of the Hölderlin Archiv.

Hopkins

E85 *Hopkins Quarterly.* Toronto: St. Michael's Coll., 1974– . 4/yr.

Carries a bibliography of international studies; published annually through 1980, in volume 16 (1989; for 1981–86), and annually since 1989.

E86 *Hopkins Research Bulletin.* Enfield, Eng.: Hopkins Soc., 1970–76.

Published an annual list of international books, reviews, articles, dissertations, theses, and newspaper items.

Hugo

(C29) *La revue des lettres modernes: Histoire des idées et des littératures Victor Hugo* is a subseries, 1983– .

Hunt

(B52) *Keats-Shelley Journal: Keats, Shelley, Byron, Hunt, and Their Circles*

Carries an annual, extensive bibliography of international books and articles. Hunt items were listed in the

Keats section of the bibliography until volume 24 (1977; for 1975), in which they were put into a separate section on Hazlitt and Hunt. Subject index.

Ibsen

E87 *Contemporary Approaches to Ibsen: Proceedings of the International Ibsen Seminar.* New York: Oxford UP, 1966– . Irregular. (Incorporates the *Ibsen Yearbook*, 1970/71– , which continues the *Ibsenårbok*, 1952–69, both published by the Universitetsforlaget, Oslo.)

"Ibsen Bibliography" lists international books and articles for 1953– and appears in most volumes, 1953– .

Jacob

(C29) *La revue des lettres modernes: Histoire des idées et des littératures Max Jacob* is a subseries, 1972– .

James

James has received a chapter in *American Literary Scholarship* (B72) since the first volume.

E90 *Henry James Review.* Baltimore: Johns Hopkins UP, 1979– . 3/yr.

"James Studies [year]: An Analytic Bibliographic Monograph," a review essay, discusses international books and articles on James from 1979 through 1984 (vols. 1–9, 1979–88).

Johnson

(B44) *Johnsonian News Letter*

In addition to its now extensive bibliography on Restoration and eighteenth-century literature, this journal includes the sections "New Books on Johnson" and "Précis of Articles on Johnson and Boswell," both listing new international studies.

Jouve

(C29)   *La revue des lettres modernes: Histoire des idées et des littératures Pierre-Jean Jouve* is an subseries, 1981– .

Joyce

E91   *James Joyce Quarterly.* Tulsa: U of Tulsa, 1963– . 4/yr.
   "Current JJ Checklist," starting in 1963, is an annual bibliography of international editions (especially translations), studies (books, reviews, articles), theatrical productions, musical settings, records, and miscellany.

E92   *Joyce Studies Annual.* Austin: U of Texas, 1990– . Annual.
   The "Annual James Joyce Checklist" for 1989– is a bibliography of international books, articles, reviews, and unpublished conference papers about Joyce, as well as new editions and translations, musical settings, theatrical productions, readings, films, and other events and materials.

(C29)   *La revue des lettres modernes: Histoire des idées et des littératures James Joyce* is a subseries, 1987– .

Kafka

E93   *Journal of the Kafka Society of America.* Philadelphia: Temple U, 1977– . 2/yr.
   Although the journal does not carry a regular bibliographic checklist, it does publish bibliographical information and news on research in progress, on dissertations, and on forthcoming projects and publications in each issue. A comprehensive bibliography of international books and articles for 1975–80 is in volume 4 (1980), and one for 1980–92 is in volume 14 (1992); these bibliographies update Angel Flores, *A Kafka Bibliography, 1908–1976* (New York: Gordian, 1976).

Keats

(B52)   *Keats-Shelley Journal: Keats, Shelley, Byron, Hunt, and Their Circles*

Carries an annual, extensive bibliography of international studies on Keats and his circle. Subject index.

Langland

E100   *The Yearbook of Langland Studies.* East Lansing: Colleagues, 1987– . Annual.
"Annual Bibliography" is an annotated list of international books, articles, dissertations from *Dissertation Abstracts International,* and book reviews dealing with Langland and related matters, excluding work on alliterative romances and on the Gawain poet.

Larbaud

E101   *Cahiers des Amis de Valéry Larbaud.* Vichy: Association des Amis de Valéry Larbaud, 1970– . Annual.
"Bibliographie larbaudienne" is a list of international books and articles about Larbaud; it also records sales and donations of manuscript materials.

La Roche

(E203) *Wieland-Studien*
Each annual volume carries an extensive bibliography of international books, articles, and dissertations about La Roche and of new editions of her works.

Lawrence

E102   *D. H. Lawrence Review.* Newark: U of Delaware, 1968– . 3/yr. (Vols. 1–16 published at the U of Arkansas, Fayetteville.)
"The Checklist of D. H. Lawrence Criticism and Scholarship," usually in the third issue, is an extensive list of international books, articles, and dissertations for 1959– . "Laurentiana," in each issue, usually includes additional recent items.

Léger

See Perse.

Lessing, Doris

E103 *Doris Lessing Newsletter*. Oakland: Mills Coll., 1976– . 2/yr.
"New Items on Doris Lessing," in each issue, is a brief
list of miscellaneous items, including recent publications
by and about Lessing.

Lessing, G. E.

E104 *Lessing Yearbook*. Detroit: Wayne State UP, 1969– . Annual.
(Vols. 1–11 published by Hueber, Munich.)
Each annual volume contains extensive reviews of books
on Lessing and on eighteenth-century German literature,
and an irregular bibliography lists international Lessing
studies starting with 1963.

Lewis

E105 *Mythlore*. Altadena: Mythopoeic Soc., 1969– . 4/yr.
"The Inklings Bibliography," in each issue, lists books,
articles, and conference papers on C. S. Lewis, J. R. R.
Tolkien, and Charles Williams; it first appeared in issue
number 12 (1976; also numbered vol. 3, no. 4).

London

E106 *Call: The Official Newsletter of the Jack London Society*. San
Antonio: U of Texas, 1991– . 2/yr.
Most issues report conference proceedings and "Re-
search Notes," a list of recent scholarly publications.

E107 *Jack London Newsletter*. Carbondale: Southern Illinois U,
1967–88. 3/yr.
"WLT[2]: Supplement," in every issue from 6.4 (1974)
through 14.1 (1981), lists new editions and translations
along with books and articles about London. Supplements

H. C. Woodbridge, John London, and G. H. Tweeney, *Jack London: A Bibliography* (Georgetown: Talisman, 1966).

Lowry

E108 *Malcolm Lowry Review*. Waterloo, ON: Wilfrid Laurier U, 1977– . 2/yr.

Regular checklists update the primary and secondary listings in William H. New, *Malcolm Lowry: A Reference Guide* (Boston: Hall, 1978).

Luther

E109 *Luther Jahrbuch*. Göttingen: Vandenhoeck, 1919– . Annual. (Suspended 1942–56.)

"Lutherbibliographie" for 1927– , in volumes 1929– , is an annual, classified, and comprehensive bibliography of international books and articles on Luther and aspects of the Reformation, on the history of books and printing, and on German language and culture. Author and selective title index.

Malraux

(C29) *La revue des lettres modernes: Histoire des idées et des littératures André Malraux* is a subseries, 1971– .

Mann

E110 *Thomas-Mann-Studien*. Frankfurt: Klostermann, 1967– . Annual. (Vol. 1–8 published by Francke, Bern.)

Each volume is devoted to a single topic and includes a bibliography of relevant secondary literature.

Martí

E111 *Anuario martiano*. Havana: Biblioteca National José Martí, 1969–77. Annual.

"Bibliografía martiana" is a bibliography of Martí studies for 1964–75.

Maupassant

(E62) *Les Amis de Flaubert*
Carries an annual bibliography of international books and articles on Maupassant, 1960– .

Mauriac

(C29) *La revue des lettres modernes: Histoire des idées et des littératures François Mauriac* is a subseries, 1974– .

Melville

Melville has received a chapter in *American Literary Scholarship* (B72) since the first volume.

Mencken

E112 *Menckeniana: A Quarterly Review.* Baltimore: Enoch Pratt Free Library, 1962– . 4/yr.
Nearly every issue lists newly published or discovered primary items along with critical books, articles, and newspaper stories.

Merton

E113 *Merton Annual: Studies in Thomas Merton, Religion, Culture, Literature, and Social Concerns.* New York: AMS, 1988– . Annual.
Carries "The Merton Phenomenon," a bibliography of new editions and international books, articles, and dissertations.

Mill

E114 *Mill News Letter.* Toronto: U of Toronto, 1965–88. 2/yr.
Each issue lists books and articles about Mill and related subjects.

Milton

A chapter has been devoted to Milton in *The Year's Work in English Studies* (B2) since 1971.

E115 *Milton Quarterly*. Athens: Ohio U, 1967– . 4/yr. (Titled *Milton Newsletter*, vols. 1–3, 1967–69.)

Most issues carry abstracts of about ten recent articles or papers.

Moore

E116 *Marianne Moore Newsletter*. Philadelphia: Rosenbach Foundation, 1977–83. 2/yr.

Each issue lists newly discovered works by Moore, translations, and critical studies (books, articles, and works in progress).

Morris

E117 *Journal of the William Morris Society*. London: William Morris Soc., 1961– . 2/yr.

Carries a biennial annotated bibliography of international books, articles, dissertations, and exhibition catalogs, covering 1978– .

Musil

E118 *Musil-Forum*. Saarbrücken: Internationale Robert-Musil-Gesellschaft, 1975– . Annual.

"Jahresbibliographie" is a list of international editions, translations, books, and articles about Musil. (Author has not examined the bibliography.)

Nabokov

E121 *Nabokovian*. Lawrence: U of Kansas, 1979– . 2/yr. (Titled *Vladimir Nabokov Research Newsletter*, nos. 1–12.)

Publishes an annual bibliography of international books, articles, reviews, and dissertations, including new editions of primary works for 1978– ; in addition, most issues provide abstracts of recent dissertations and conference papers.

Nerval

E122 *Cahiers Gérard de Nerval*. Paris: Société Gérard de Nerval, 1978– . Annual.
    A list of international books, articles, dissertations, and new editions for 1978– appears in most volumes starting with volume 3 (1980).

Newman

E123 *Internationale Cardinal Newman Studien*. Sigmaringendorf: Glock, 1988– . Irregular. (Continues *Newman Studies*, 1948–80.)
    "Newman-Bibliographie" lists new international books, articles, editions, and translations. (Author has not examined the bibliography.)

Nietzsche

E124 *Nietzsche-Studien: Internationales Jahrbuch für die Nietzsche-Forschung*. Berlin: Gruyter, 1972– . Annual.
    "Literatur-Register" in each volume lists new editions of Nietzsche's work and international books and articles about Nietzsche, including items from earlier years.

Nin

E125 *Anaïs: An International Journal*. Los Angeles: Anaïs Nin Foundation, 1983– . Annual.
    "Readings," in each volume starting with volume 5 (1987), is in part a checklist of recent publications of interest to readers—books by Nin contemporaries and sympathizers as well as critical studies.

E126   *Under the Sign of Pisces: Anaïs Nin and Her Circle.* Columbus: University Libraries, Ohio State U, 1970–81. 4/yr.

Most issues list new critical books and articles, works by Nin, related books, articles, and other media, as well as news and notes of interest to collectors and scholars.

Norris

E127   *Frank Norris Studies.* Tallahassee: Frank Norris Soc., 1986– . 2/yr.

"Current Publications Update" in each issue lists recent books and articles.

O'Casey

E130   *O'Casey Annual.* London: Macmillan, 1982–85. Annual.

"Sean O'Casey: An Annual Bibliography" appears in each volume and covers international books, articles, dissertations, new editions of O'Casey's works, and reviews of productions for 1980–84. Continues coverage formerly in the *Sean O'Casey Review* (E131).

E131   *Sean O'Casey Review.* Holbrook: O'Casey Studies, 1974–82. 2/yr.

An annual list of international books and articles on O'Casey is carried in the fall issue.

O'Neill

E132   *Eugene O'Neill Review.* Boston: Suffolk U, 1977– . 3/yr. (Titled *Eugene O'Neill Newsletter,* vols. 1–12.)

Each issue lists abstracts, articles, papers, and dissertations, along with notices of recent performances and news of upcoming conferences.

Peguy

(C29)   *La revue des lettres modernes: Histoire des idées et des littératures Charles Péguy* is a subseries, 1980– .

Pérez Galdós

E135 *Anales galdósianos.* Austin: Asociación Internacional de Galdósianos, 1966– . Annual.

Carries an annual, classified bibliography of international books, articles, dissertations, and conferences on Pérez Galdós, his works, and his social and cultural context.

Perse (Léger)

E136 *Cahiers Saint-John Perse.* Paris: Centre National des Lettres, 1978– . Biennial.

Each volume carries a bibliography of international books and articles about Perse.

(C29) *La revue des lettres modernes: Histoire des idées et des littératures Saint-John Perse* is a subseries, 1987– .

Pinter

E137 *Pinter Review.* Tampa: U of Tampa, 1987– . Annual.

The "Harold Pinter Bibliography" for 1987– is a classified list of new works by Pinter and of international books, articles, book and production reviews, dissertations, productions, news stories, and radio and television programs.

Poe

Poe has received a chapter in *American Literary Scholarship* (B72) since the volume for 1973.

E138 *Poe Studies / Dark Romanticism: History, Theory, Interpretation.* Pullman: Washington State U, 1968– . 2/yr. (Titled *Poe Newsletter,* 1968–69.)

"International Poe Bibliography," in most issues, is an extensive list of international books, articles, dissertations, and editions. It is supplemented by notes about recent publications and by useful subject indexes for 1969–83 (in 17.2) and for 1983–88 (in 24.1–2). Preceded by checklists for 1962–66 in *Emerson Society Quarterly,* numbers 38 (1965) and 47 (1967).

Poirier

See Gracq.

Pound

Pound, along with Eliot, has received a chapter in *American Literary Scholarship* (B72) since the volume for 1974.

Proust

E139   *Bulletin Marcel Proust.* Paris: Société des Amis de Marcel Proust et des Amis Combray, 1950– . Annual.

Each volume since 1951 carries a bibliography of recent international books, articles, and dissertations.

E140   *Etudes proustiennes.* Paris: Gallimard, 1973– . Approximately biennial.

Part of the Gallimard series *Cahiers Marcel Proust.* Each volume for 1971– carries a bibliography of international books, articles, and dissertations from *Dissertation Abstracts International*; includes new editions.

E141   *Proust Research Association Newsletter.* Lawrence: Proust Research Assn., 1969– . 2/yr.

Each issue lists editions, books, articles, dissertations, works in progress, and selected abstracts of papers and of forthcoming books.

E142   *Bulletin d'informations proustiennes.* Paris: Presses de l'Ecole Normale Supérieure, 1975– . 2/yr.

"Les activités proustiennes," in each issue, lists new international studies, works in progress, and miscellaneous news.

(C29)   *La revue des lettres modernes: Histoire des idées et des littératures Marcel Proust* is a subseries, 1992– .

Pynchon

E143   *Pynchon Notes.* Eau Claire: U of Wisconsin, 1979– . 2/yr.
Each issue contains a bibliography of international
books, reviews, articles, and dissertations, as well as "News,"
a section that lists books, articles, and forthcoming meetings and projects.

Raabe

E145   *Jahrbuch der Raabe-Gesellschaft.* Braunschweig: Waisenhaus,
1960– . Annual. (Continues *Raabe-Jahrbuch,* 1950–59.)
Starting with 1974, the annual carries a list of interna-
tional books, articles, and dissertations, which updates Fritz
Meyen, *Wilhelm Raabe: Bibliographie* (2nd ed., Göttingen:
Vandenhoeck, 1973).

Racine

E146   *Cahiers raciniens.* Neuilly-sur-Seine: Société Racinienne,
1957–74. 2/yr.
The second issue of each volume contains a list of international editions, books, articles, and dissertations; the lists
cover 1957–71.

Ramuz

(C29)   *La revue des lettres modernes: Histoire des idées et des littératures
Charles-Ferdinand Ramuz* is a subseries, 1982– .

Rhys

E147   *Jean Rhys Review.* New York: Columbia U, 1987– . 2/yr.
Each fall issue contains a bibliography of new editions
and international books, articles, and dissertations. Updates Elgin Mellown, *Jean Rhys: A Descriptive and Annotated
Bibliography of Works and Criticism* (New York: Garland,
1984).

Rimbaud

E148 *Rimbaud vivant: Bulletin des Amis de Rimbaud*. Paris: Amis
      de Rimbaud, 1973– . 2/yr.
      A bibliography in each issue, starting with number 16
      (1979), lists new editions and current studies, mainly
      French.

(C29) *La revue des lettres modernes: Histoire des idées et des littératures*
      Arthur Rimbaud is a subseries, 1972– .

Rousseau

E149 *Annales de la Société Jean-Jacques Rousseau*. Geneva: Jullien,
      1905– . Irregular.
      Each volume carries an extensive, classified bibliography
      of international books and articles for 1904– . See both
      "Bibliographie" and "Chronique."

Sauser

See Cendrars.

Schiller

E150 *Jahrbuch der deutschen Schillergesellschaft*. Stuttgart: Alfred
      Kröner, 1957– . Annual.
      "Schiller-Bibliographie" is a classified list of international
      books, articles, and dissertations for 1966– that appears
      approximately every four years starting with volume 4
      (1970).

Schnitzler

E151 *Modern Austrian Literature: Journal of the International Arthur*
      Schnitzler Research Association. Riverside: Intl. Arthur
      Schnitzler Research Assn., 1961– . 4/yr.
      "Arthur Schnitzler Bibliography," in volume 4 and vol-
      umes 6–10 (1971–77), is an annual, annotated list of inter-
      national books, articles, and dissertations, new editions and

translations, and research in progress for 1966–77. Volumes 11– (1978–) carry an annual list of North American dissertations on Austrian literature for 1977– .

Shakespeare

The *World Shakespeare Bibliography* issue of the *Shakespeare Quarterly* (E155) now lists over 5,000 items a year and is well indexed and comprehensive. It can be supplemented with items from the current indexes listed in chapter 2 and from the *Shakespeare Newsletter* (E162) and made more comprehensible by an examination of the evaluative bibliographic essays in *Shakespeare Survey* (E157) and *The Year's Work in English Studies* (B2). The *MLA International Bibliography* (A1) and the *Annual Bibliography of English Language and Literature* (B1) continue to list some 700 and 600 items a year respectively.

E155   *Shakespeare Quarterly*. Washington: Folger Shakespeare Library, 1950– . 5/yr. (Supersedes *Shakespeare Association Bulletin*, New York, 1924–49.)

Electronic format: CD-ROM (Cambridge UP, 1900–).

World Shakespeare Bibliography, which appears annually as the fifth issue, is a comprehensive, classified list of international books, reviews, articles, dissertations, selected papers, reprints, productions, and reviews of productions. There were 5,425 items in the 1993 bibliography. Most items are given brief descriptive annotations; one section covers general studies (with subdivisions for biography, milieu studies, paleography, etc.), and the other covers individual plays and includes criticism, information on productions, and reviews of productions. Subject and name indexes. Coverage has been continuous and increasingly comprehensive for 1924– .

The CD-ROM version, *World Shakespeare Bibliography on CD-ROM* (Cambridge UP, 1996–), consists of one retrospective disk containing 10,000 studies (international books, articles, and dissertations) and several thousand reviews of books, productions, films, and recordings,

1900–93, and a second disk with annual updatings of the *World Shakespeare Bibliography.*

E156 *Shakespeare-Jahrbuch.* Weimar: Böhlaus, 1865–1992. Annual.

"Shakespeare-Bibliographie," in volumes 1–128 (1865–1992), is a comprehensive, classified bibliography of international editions and translations, books, reviews, articles, and dissertations, containing some 1,400 items a year and including an author index.

The yearbook was published by the Shakespeare-Gesellschaft, formed in 1864, which retained the original yearbook and continued its numbering after the Deutsche Shakespeare-Gesellschaft West (DSG) formed in 1964 and began publishing its own yearbook (E160). In 1993 the two societies rejoined and began publishing a single yearbook, the *Deutsche Shakespeare-Gesellschaft, Deutsche Shakespeare-Gesellschaft West. Jahrbuch* (E159), with no bibliography. Volumes 83–99 (1950–63) were published by Quelle, Heidelberg; volumes 72–82/83 (1936–48) by Böhlaus, Weimar; and volumes 61–71 (1925–35) by Tauchnitz, Leipzig. Publication of earlier volumes shifted between Weimar and Berlin and among several publishers. Following the formation of the DSG West and the simultaneous publication of two yearbooks, the bibliography for 1964/65 was published separately (Weimar: Böhlaus, 1967) and then continued with volume 104 (1968). Meanwhile a similar bibliography was published in the *Deutsche Shakespeare-Gesellschaft West. Jahrbuch* for 1964–68 (1965–69). After 1968 the latter bibliography was considerably reduced in size and limited mainly to German or German-language publications.

(A1) *MLA International Bibliography*
       Extensive list of international books, articles, and dissertations.

(B1) *Annual Bibliography of English Language and Literature*
       Extensive list of international books, articles, and dissertations.

(B2) *The Year's Work in English Studies*
       A separate chapter is devoted to Shakespeare studies.

E157   *Shakespeare Survey.* Cambridge: Cambridge UP, 1948– . Annual.

   "The Year's Contributions to Shakespearian Study," 1948– , is a selective bibliographic essay, with chapters on critical studies; Shakespeare's life, times, and stage; and textual studies. Critic index.

E158   *Shakespeare Bulletin: A Journal of Performance Criticism and Scholarship.* Easton: Lafayette Coll., 1982– . 4/yr. (Incorporated the *Shakespeare on Film Newsletter* in 1992.)

   Each issue includes reviews of Shakespeare productions in New York and in professional theaters and major festivals throughout the United States and Canada.

E159   *Deutsche Shakespeare-Gesellschaft, Deutsche Shakespeare-Gesellschaft West. Jahrbuch.* Bochum: Kamp, 1993– . Continues *Shakespeare-Jahrbuch* (E156) and *Deutsche Shakespeare-Gesellschaft West. Jahrbuch* (E160).

   The "Verzeichnis der Shakespeare Inszenierungen und Bibliographie der Kritiken" is a list of the year's productions, 1991/92– , in Germany, Switzerland, and Austria, with production credits and reviews. Continues a similar listing in the *Deutsche-Shakespeare Gesellschaft West. Jahrbuch.*

E160   *Deutsche Shakespeare-Gesellschaft West. Jahrbuch.* Heidelberg: Quelle, 1964–92. Annual.

   Includes a selective, classified list of editions and books, reviews, and articles written in German, published in Germany, or about Shakespeare and Germany (including translations) and lists German, Swiss, and Austrian stage productions, with reviews.

E161   *Shakespeare in Southern Africa: Journal of the Shakespeare Society of Southern Africa.* Grahamstown, S. Afr.: Shakespeare Soc. of Southern Africa, Rhodes U, 1987– . Annual.

   "A Shakespeare Bibliography of Periodical Publications in South Africa" for 1987– , in volumes 2– (1988–), lists some 40 items in each annual installment. (Author has not examined the bibliography.)

E162   *Shakespeare Newsletter.* New Rochelle: Iona Coll., 1951– . 4/yr. (Place, publisher, and frequency have varied.)

   Each issue includes bibliographical material of various

kinds, which has included abstracts of about 5 to 10 articles an issue, of dissertations, and of conference papers.

E163 Hamlet *Studies: An International Journal of Research on* The Tragedie of Hamlet, Prince of Denmarke. New Delhi: Vikas, 1979– . 2/yr. (Usually as one.)

"A Review of Periodical Articles" annually covers 10–20 English-language articles on *Hamlet* not published in Hamlet *Studies*, 1978– .

(B38) *Shakespearean Research and Opportunities*

Includes an annual, annotated bibliography international books and articles on a great variety of Renaissance intellectual issues for 1966–71. Also provides an annual author list of works in progress by North American critics (books, editions, articles, and dissertations).

Shaw

E165 *Shaw: The Annual of Bernard Shaw Studies.* University Park: Pennsylvania State UP, 1981– . Annual. (Formerly *Shaw Review*, 1957–80, and *Shaw Bulletin*, 1951–56.)

Carries a "Continuing Checklist of Shaviana" with international coverage of editions, books, articles, pamphlets, dissertations, and recordings, as well as new editions of Shaw's work. Now annual, this list appeared in each issue through 1980.

E166 *Shavian.* Dagenham, Eng.: Shaw Soc., 1946– . 4/yr. (Titled *Bernard Shaw Society Bulletin*, 1946–53.)

Each issue includes "Literary Survey," an essay covering recent relevant publications on Shaw or related matters and individuals.

Shelley, Mary

(B52) *Keats-Shelley Journal: Keats, Shelley, Byron, Hunt, and Their Circles*

Carries an annual, extensive bibliography of international studies on Mary and Percy Shelley and their circles. Subject index.

Shelley, Percy

(B52) *Keats-Shelley Journal: Keats, Shelley, Byron, Hunt, and Their Circles*
Carries an annual, extensive bibliography of international studies on Percy and Mary Shelley and their circles. Subject index.

Sidney

E167 *Sidney Newsletter and Journal.* Guelph, ON: U of Guelph, 1980– . 2/yr. (Titled *Sidney Newsletter*, vols. 1–10.)
Most issues list abstracts of recent papers, conference proceedings, and dissertations, and the *Journal* regularly publishes bibliographic articles.

Spenser

E168 *Spenser Newsletter.* Pittsburgh: Duquesne U, 1970– . 3/yr.
Each issue prints book reviews and abstracts of recent articles, dissertations, and papers.

Staël

E169 *Cahiers staëliens.* Paris: Attinger, 1962– . Annual. (Supersedes *Occident et cahiers staëliens*, 1930–39.)
Bibliographies in nearly every issue list international books, articles, and dissertations.

Stendhal (Beyle)

E170 *Stendhal Club: Revue internationale d'études stendhaliennes.* Grenoble: Stendhal Club, 1958– . 4/yr.
"Bibliographie stendhalienne," in each October issue, is a comprehensive bibliography of international books, reviews, articles, and notes for 1957– ; it includes new editions (including translations), sales, and radio and television programs. Critic and subject index.

Stevens

E171   *Wallace Stevens Journal.* Northridge: Wallace Stevens Soc., 1977– . 4/yr.
"Current Bibliography" in every other issue lists international books, articles, and dissertations.

Stifter

E172   *Adalbert-Stifter Institut des Landes Oberösterreich. Vierteljahresschrift.* Linz: Adalbert-Stifter Institut, 1952– . 4/yr.
Most issues carry an international checklist of international books, articles, dissertations, and reviews.

Storm

E173   *Schriften der Theodor-Storm Gesellschaft.* Heide: Theodor-Storm Gesellschaft, 1952– . Annual.
"Storm Bibliographie" lists editions, translations, letters, and studies (mainly German books, articles, and dissertations).

Stuart, Jane and Jesse

(E107) *Jack London Newsletter*
"Jesse and Jane Stuart: A Bibliography Supplement," in each issue from 2.3 (1969) through 15.1 (1982), lists works by and about Jesse Stuart and his daughter Jane Stuart; it supplements Hensley C. Woodbridge, *Jesse and Jane Stuart: A Bibliography* (2nd ed., Murray: Murray State U, 1969).

Suarès

(C29)   *La revue des lettres modernes: Histoire des idées et des littératures André Suarès* is a subseries, 1973– .

Tasso

E180   *Studi tassiani.* Bergamo: Centro di Studi Tassiani, 1951– . Annual.

Carries a comprehensive, annotated bibliography of international books and articles for 1952– starting with number 3 (1953).

"Bibliografia tassiana," an appendix to each volume starting with 3 (1953), attempts to record all published commentary on Tasso.

Tennyson

E181 *Tennyson Research Bulletin.* Lincoln: Tennyson Research Centre, 1967– . Annual.

Starting with 1987, carries "Tennyson: A Select Bibliography," which lists current international books, articles, and work in progress; earlier volumes also list recent publications.

Thackeray

E183 *Thackeray Newsletter.* Mississippi State: Mississippi State U, 1977– . 2/yr.

"Thackeray Studies: Recent and Forthcoming," in each issue, is a list of international books, articles, and conference papers published, given, or forthcoming. The *Newsletter* also lists work in progress (including theses and dissertations) and publishes abstracts of dissertations and some recent and forthcoming publications.

See also *Dickens Studies Annual* (E41) for coverage of 1978–82 in volumes 8 (1980) and 12 (1983).

Thoreau

Thoreau has received a chapter in *American Literary Scholarship* (B72) since the first volume.

E184 *Thoreau Society Bulletin.* Geneseo: Thoreau Soc., 1941– . 4/yr.

"Additions to the Thoreau Bibliography," in each issue, is a list of international books, reviews, pamphlets, and articles. The bibliography is cumulated in *Bibliography of the* Thoreau Society Bulletin*s, 1941–1969: A Cumulation and Index* (Troy: Whitston, 1971).

Tolkien

(E105) *Mythlore*
"The Inklings Bibliography," in each issue, lists books, articles, and conference papers on C. S. Lewis, J. R. R. Tolkien, and Charles Williams. First appeared in issue number 12 (1976; also numbered vol. 3, no. 4).

Twain

See Clemens.

Unamuno

E188   *Cuadernos de la catédra Miguel de Unamuno.* Salamanca: Universidad de Salamanca, 1948–83. Annual.
"Bibliografia unamuniana" for 1937–83 appeared in most volumes and listed international books, articles, dissertations (including those in progress), new editions, and upcoming conferences.

Valéry

E191   *Forschungen zu Paul Valéry / Recherches valéryennes.* Kiel: Christian Albrechts Universität, 1988– . Frequency not known.
"Bibliographie des Jahres zu Paul Valéry" is an author list of international books, articles, and miscellaneous items in newspapers and magazines, including new editions and translations, for 1987– .
(C29) *La revue des lettres modernes: Histoire des idées et des littératures Paul Valéry* is a subseries, 1974– .
E192   *Cahiers Paul Valéry.* Paris: Gallimard, 1975– . Irregular.
Each number has carried a checklist of international

books, articles, and conferences, along with new editions, translations, and anthology selections.

Verne

(C29) *La revue des lettres modernes: Histoire des idées et des littératures Jules Verne* is a subseries, 1975– .

Villon

E193 *Fifteenth-Century Studies.* Detroit: Marygrove Coll., 1978– . Annual.

"The Current State of Villon Studies" for 1982– , in volume 14 (1988) and 18 (1991), lists international books, articles, reviews, and conference papers, mainly items not found in, or published too recently to have been included in, the *MLA International Bibliography* (A1).

Waugh

E198 *Evelyn Waugh Newsletter.* Garden City: Nassau Community Coll., 1967– . 3/yr.

"Evelyn Waugh: A Supplementary Checklist of Criticism," beginning in volume 2 (1968), is a list of international books, articles, and dissertations.

Weiss

E199 *Peter Weiss Jahrbuch.* Wiesbaden: Westdeutscher, 1992– . Annual.

Starting with volume 2 (1993), the yearbook carries a bibliography of Weiss studies. (Author has not reviewed the yearbook.)

Welty

E200 *Eudora Welty Newsletter.* Toledo: U of Toledo, 1977– . 2/yr.

An annual "Checklist of Welty Scholarship" in the second issue of each volume covers international books, articles, and dissertations; most issues also list new publications by Welty.

Whitman

A chapter is devoted to Whitman and Dickinson in *American Literary Scholarship* (B72).

E201   *Walt Whitman Quarterly Review.* Iowa City: U of Iowa, 1955– . 4/yr. (Formerly *Walt Whitman Newsletter*, 1955–58, and *Walt Whitman Review*, 1959–82, and published at Wayne State U, Detroit, 1955–82.)

   Each issue since 1955 carries a list of international books, reviews, articles, dissertations, and theses, as well as of editions, translations, letters, and other manuscript materials.

Whittier

E202   *Whittier Newsletter.* Haverill: Haverill Public Library, 1966– . 2/yr. (Vols. 1–20 published by U of Florida, Gainesville.)

   Carries an annual review of Whittier scholarship and work in progress.

Wieland

E203   *Wieland-Studien.* Sigmaringen, Ger.: Thorbecke, 1991– . Annual.

   "Wieland-Bibliographie" is an extensive bibliography of international books, articles, and dissertations, including new editions of Wieland's works, for 1983– (1983–88 covered in vol. 1).

(E104) *Lessing Yearbook*

   Includes an annual, extensive bibliography of international books and articles on Wieland for 1980– , starting in volume 16 (1984), with selective coverage for 1945–79 in the first installment.

Williams, Charles

(E105) *Mythlore*

"The Inklings Bibliography," in each issue, lists books, articles, and conference papers on C. S. Lewis, J. R. R. Tolkien, and Charles Williams. First appeared in issue number 12 (1976; also numbered vol. 3, no. 4).

Williams, Tennessee

E204   *Tennessee Williams Literary Journal.* Metairie: Tennessee Williams Lit. Journal, 1989– . 2/yr.

Carries an annual bibliography of books, articles, dissertations, and reviews of performances, covering 1980– .

E205   *Tennessee Williams Review.* Boston: Northeastern U, 1979–82. 2/yr. (Titled *Tennessee Williams Newsletter*, 1979–81, and published by Dept. of Humanities, Coll. of Engineering, U of Michigan, Ann Arbor.)

Most issues listed recent publications and recent and forthcoming productions.

Williams, William Carlos

E206   *William Carlos Williams Review.* Austin: U of Texas, 1975– . 2/yr. (Titled *William Carlos Williams Newsletter*, vol. 1–5; vols. 1–8 published at Capitol Campus, Pennsylvania State U, Middletown, and vols 9–17 at Swarthmore Coll., Swarthmore.)

Starting with volume 12 (1986), each issue lists recent books, articles, and dissertations; earlier issues listed dissertations in progress or recently completed.

Wolfe

E207   *Thomas Wolfe Review.* Akron: U of Akron, 1977– . 2/yr. (Vol. 1–11 titled *Thomas Wolfe Newsletter*.)

"The Wolfe Pack: Bibliography," in each issue, is a list of international books and articles, with brief annotations.

Wordsworth

E208 *Wordsworth Circle.* Philadelphia: Temple U, 1970– . 4/yr.
"Wordsworth Scholarship: An Annual Register," in volumes 3–11 (1972–80), is a bibliographic essay for 1971–79 covering international books, articles, and dissertations, with less formal listings of scholarship in volumes 1–2.

Yeats

E210 *Yeats Annual.* Atlantic Highlands: Humanities, 1982– . Annual.
The "Recent Yeats Bibliography" covers 1981– (starting in vol. 3, 1985) and lists books, articles, and dissertations from *Index to Theses* and *Dissertation Abstracts International*; it includes items from earlier years not previously listed, recordings and graphics, and some material by Yeats. Dissertations for 1980–83 were listed separately in volumes 1–3, and volume 4 carried a list of European dissertations, 1969–80.

E211 *Yeats: An Annual of Critical and Textual Studies.* Ann Arbor: U of Michigan P, 1983– . Annual. (Vols. 1–3, 1983–85, Ithaca: Cornell UP, and vols. 4–5, 1986–87, Ann Arbor: UMI.)
"A Yeats Bibliography," which covers 1981– , is a list of English-language books, articles, and book reviews, including sound recordings, graphics, newly republished essays, and some material by Yeats; it updates K. P. S. Jochum, *W. B. Yeats: A Classified Bibliography of Criticism* (2nd ed., Urbana: U of Illinois P, 1990), which had itself drawn on earlier lists. In addition, "Dissertation Abstracts" for 1982– reprints abstracts from *Dissertation Abstracts International*.

(E56) *Yeats Eliot Review: A Quarterly Journal of Scholarship, Criticism, and Opinion*

"Bibliographical Update," in each issue of volumes 1–7 (1974–82), lists current international books, articles, and dissertations.

Zola

E215   *Les cahiers naturalistes. Bulletin.* Paris: Société Littéraire des Amis d'Emile Zola, 1955– . Annual.

"Bibliographie" is a classified compilation of new international editions and translations and of books, articles, and dissertations on Zola and naturalism.

Appendix

Electronic Bibliographies and Indexes

The electronic versions of serial bibliographies described in chapters 2 through 6 are listed again here, along with dates of coverage and frequency of updates for each (if known). They are listed alphabetically by title of the print version; if the electronic version's title is the same, it is not repeated. See the main entries for more information about coverage of each bibliography, and see the *Gale Directory of Databases, CD-ROMs in Print,* and the *CD-ROM Directory with Multimedia CD's* (listed in the bibliography) for additional information about specific databases.

ABC Pol Sci: Bibliography of Contents: Political Science and Government. D261.

  CD-ROM. *ABC Pol Sci on Disc.* Santa Barbara: ABC-Clio, 1992– .
ABI/Inform. D202.

  CD-ROM. *ABI/Inform Ondisc.* Ann Arbor: UMI, 1971– . 12/yr.

  Online. File 15. Palo Alto: Dialog, 1971– . 52/yr.

  Online. Epic file 30; FirstSearch. Dublin: OCLC, 1970– . 12/yr.
America: History and Life. D257.

  CD-ROM. *America: History and Life on Disc.* Santa Barbara: ABC-Clio, 1982– . 3/yr.

  Online. File 38. Palo Alto: Dialog, 1964– . 4/yr.
L'année philologique: Bibliographie critique et analytique de l'antiquité gréco-latine. D75.

  CD-ROM. *The Database of Classical Bibliography on CD-ROM.* Atlanta; Scholars, 1976– . Annual.
Annual Bibliography of English Language and Literature. B1.

  Online. *ABELL On-line.* Cambridge: Cambridge U libraries catalog, 1995– .

Applied Science and Technology Index. A19.

    CD-ROM and online. New York: Wilson, 1983– . 12/yr.

    Online. Epic file 61; FirstSearch. Dublin: OCLC, 1983– . 12/yr.

Artbibliographies Modern. D22.

    Online. File 56. Palo Alto: Dialog, 1974– . 2/yr.

Art Index. D20.

    CD-ROM and online. New York: Wilson, 1984– . 4/yr.

    Online. Epic file 61; FirstSearch. Dublin: OCLC, 1983– . 12/yr.

Arts and Humanities Citation Index. A6.

    CD-ROM. *Arts and Humanities Citation Index: Compact Disc Edition.* Philadelphia: Inst. for Scientific Information, 1990– . Annual.

    Online. *Arts and Humanities Search.* Epic file 62; FirstSearch. Dublin: OCLC, 1980– . 52/yr.

    Online. *Arts and Humanities Search.* File 439. Palo Alto: Dialog, 1980– . 52/yr.

Avery Index to Architecture. D26.

    Online. Mountain View: RLIN, 1979– . Continual updating.

    Online. File 178. Palo Alto: Dialog, 1979– . 2/yr.

BHA: Bibliography of the History of Art. D21.

    Online. *Art Literature International.* File 191. Palo Alto: Dialog, 1973– . 2/yr.

Bibliografia generale della lingua e della letteratura italiana. C42.

    CD-ROM. Rome: Salerno, 1994– .

Bibliographic Index: A Cumulative Bibliography of Bibliographies. D35.

    Online. New York: Wilson, 1984– . 52/yr.

Bibliographie linguistischer Literatur (BLL): Bibliographie zur allgemeinen Linguistik und zur anglistischen, germanistischen und romanistischen Linguistik. D287.

    Online. Karlsruhe, Ger.: STN, 1971– . Annual.

Bibliographie van de Nederlandse Taal- en Literaturwetenschap. C102.

    Online. Leiden: Nederlands Centrum voor Bibliotheekautomatisering Pica, 1940–45, 1960– . 52/yr.

Biography and Genealogy Master Index. D43.

    CD-ROM. *Biography and Genealogy Master Index CD-ROM.* Detroit: Gale, 1976– . Annual.

    Online. *Biography Master Index.* Files 287–288. Palo Alto: Dialog, 1980– . Annual.

Biography Index: A Cumulative Index to Biographical Material in Books and Magazines. D42.

CD-ROM and online. New York: Wilson, 1984– . 4/yr.

Online. Epic file 12; FirstSearch. Dublin: OCLC, 1984– . 12/yr.

Biological and Agricultural Index. A18.

CD-ROM and online. New York: Wilson, 1983– . 12/yr.

Online. Epic file 54; FirstSearch. New York: Wilson, 1983– . 12/yr.

Book Review Digest. D47.

CD-ROM and online. New York: Wilson, 1983– . 4/yr.

Online. Epic file 21; FirstSearch. Dublin: OCLC, 1983– . 12/yr.

Book Review Index. D45.

CD-ROM. Detroit: Gale, 1969– . Annual.

Online. File 137. Palo Alto: Dialog, 1969– . 3/yr.

British Education Index. D209.

Online. File 121. Palo Alto: Dialog, 1976– . 4/yr.

British Humanities Index. A9.

CD-ROM. *BHI Plus.* London: Saur, 1985– . 4/yr.

Broadcast News. A45.

CD-ROM. Woodbridge: Research, 1993– . 12/yr.

Business Periodicals Index. D201.

CD-ROM and online. New York: Wilson, 1984– . 4/yr.

Online. Epic file 33; FirstSearch. Dublin: OCLC, 1984– . 12/yr.

Canadian Literary Periodicals Index. B92.

CD-ROM. Teeswater, ON: Reference, 1984–87, 1992– . Annual.

Canadian Periodical Index / Index de périodiques canadienne. B97.

CD-ROM. Toronto: Globe and Mail, 1988– . 2/yr.

Chicano Index. D217.

CD-ROM. *Chicano Database on CD-ROM.* Berkeley: Chicano Studies Library, U of California, 1967– . 2/yr.

CIS / Index to Publications of the United States Congress. D252.

CD-ROM. *Congressional Masterfile.* Bethesda: Congressional Information Service, 1789– . 4/yr.

Online. File 101. Palo Alto: Dialog, 1970– . 12/yr.

Cumulated Index Medicus. D445.

CD-ROM. *Medline Standard.* Norwood: SilverPlatter, 1966– . 12/yr.

Online. *Medline.* Files 152–155. Palo Alto: Dialog, 1966– . 52/yr.

Online. *Medline.* Epic file 48; FirstSearch. Dublin: OCLC, 1985– . 12/yr.

Dissertation Abstracts International. D154.

CD-ROM. Ann Arbor: UMI, 1861– . 2/yr.

Online. File 35. Palo Alto: Dialog, 1861– . 12/yr. Includes records from *Master's Abstracts International,* 1988– .

Education Index. D208.

CD-ROM and online. New York: Wilson, 1984– . 4/yr.

Online. Epic file 6; FirstSearch. Dublin: OCLC, 1983– . 12/yr.

Environment Abstracts. D442.

CD-ROM. Congressional Information Service, 1971– . 4/yr.

Online. *Enviroline.* File 40. Palo Alto: Dialog, 1971– . 12/yr.

ERIC. D205.

CD-ROM. *ERIC on SilverPlatter.* Norwood: SilverPlatter, 1966– . 4/yr.

CD-ROM. *Dialog Ondisc: ERIC.* Palo Alto: Dialog, 1966– . 4/yr.

Online. File 1. Palo Alto: Dialog, 1966– . 12/yr.

Online. Epic file 1; FirstSearch. Dublin: OCLC, 1966– . 12/yr.

Essay and General Literature Index. A10.

CD-ROM and online. New York: Wilson, 1983– . Annual.

Online. Epic file 72. Dublin: OCLC, 1983– . Annual.

Ethnic Newswatch: A Multicultural Database. D215.

CD-ROM. Stamford: Softline, 1991– . Annual.

FRANCIS bulletin signalétique. A2.

CD-ROM. *FRANCIS CD-ROM.* Paris: Centre National de la Recherche Scientifique et Technique, 1972– . Annual.

Online. Paris: Questel, 1984– . Annual.

General Science Index. D437.

CD-ROM and online. New York: Wilson, 1984– . 4/yr.

Online. Epic file 55; FirstSearch. Dublin: OCLC, 1984– . 12/yr.

Handbook of Latin American Studies. C62.

Online. Mountain View: RLIN, 1983– . Annual.

HAPI: Hispanic American Periodicals Index. C60.

CD-ROM. Los Angeles: U of California, Los Angeles, Library Information Systems, 1970– . Annual.

Online. Mountain View: RLIN, 1970– . Annual.

Historical Abstracts: Bibliography of the World's Periodical Literature. D256.

CD-ROM. *Historical Abstracts on Disc.* Santa Barbara: ABC-Clio, 1982– . 3/yr.

History of Science and Technology. D436.

Online. Mountain View: RLIN, 1983– . Annual.

Humanities Index. A8.

CD-ROM and online. New York: Wilson, 1974– . 4/yr.

Online. Epic file 60; FirstSearch. Dublin: OCLC, 1984– . 12/yr.

IFB Abstracts. See D406.

Online. Internet, 1994– . Available http://library.upenn.edu/ifba.

Index to American Periodicals of the 1700s and 1800s. A50.

CD-ROM. Indianapolis: Computer Indexed Systems, 1986– . Irregular.

Index to English Literary Periodicals, 1681–1914. A49.

CD-ROM. Indianapolis: Computer Indexed Systems, 1989– . Irregular.

Index to Legal Periodicals. D264.

CD-ROM and online. New York: Wilson, 1981– . 4/yr.

Online. Epic file 80; FirstSearch. Dublin: OCLC, 1981– . 12/yr.

Index to South African Periodicals / Repertorium van Suid-Afrikaanse tydskrifartikels. B83.

Online. Pretoria: SABINET (South African Library Network System), 1986– .

Index to Theses with Abstracts Accepted for Higher Degrees by the Universities of Great Britain and Ireland and the Council for National Academic Awards. D162.

CD-ROM. London: Learned Information, 1970– . Annual.

Internationale Bibliographie der Zeitschriftenliteratur aus allen Gebieten des Wissens. A17.

CD-ROM. *IBZ CD-ROM.* Osnabrück, Ger.: Zeller, 1989–93.

Journal of Economic Literature. D203.

CD-ROM. *Econlit.* Norwood: SilverPlatter, 1969– . 4/yr.

Online. *Economic Literature Index.* File 139. Palo Alto: Dialog, 1969– . 4/yr.

Online. *Econlit.* Epic file 37; FirstSearch. Dublin: OCLC, 1969– . 12/yr.

Library and Information Science Abstracts. D281.

CD-ROM. *LISA.* Norwood: SilverPlatter, 1969– . Annual.

Online. *LISA*. File 61. Palo Alto: Dialog, 1969– . 12/yr.

Library Literature: An Index to Library and Information Science. D280.
    CD-ROM and online. New York: Wilson, 1984– . 4/yr.
    Online. Epic file 5; FirstSearch. Dublin: OCLC, 1984– . 12/yr.

Linguistics and Language Behavior Abstracts. D286.
    CD-ROM. Norwood: SilverPlatter, 1974– . 4/yr.
    Online. File 36. Palo Alto: Dialog, 1973– . 4/yr.

MLA International Bibliography of Books and Articles on the Modern Languages and Literatures. A1.
    CD-ROM. Norwood: SilverPlatter, 1963– . 4/yr.
    Online. Epic file 71; FirstSearch. 1963– . Dublin: OCLC, 10/yr.

Monthly Catalog of United States Government Publications. D250.
    CD-ROM. *GPO on SilverPlatter*. Norwood: SilverPlatter, 1976– . 6/yr.
    CD-ROM. *Government Documents Catalog Service*. Pomona: Auto-Graphics, 1976– . 12/yr.
    Online. *GPO Monthly Catalog*. Epic file 10; FirstSearch. Dublin: OCLC, 1976– . 12/yr.

Muse: Music Search. D342.
    CD-ROM. Baltimore: Natl. Information Services, 1970– . Annual.

Music Index: A Subject-Author Guide to Current Music Periodical Literature. D340.
    CD-ROM. Arlington: Chadwyck-Healey, 1981– . Annual.

NewsBank Electronic Index. A41.
    CD-ROM. New Canaan: NewsBank, 1980– . 12/yr. NewsBank, 1980– . 12/yr.

Newspaper Abstracts. A40.
    CD-ROM. Ann Arbor: UMI, 1985– . 12/yr.
    Online. Epic file 28; FirstSearch. Dublin: OCLC, 1989– . 12/yr.
    Online. *Newspaper and Periodical Abstracts*. File 484. Palo Alto: Dialog, 1988– . 52/yr. Also file 603 for 1984–88, newspapers only.

PAIS International in Print. C3.
    CD-ROM. *PAIS International*. Norwood: SilverPlatter, 1972– . 4/yr.
    CD-ROM. *PAIS on CD-ROM*. New York: Public Affairs Information Service, 1972– . 4/yr.

Online. File 49. Palo Alto: Dialog, 1972– . 12/yr.

Online. *PAIS International,* Epic file 2, 1972– ; *PAIS Decade,* FirstSearch, latest 10 years. Dublin: OCLC. 12/yr.

Periodical Abstracts. A16.

CD-ROM. Ann Arbor: UMI, 1986– . 4/yr.

Online. Epic file 29; FirstSearch. Dublin: OCLC, 1986– . 12/yr.

Online. *Newspaper and Periodical Abstracts.* File 484. Palo Alto: Dialog, 1988– . 52/yr.

Philosopher's Index: An International Index to Periodicals and Books. D365.

CD-ROM and online. File 57. Palo Alto: Dialog, 1940– . 4/yr.

Poem Finder. D126.

CD-ROM. Great Neck: Roth, 1991– . Annual.

Point de repère: Index analytique d'articles de périodiques de langue française. C22.

Online. *Repère.* Montreal: Services Documentaires Multimedia, 1972– . Daily.

Psychological Abstracts. D392.

CD-ROM. *Psyclit.* Norwood: SilverPlatter, 1974– for articles and 1987– for books. 4/yr.

CD-ROM. *Psyclit.* Palo Alto: Dialog, 1974– for articles and 1987– for books. 4/yr.

Online. *Psycinfo.* File 11. Palo Alto: Dialog, 1967– . 12/yr.

Online. *Psycinfo.* Epic file 3, 1967– ; *Psycfirst,* FirstSearch, latest 3 years. Dublin: OCLC, 12/yr.

Readers' Guide to Periodical Literature. A20.

CD-ROM and online. New York: Wilson, 1983– . 4/yr.

Online. FirstSearch. Dublin: OCLC, 1983– . 12/yr.

Religion Index One: Periodicals. D420.

CD-ROM and online. *ATLA Religion Database.* New York: Wilson, 1949– . 4/yr.

Online. *Religion Index.* File 190. Palo Alto: Dialog, 1949– . 12/yr.

CD-ROM. *Religion Indexes: RIO/RIT/IBRR, 1975– , on CD-ROM.* Evanston: ATLA, 1975– .

Religious and Theological Abstracts. D424.

CD-ROM. Myerstown: Religious and Theological Abstracts, 1957– . Annual.

RILM Abstracts: Répertoire Internationale de Littérature Musicale / International Repertory of Music Literature. D341.

CD-ROM. See *Muse*, above.

Scholarly Book Reviews on CD-ROM. D48.

CD-ROM. Bethesda: University Publications of America, 1991– . 4/yr.

Shakespeare Quarterly. E155.

CD-ROM. *World Shakespeare Bibliography on CD-ROM.* Cambridge: Cambridge UP, 1996– . Annual.

Social Sciences Citation Index. D456.

CD-ROM. *Social Sciences Citation Index: Compact Disc Edition.* Philadelphia: Inst. for Scientific Information, 1989– . Annual.

Online. *Social Scisearch.* File 7. Palo Alto: Dialog, 1972– . 52/yr.

Online. FirstSearch. Dublin: OCLC, 1980– . 52/yr.

Social Sciences Index. D455.

CD-ROM and online. New York: Wilson, 1983– . 4/yr.

Online. Epic file 4; FirstSearch. Dublin: OCLC, 1984– . 12/yr.

Sociological Abstracts. D457.

CD-ROM. *Sociofile.* Norwood: SilverPlatter, 1974– . 5/yr.

Online. File 37. Palo Alto: Dialog, 1963– . 5/yr.

Online. Epic file 7; FirstSearch. Dublin: OCLC, 1963– . 6/yr.

Zeitungs-Index: Verzeichnis wichtiger Aufsätze aus deutschsprachigen Zeitungen. C92.

CD-ROM. New Providence: Bowker, 1974– .

Bibliography

The two chief sources of information about current serial bibliographies for this guide were library catalogs and reference collections, particularly those at Columbia University, the New York Public Library, the Ohio State University, the University of Cincinnati, and Miami University, and serial bibliographies themselves. The *MLA International Bibliography*, the *Annual Bibliography of English Language and Literature*, and the *Bibliographic Index* were especially useful, as was OCLC's *Worldcat*. Additional sources are listed here.

Abstracting Services: Annotated Directory. 2 vols. The Hague: Intl. Federation for Documentation, 1969.

Bassan, Fernande, Paul F. Reed, and Donald C. Spinelli. *An Annotated Bibliography of French Language and Literature.* New York: Garland, 1976.

Bell, Inglis F., and Jennifer Gallup. *A Reference Guide to English, American, and Canadian Literature: An Annotated Checklist of Bibliographical and Other Reference Materials.* Vancouver: U of British Columbia P, 1971.

Bibliography, Documentation, Terminology. Paris: UNESCO, 1961–79.

Blazek, Ron, and Elizabeth Aversa. *The Humanities: A Selective Guide to Information Sources.* 4th ed. Englewood: Libraries Unlimited, 1994.

Bleznick, Donald W. "A Guide to Journals in the Hispanic Field: A Selected Annotated List of Journals Central to the Study of Spanish and Spanish American Language and Literature." *Hispania* 49 (1966): 569–83; 52 (1969): 723–37; 55 (1972): 207–21.

———. *A Sourcebook for Hispanic Literature and Language: A Selected,*

Annotated Guide to Spanish, Spanish-American, and Chicano Bibliography, Literature, Linguistics, Journals, and Other Source Materials. 2nd ed. Metuchen: Scarecrow, 1983.

Bracken, James K. *English and American Writers.* Englewood: Libraries Unlimited, 1991. Vol. 2 of *Reference Works in British and American Literature.*

The CD-ROM Directory with Multimedia CD's: International. 9th ed. London: TFPL, 1992.

CD-ROMs in Print: An International Guide to CD-ROM, CD-I, CDTC, Multimedia, and Electronic Book Products. Westport: Meckler, 1994.

Chalcraft, Anthony, Ray Prytherch, and Stephen Willis, eds. *Generalia, Language and Literature, the Arts.* 5th ed. London: Library Assn., 1991. Vol. 3 of *Walford's Guide to Reference Material.*

Chicorel Index to Abstracting and Indexing Services: Periodicals in Humanities and the Social Sciences. 2 vols. New York: Chicorel, 1974.

Couch, Nena, and Nancy Allen, eds. *The Humanities and the Library.* 2nd ed. Chicago: Amer. Library Assn., 1993.

Faulhaber, Uwe K., and Penrith B. Goff. *German Literature: An Annotated Reference Guide.* New York: Garland, 1979.

Fisher, Benjamin Franklin, IV. *The Gothic's Gothic: Study Aids to the Tradition of the Tale of Terror.* New York: Garland, 1988.

Fisher, John H. "Serial Bibliographies in the Modern Languages and Literatures." *PMLA* 66 (1951): 138–53.

"From Seattle to Schenectady: More Book Reviews." *Coda: Poets and Writers Newsletter* 6 (1978): 21–24.

Gale Directory of Databases. Detroit: Gale, 1993.

Gorman, Gary E., and J. J. Mills. *Guide to Indexing and Abstracting Services in the Third World.* London: Zell, 1993.

Gray, Richard A. *Serial Bibliographies in the Humanities and Social Sciences.* Ann Arbor: Pierian, 1969.

Greene, Donald. "'More Than a Necessary Chore': The Eighteenth-Century Current Bibliography in Retrospect and Prospect." *Eighteenth-Century Studies* 10 (1976–77): 94–110.

Harner, James L. *Literary Research Guide.* 2nd ed. New York: MLA, 1993.

Hartman, Charles. "Recent Publications on Chinese Literature: I: The Republic of China (Taiwan)." *Chinese Literature: Essays, Articles, Reviews* 1 (1979): 81–86.

Harzfeld, Lois A. *Periodical Indexes in the Social Sciences and Humanities: A Subject Guide*. Metuchen: Scarecrow, 1978.

Horecky, Paul, ed. *East Central Europe: A Guide to Basic Publications*. Chicago: U of Chicago P, 1969.

————, ed. *Southeastern Europe: A Guide to Basic Publications*. Chicago: U of Chicago P, 1969.

Kasten, Seth. "Religious Periodical Indexes: A Basic List." *Reference Services Review* 9.1 (1981): 53–55.

Kieft, Robert. "Reference Works for Literary Theory." *Reference Services Review* 20.4 (1992): 49 +.

Kujoth, Jean Spealman. *Subject Guide to Periodical Indexes and Review Indexes*. Metuchen: Scarecrow, 1969.

Llorens, Ana M. R. "Bibliographic Indexes to Periodical Literature in the Romance Languages." *Modern Language Journal* 60 (1976): 23–30.

Marcuse, Michael J. *A Reference Guide for English Studies*. Berkeley: U of California P, 1990.

McMallin, B. J. "Indexing the Periodical Literature of Anglo-American Bibliography." *Studies in Bibliography* 33 (1980): 1–17.

McPheron, William, ed. *English and American Literature: Sources and Strategies for Collection Development*. Chicago: Amer. Library Assn., 1987.

Mesplay, Deborah, and Loretta Koch. "An Evaluation of Indexing Services for Women's Studies Periodical Literature." *RQ* 32 (1993): 404–10.

Nitkina, N. V., and G. V. Mikheeva, eds. *Guide to Bibliographies of Russian Periodicals and Serial Publications, 1728–1985*. 2nd ed. Commack: Nova Science, 1993.

Palfrey, Thomas B., Joseph G. Fucilla, and William C. Holbrook. *Bibliographical Guide to the Romance Languages and Literatures*. 8th ed. Evanston: Chandler's, 1971.

Patterson, Margaret C. *Author Newsletters and Journals: An International Annotated Bibliography of Serial Publications Concerned with the Life and Works of Individual Authors*. Detroit: Gale, 1979. Supps. in *Serials Review* 8.4 (1982): 61–72; 10.1 (1984): 51–59; and 11.3 (1985): 31–44.

Perry, Stephen L. "The MLA Database as a Source of Film Criticism." *Journal of Academic Librarianship* 7 (1992): 146–50.

Reynolds, Michael M. *A Guide to Theses and Dissertations: An Annotated, International Bibliography of Bibliographies.* Detroit: Gale, 1975.

Rouse, Richard H., J. H. Claxton, and M. D. Metzger. *Serial Bibliographies for Medieval Studies.* Berkeley: U of California P, 1969.

Scheven, Yvette. *Bibliographies for African Studies, 1980–1983.* New York: Zell, 1984.

Schweik, Robert C., and Dieter Riesner. *Reference Sources in English and American Literature: An Annotated Bibliography.* New York: Norton, 1977.

Scott, Patrick. "Bibliographical Problems in Research and Composition." *College Composition and Communication* 37 (1986): 167–77.

Sheehy, Eugene P., ed. *Guide to Reference Books.* 10th ed. Chicago: Amer. Library Assn., 1986; supp. 1992.

Shilstone, Marion, and Wojczech Zalewski. "Current Bibliographies in Russian and Soviet Area Studies." *Russian Review* 37 (1978): 313–22.

Totok, Wilhelm, Karl-Heinz Weismann, and Rolf Weitzel, eds. *Handbuch der bibliographischen Nachschlagewerke.* 4th ed. Frankfurt: Klostermann, 1972.

Ulrich's International Periodicals Directory. 33rd ed. New Providence: Bowker, 1994.

Vesenyi, Paul E. *An Introduction to Periodical Bibliography.* Ann Arbor: Pierian, 1974.

Worldcat. Dublin: OCLC.

Index

Before consulting this index, note the table of contents with its detailed, alphabetical list of the subjects and authors covered by serial bibliographies (ch. 5–6) and its outline of the regional and national literatures (ch. 3–4). Note also the topics covered in the introduction (ch. 1) and the categories of comprehensive bibliographies and general indexes in chapter 2.

Indexed here are the titles of all books and periodicals mentioned in chapters 1 through 6; the names of authors, editors, and compilers of bibliographies mentioned in the text; and descriptive titles of the serial bibliographies contained in the books and periodicals. Titles such as "Checklist," "Recent Studies," and "Annual Bibliography" are not descriptive, but those such as "Annual James Joyce Checklist" are; descriptive titles are indexed by keyword (*Joyce* in this case). Most of the people indexed are compilers of cumulations and single-issue bibliographies; unfortunately, it was impossible to identify and list all the bibliographers whose important ongoing work this guide records.

Numbers preceded by capital letters are item numbers for entries; those not preceded by letters are page numbers. Page numbers followed by item numbers in parentheses refer to cross-reference entries.